DISCARD

RIDING FOR AMERICA

RIDING FOR AMERICA

The United States Equestrian Team

Edited by Nancy Jaffer

Foreword by John H. Fritz

Introduction by William Steinkraus

D O U B L E D A Y

New York   London   Toronto   Sydney   Auckland

The editor is grateful to her husband, Lawrence Nagy, for his vital support in this project, including technical expertise in producing the manuscript, and the encouragement that kept her going.

PUBLISHED BY DOUBLEDAY
a division of Bantam Doubleday Dell Publishing Group, Inc.
666 Fifth Avenue, New York, New York 10103

DOUBLEDAY and the portrayal of an anchor
with a dolphin are trademarks of Doubleday,
a division of Bantam Doubleday Dell
Publishing Group, Inc.

Library of Congress Cataloging-in-Publication Data

Riding for America : the United States Equestrian Team / edited by
Nancy Jaffer.—1st ed.
p.   cm.
1. United States Equestrian Team.   2. Horse sports—United States.
I. Jaffer, Nancy.
SF294.25.R53   1990
89-77135
CIP

ISBN 0-385-26798-3
Copyright © 1990 by The U.S. Equestrian Team

ART DIRECTOR: CAROL MALCOLM

BOOK DESIGN BY RICHARD ORIOLO

All Rights Reserved
Printed in the United States of America
October 1990
First Edition

EDITOR'S PREFACE

As a fan of the USET almost from the time that it was created, I used to watch worshipfully when the Team competed in the international jumping classes at Madison Square Garden.

Attending the National Horse Show there was an annual treat during my childhood, when I never dreamed that I would meet—much less get to know—such luminaries as Billy Steinkraus and Frank Chapot.

They, and the other members of the USET I have since chronicled around the world, are remarkable for their contributions to their sport and their country. I so enjoyed working on this book because it offered the privilege of learning about equestrian history as it was made, in the words of those who made it.

NOTE

Although the volume is called *Riding for America*, driving for America is also an important element of the USET program. The USET's newest discipline is attracting an increasing number of participants and spectators.

The three organizations involved in American international equestrian sport are commonly referred to by their initials, and we have followed that practice in this book. The names of the organizations are:

USET—United States Equestrian Team, the nonprofit, voluntary group that exists for the purpose of training, selecting, and financing the equestrian teams that represent the United States in world competition, including the Olympics.

FEI—Fédération Equestre Internationale, the Swiss-based governing body of international equestrian sport, which formulates its rules.

AHSA—American Horse Shows Association, the national federation of the United States. It is the governing body of horse shows in this country and is our official member of the FEI and the U.S. Olympic Committee.

FOREWORD

When a group of American sportsmen established the United States Equestrian Team in 1950, they had a twofold purpose in mind: to ensure that the United States would continue to be represented in the equestrian events of the Olympic Games and that there would be an American team in the international show jumping classes at the National Horse Show in New York and the Toronto Winter Fair in Canada. During the past four decades the responsibilities of the Team have grown considerably beyond those two objectives.

In 1950 the USET's responsibilities were limited. In 1950 there were no Pan American Games, no World or Continental Championships, no World Cups, no combined driving competitions, no Young Rider events. There were only a few riders and horses in the United States capable of competing at the international level in the Olympic disciplines.

The USET's program in the late 1980s reflected the great growth in horse sport activities in the United States and the rest of the world since 1950, especially during the decades of the 1970s and '80s. In 1950 the American Horse Shows Association, the national equestrian federation of the United States, recognized 276 shows—compared to more than 2,500 shows in 1989. By 1989 the association had in excess of 54,000 members, compared to 2,990 individual members in 1950. Similarly, there were 452 AHSA recognized officials and ten high score awards in 1950, and by 1989 there were more than 3,000 AHSA officials and more than 70 national high score awards.

In the 1950s and '60s the USET relied on full-time coaches in show jumping and three-day eventing to conduct programs for a small number of riders and horses, from which teams for international competitions were selected. Today we have long lists of dozens of riders and horses competing in the Olympic disciplines at the international level, and the Team holds training programs in all parts of the country, as well as at its headquarters in Gladstone, New Jersey, to develop and refine riders, drivers, and horses to represent the United States year after year on the international equestrian scene. An executive vice president with a secretary could easily administer the affairs of the Team during its developing years. By 1990 it took a staff of more than fifteen people and an annual budget of close to three million dollars to conduct the USET's program and fulfill its obligations.

In 1976 a book entitled *The U.S. Equestrian Team Book of Riding* was published. It covered the first quarter-century of the USET's existence, with articles by those associated with the Team during its developing years. This new book, *Riding for America*, includes an Introduction by William Steinkraus, chairman of the USET board, who rode for the Team from 1951 through 1972 and who was the first American to win an Olympic individual gold medal. Bill discusses American participation in international equestrian competition from the early part of this century through the 1976 Olympic Games.

The book further includes contributions from those who have competed for the USET (or in other ways been associated with the Team) in the busy years since 1975, during which time American equestrians have won eleven Olympic medals, including five golds; sixteen Pan American medals, including nine golds; six World Championship medals, including two golds; and have won the Show Jumping World Cup seven out of eleven times.

November 1989

JOHN H. FRITZ
Vice President
The United States Equestrian Team

CONTENTS

Contents

Introduction: The First Quarter-Century

William Steinkraus
USET Chairman

"Riding for America." The words have a romantic ring, conjuring up images from Paul Revere to Custer's Seventh Cavalry and Teddy Roosevelt's Rough Riders. But, in fact, our country's mounted cavalry tradition was relatively short. Although the Continental Congress formed dragoon regiments, which existed until after the War of 1812 and were later revived in the 1830s, the earliest cavalry regiments to be so called trace back no further than 1855. (And as it happens, I myself had the honor of serving in World War II with the last surviving mounted cavalry regiment, the 124th Cavalry from Texas. We escaped being mechanized, but suffered what is perhaps an even worse fate for cavalrymen: we marched into Burma on foot, using pack mules to carry our heavy weapons and equipment. The regiment was disbanded in China in 1945.)

For most of the present century, the words "Riding for America" have assumed an additional connotation, one associated not with the battlefield but with the pistes of equestrian sport.

There was a high jump and long jump at the 1900 Olympics in Paris, but Turin, Italy, enjoys the distinction of having organized, in 1902, the first horse show in which officers from various nations officially represented their countries; and to judge from the subsequent growth of this kind of activity, it was clearly an idea whose time had come. London's very first indoor horse show at Olympia in 1907 (following some decades of outdoor shows) offered international jumping, and the 1908 Olympic Games in St. Louis also featured demonstrations of equestrian sport, though no official competitions. Show jumping as we know it today, dressage, and three-day eventing were not part of the Olympics until 1912.

In 1909, a team of British officers came to New York's National Horse Show to compete against a team of American officers drawn from our Seventh, Eleventh, and Fourteenth Cavalry regiments. Thus commenced a tradition of military equestrian representation for our country at the National—and, from 1912 on, at the Olympic Games—that was to end only with the dissolution of our mounted cavalry in 1948. (International equestrian competition was pretty much an exclusively military prerogative around the world prior to World War II, and at the biggest of all the prewar Olympic Games, Berlin in 1936, the only "civilian" who competed was Eddy Kahn, a Dutch three-day event rider.)

By 1911, the National boasted five international teams—officers from France, Great Britain, and Holland taking on a North American contingent from Canada and their U.S. host. Two members of the U.S. team were named the following year to our first Olympic equestrian team for the Games at Stockholm: Captain (later Major General) Guy V. Henry and Lieutenant E. R. Graham. Henry went on to become not only commanding officer of the cavalry school and chief of cavalry, but also president of the International Equestrian Federation (FEI). At Stockholm, where sixty-two riders and seventy horses from ten nations took part, Henry finished eleventh individually in the "Military" (as the three-day event was then called) and shared a team bronze medal. He was also thirteenth in dressage (riding the same horse!) and a member of the fourth-place jumping team, this time riding Graham's horse.

The New York National was cancelled in 1914 because of the world conflict that was beginning to erupt in Europe, and though the show resumed the following year with class conditions still open to foreign officers, World War I meant they would not again compete in New York until 1925. What should have been the 1916 Olympic Games also fell victim to World War I, but after the Armistice, Antwerp bravely went ahead and organized the first postwar Olympics in 1920. Only eight nations, including the United States, took part in the equestrian events, and though our riders failed to win a medal, they came tantalizingly close. They were fourth in the Military as a team, and fifth in team jumping (the best-scoring rider on both occasions being Captain Harry D. Chamberlin). Only in dressage were our riders clearly outclassed, finding themselves tied for fourteenth and last place. The U.S. team captain tersely reported after the Games that the competition seemed to be pretty much a matter for specialists, rather than something an officer could develop in his spare time.

Four years later, the results at the Paris Olympics underlined this conclusion. This time the U.S. team was eliminated both in the Military and in the team jumping, and no dressage team was even entered, as a result of the dismal showing four years earlier. The one bright spot was the winning of an individual bronze in the three-day event by Major Sloan Doak. The chief of cavalry, General Kromer, responded to the disappointing results by launching a serious effort to obtain special training abroad for a select group of officers, Chamberlin among them, and to expand their competitive experience.

One of the "officers" on the 1924 Olympic team was actually a Millbrook, New York, foxhunter named Frederic Bontecou, who was riding in uniform as a reserve officer. Although he was eliminated in Paris, the following year he showed American promise by

Arguably the finest horseman the Army ever produced, Major (later Brigadier General) Harry D. Chamberlin comes off the bank with Nigra at the 1928 Olympic Games in Amsterdam. Four years later, Chamberlin was to win three Olympic medals, including the individual show-jumping silver, at the Los Angeles Olympics. USET PHOTO

winning the coveted George V Gold Cup in Britain with his giant gray gelding, Ballymacshane, thus scoring the first major international victory for an American rider. (It was a thrill for me to duplicate his feat thirty years later.)

Notwithstanding efforts to provide more thorough preparation for the American riders, results in the Amsterdam Olympic Games of 1928 were again disappointing. The United States finished no higher than ninth out of fifteen teams in jumping, while the best individual finishes were two seventeenths, by Majors Harry Chamberlin and Sloan Doak in the jumping and Military, respectively. Even so, there was growing reason to believe that General Kromer's initiatives were beginning to bear fruit. The following year, Lieutenant Earl "Tommy" Thomson became the first American officer to win the Individual Championship in New York, and the United States won its first Nations' Cup at Boston, which was then also an international show.

By the time the Olympic Games came back to American shores in 1932, the ravages of worldwide economic depression severely limited equestrian participation, holding the field at Los Angeles to only thirty-one riders from six nations. Against this admittedly weakened field, the host nation still produced some stirring performances and its first Olympic equestrian medals since 1912, including its first gold ever. Lieutenant Thomson and Jenny Camp were only narrowly defeated for the individual three-day gold medal by the defending champions, Holland's Lieutenant Charles Pahud de Mortanges with

Marcroix—the United States handily dispatching Holland, the only other team to finish, for the team gold. In jumping, Harry Chamberlin, now a major, earned the individual silver medal, a single knockdown behind Japan's Lieutenant Baron Takeishi Nishi, no team finishing as only five riders completed the course. With only three full dressage teams competing, the United States was assured at least a team bronze, but a surprising bonus came our way; a Swedish officer was dropped from second place to last for clucking at his horse, thus elevating Captain Hiram Tuttle to the individual bronze behind Commandants Xavier Lesage and Charles Marion from France. (This bronze remains, to this day, the only U.S. individual medal in dressage.)

In contrast to Los Angeles's restricted equestrian field, participation at Berlin in the 1936 Olympic Games broke all previous records, no fewer than 127 riders from twenty-one nations taking part. As was more or less expected, the German team proved completely dominant, winning all six team and individual gold medals. But even against the strongest teams in the world, there were some very gratifying results for our American officers. Earl Thomson, now a captain, and Jenny Camp proved that their individual silver in Los Angeles was no fluke by doing it again in a field of fifty, while Captain Carl "Rags" Raguse and Dakota jumped off for the individual bronze in show jumping and had the fastest time, only to have a fence down. Even so, the jumping team's fourth-place finish was distinctly encouraging, while the three-day team was considered very unlucky not to have

Captain (later Colonel) Earl F. Thomson and Jenny Camp negotiate the last cross-country fence in the 1932 Los Angeles Olympic three-day event. They finished with the first of two successive Olympic individual silver medals, and a share in the team gold as well. USET PHOTO

The American Equestrian Team for the 1936 Olympic Games in Berlin (left to right) (front row): *Captain C. C. Jadwin, Major W. B. Bradford, Major Hiram Tuttle, Captain I. L. Kitts, Captain C. S. Babcock;* (second row) *Lieutenant H. S. Isaacson, Lieutenant R. W. Curtis, Captain E. F. Thomson, Captain M. H. Matteson;* (third row) *Captain J. M. Willems, Major A. H. Moore, Captain C. W. A. Raguse.* USET PHOTO

finished at least that high because of the tragic accident to Captain Willems's mount, Slippery Slim, who had to be destroyed after a fall at the infamous pond obstacle. In dressage, we finished ninth and last behind eight European teams, but this was pretty much to be expected; as subsequent events would prove, only European-trained dressage riders could hope to score well in Europe.

Though Olympic tradition required wars to be suspended in ancient Greece so that the Olympic Games could take place, modern times have proved less respectful in observing the ritual. The United States had prepared a strong squad for the 1940 Olympics originally scheduled for Helsinki, but these were cancelled; and then the XIII Olympiad, which should have culminated in the 1944 Olympic Games, was preempted, too, as the globe was consumed by World War II. But just as Antwerp had revived the Olympics close on the heels of World War I, so did London undertake to put the "Blitz" behind it and stage the Olympic Games of 1948. This time, the American officers proved that they had learned a bit about specialized European equestrian sports, for they came to London not only with some of the horses that had been in training for the 1940 Olympics at home, but also with some "liberated" horses from the German Olympic stables and the most cele-brated of all the German dressage trainers, Otto Löhrke.

London's results projected our officers solidly into the front echelon of equestrian powers. By the time the Games were over, our riders had accounted for team gold and silver medals in the three-day event and in dressage (thanks to a fine fourth-place finish by Captain Robert Borg). In addition, Lieutenant Colonel Frank S. Henry had won the individual silver medal in three-day, while "Tommy" Thomson, the hero of 1932–36 and now a colonel, rode on both the dressage and three-day teams to earn his fourth and fifth Olympic medals. The jumping team was eliminated; all three rounds counted in those days, and if any horse had a problem, you were dead. However, Colonel F. F. Wing (who later, as Brigadier General Wing, became executive vice president of the USET) jumped off on Democrat for the silver medal with two others. He missed the bronze by just over a second to finish fourth. But if these near misses were no doubt frustrating for the jumping team, they had their moments of glory elsewhere in Europe that summer. Wing and Totilla won the Grand Prix of Aachen and the team won the Nations' Cups of Lucerne, London, and Dublin, all first-time wins for the United States; on overall form, our team was equal to any in the world that year.

(As a senior in college I made a grand tour of Europe that summer, and was present for the Games, and also for the London and Dublin team victories. I was thrilled to death, but cheeky enough to think that I'd sat on horses that could have coped with the Games course. The last thing in my mind was that four years hence I might have a chance to find out if I was right, or be granted the extraordinary privilege of riding Democrat in his last three international competitions!)

The riding community's euphoria over the splendid 1948 results did not last long. Shortly after the Olympics, the Pentagon determined that horse cavalry was no longer viable in "modern" warfare, and a stroke of some general's pen officially terminated our mounted cavalry. The triumph of armor over the horse was finally complete. One con-sequence of this act, as the management of the National Horse Show was shocked to learn, was that there would be no official U.S. team for our own official international horse show, and Canada, France, and Mexico were obliged to compete among themselves for our own Nations' Cup.

The following year, nothing had changed, though several reserve officers (Gordon Wright among them) competed in uniform as individuals to give the show at least an American presence, and the Mexican Olympic champions from 1948 continued to win everything. It was unthinkable that this situation could be permitted to continue for much longer, yet our national federation—the American Horse Shows Association—was hardly situated to do very much about it. Under the tax code of that era, it was not considered a nonprofit organization (and hence in no position to act as a fund-raiser); in addition, a substantial part of its basic constituency had little, if any, interest in the Olympic disciplines or international competition.

Ultimately, an answer to this dilemma was found in the creation of an ad hoc orga-nization whose sole purpose in life would be to select, train, equip, and finance our nation's international equestrian representation, with special emphasis on our own North American fall circuit of international shows and the Olympic Games. (With the first revision of the charter, the list was expanded to include the newly created Pan American Games as well.)

Thus the second half of the twentieth century commenced with an entirely new system of equestrian representation for our country—"a whole 'nother ball game," as our vernacular puts it.

The infant International Equestrian Competition Corporation (as the USET first termed itself) started completely from scratch under the guidance of Colonel John "Gyp" Wofford, a veteran of the 1932 Olympic Games who was elected the first president. Wofford was not only an Olympian himself, but also the father of Olympic riders, for all three of his sons were later to represent the USET in international competition, and two of them in the Olympics. Other key personages in the creation of the USET were Whitney Stone; Amory Haskell and Walter Devereux of the National; and General John Tupper Cole, a fine horseman and great gentleman who had been trainer of the 1948 Army Olympic Team.

The very first "civilian" U.S. Equestrian Team had a distinctly non-army look, for it consisted of two lady riders, Carol Durand and Norma Matthews (now Shiley), and the veteran amateur steeplechase and open jumper rider, Arthur McCashin. It was truly a team that represented our whole country, for McCashin hailed from New Jersey, Durand from Missouri, and Matthews from California, and they acquitted themselves admirably

Key figures from the administration of the USET in its early years: Whitney Stone, president from 1951 through 1972; Brigadier General Frederic W. Boye, the Team's first executive vice president; Andrew M. Montgomery, the founding secretary; James M. R. Glaser, an early West Coast vice president. USET PHOTO

Bertalan de Némethy (at right) with the very first U.S. Prix de Nations team he coached, at Ostend, Belgium, in 1955. Left to right: Arthur McCashin, the team's first riding captain; Bill Steinkraus, who succeeded him in that role the following year; Major (later Colonel) J. W. Russell, and Hugh Wiley. USET PHOTO BY JEAN BRIDEL

in their first appearance on the fall circuit of 1950. Despite the presence of the Mexican Olympic champions, who had seemed invincible the year before, they won the major team classes at New York and Toronto, as well as three other competitions, and even the staunchest cavalrymen were compelled to admit that some vestige of equestrian life might be possible without an army team.

The following year, 1951, was primarily concerned with selecting an Olympic team—the trials were held, as in 1948, at Fort Riley, Kansas—and putting it into training. This was not an easy task, as we had no domestic competitions at all in two of the three Olympic disciplines—dressage and eventing—and riders with the very slightest professional taint were then summarily excluded from eligibility. Among the three Olympic disciplines, only show jumping felt comfortable to the American civilian rider, but even there the international rules in which touches never counted but time did were distinctly novel, as were the wider range of obstacles and the emphasis on water jumps, ditches, and banks.

Colonel Wofford was named overall non-riding team captain for the 1952 Olympics, assisted by Arthur McCashin as the riding captain of the jumpers, and Bob Borg (now a civilian) as trainer of the three-day and dressage squads. Only Borg and his teammate from the 1948 Olympic team, Major John Russell (who had ridden on the jumping team), had any previous Olympic experience.

The 1952 Olympic Games were held in Helsinki, Finland (to make up for 1940), and considering the odds, the novice U.S. team did surprisingly well both in pre-Olympic competitions in Europe and in the Games themselves—thanks in no small measure to the loan of several old army horses (Democrat, Rattler, Bill Biddle among them), which were leased to the USET for one dollar apiece. The U. S. jumping riders won Germany's pre-Olympic team competition at Düsseldorf over all the leading teams, while Russell and Rattler were the first foreigners ever to win the coveted Hamburg Jumping Derby; Borg and Bill Biddle won its dressage counterpart on the same weekend.

In the Helsinki Games themselves our jumpers and eventers both won team bronze medals, competing against fifteen and eighteen other teams, respectively, and though our dressage team dropped to sixth for the same old reasons, we hoped to be able to cope with European conditions eventually. But we never thought it would be easy!

After returning to the United States for our fall circuit of indoor shows, I was lucky enough to get the ride on Russell's (and Wing's) Olympic mount, the then-nineteen-year-old Democrat, since Russell remained in Europe on active duty. In his last three shows before retirement, Democrat went out in a real blaze of glory, winning all eight of the individual classes we showed him in and sharing in several team victories as well. Just imagine what he might have been able to do at age eleven, had the 1944 Olympics been held!

After this promising start, the metaphoric roof fell in on the USET. We had hoped that by doing all the same things a little better in preparing for the next Games we could produce even better results, but we had to learn the hard way what the Army had learned several decades earlier—international equestrian competition under international rules is very much a European specialty, and it takes continuous training and competition under those conditions to have any hope of keeping up with them.

We had not sent a team to the very first Pan American Games in 1951, since the cost of getting to the first venue, Buenos Aires, would have been twice the overall budget for Helsinki. But with the 1955 renewal actually on our borders, in Mexico, it looked like a good opportunity to gain some Games experience. In the actual event there were some bright spots—Borg was the dressage silver medalist, and Walter Staley, Jr., won the three-day individual gold—but now that they had no old army horses to fall back on, the jumpers failed to impress their staunchest supporters, and there were no team medals for us at all.

We tried hard to regroup for the Stockholm Olympic Games in 1956, but the fact that I rode a six-year-old in the Games (even though it was a very good one, my own Night Owl) while Frank Chapot rode a horse that was blind in one eye should tell you something. The jumping team ended up fifth out of twenty, but we were disappointed because we had really hoped for another medal. None of our three-day horses started the last day, and we didn't even have a full dressage team (Borg and an aging Bill Biddle could place no higher than seventeenth), so there was not an awful lot to be thrilled about.

Yet just as the Paris Olympic Games in 1924 had proven to be a turning point for our Army riders, so did Stockholm for those of the USET. Following the Mexico City debacle for the jumpers, the Team had been lucky enough to engage the now-celebrated former Hungarian team rider, Captain Bertalan de Némethy, as a full-time jumping coach. And after Stockholm, it committed itself, as nearly as possible, to getting top coaches in every

Another era of show jumpers, the 1962 squad: Carol Hofmann, Bill Robertson, Mary Mairs, Bill Steinkraus, Frank Chapot, Kathy Kusner, and coach Bertalan de Némethy. USET PHOTO

discipline. Of course, the USET budget had to be enlarged to accommodate this new year-round commitment—something that has become, like the U.S. federal budget deficit, very much an annual affair—in order to provide not only for a much better sustained training program, but for competition abroad even in non-Olympic years.

The new tactic was rewarded almost from the beginning. The USET sent jumping teams abroad in both 1958 and 1959, and they returned with thirty-two international wins, including the Nations' Cups of London (twice) and Rome, and backed this up with another thirty-three victories on the fall circuit. By the time the 1959 Pan American Games arrived in Chicago, the U.S. squads were considered solid contenders in every discipline and the results justified this optimism. Michael Page and Trish Galvin won what would prove for each to be the first of two consecutive individual Pan American gold medals in eventing and dressage, respectively, and Hugh Wiley and his famous Nautical would have won the jumping individual gold, had one been offered. The jumping squad won its team gold medal, while the other two teams both won silvers, and all in all, the progress accomplished since the Mexico City rout four years earlier was considered very gratifying.

Off this solid prep, results from the Rome Olympic Games in 1960 were perhaps not quite what we had hoped for, yet our riders were very much in contention in every discipline.

Trish Galvin and Rath Patrick, who had won the Grand Prix of Aachen in dressage en route to Rome, finished sixth out of seventeen competitors there, truly an astonishing feat for someone who took up dressage only when the proposal to permit women to ride in the three-day event failed. (Four years later, it finally passed, enabling Lana du Pont to become the very first woman to ride in an Olympic three-day in the Tokyo Games.)

Two eliminations killed the chances of our three-day team, though Mike Page and Mike Plumb both finished with useful scores.

In jumping, George Morris and Sinjon missed a medal by only one point in the individual test over a course so difficult that it admitted just a single clear round. In team jumping, our riders finished second to West Germany, once again firmly established as the leading equestrian power, over a course that yielded no clears and only three four-faulters for the eighteen starting teams.

Preparations for Rome had taken place in a variety of borrowed facilities ranging from Alvin Untermyer's stables in Greenwich, Connecticut, to John Galvin's Rancho San Fernando Rey in California. Now at last, however, the Team was able to establish a full-time, year-round training center in Gladstone, New Jersey, thanks to the generosity of James Cox Brady. There the Team was able to offer not only jumper training under de Némethy, but also three-day training under de Némethy's countryman, Stefan von Visy (later succeeded by Major Joseph Lynch), and assistance in dressage from time to time by such distinguished coaches as Richard Wätjen and Bengt Ljungquist.

The improved continuity of training paid off handsomely at the next Pan American Games in São Paulo, Brazil, where the Team won all five gold medals on the program.

Three-day event individual medal ceremony from the 1959 Pan American Games: Norman Elder of Canada, bronze medal; Michael Page (gold); and J. Michael Plumb (silver). This was the first of two successive individual Pan American gold medals for Page, who triumphed again in São Paulo with the same remarkable little horse, Mrs. John Galvin's Grasshopper. USET PHOTO

(There was no team dressage.) Mary Mairs (later Mrs. Frank Chapot) became the first Games individual gold medalist for the jumping squad, joining Michael Page (three-day) and Trish Galvin (dressage) in a clean sweep of the individual medals.

After this impressive showing, much was expected from the team that journeyed to Tokyo for the 1964 Olympic Games, but not much went our way. Our strongest three-day horse, Mike Plumb's Markham, had to be destroyed on the plane going to Japan, and Sinjon (whom I had inherited when George Morris left the team for a brief acting career) reinjured a leg the very last school before competition and could not be used. In the actual competition, the dressage team placed a commendable fourth, but the jumping team slipped back to sixth. The best performance for the United States was that of the three-day team, led by Michael Page (fourth individually), whose fine effort put at least one of our teams on the medalists' podium and gave us something to cheer about as they accepted the silver. (Mike Plumb had ridden Billy Haggard's Bold Minstrel, sportingly sent over by his owner at the last minute as a replacement for Markham to make the medal possible.)

The 1967 Pan American Games in Winnipeg produced more satisfactory results, however. There were individual gold medals in dressage (Kyra Downton) and the three-day event (Michael Plumb), and a team gold in three-day along with two team silvers. Accordingly, we were once again optimistic about our chances for the 1968 Olympic Games in Mexico City, notwithstanding concerns about the effects of altitude on our horses' performance. On balance it proved a good Games for us, despite the inevitable surprises. Torrential rains turned the cross-country course into a quagmire, and this phase had to be concluded under the most appalling conditions I have ever witnessed. Even so, Mike Page, who had missed the individual bronze by less than two points in 1964, was able to connect with it this time, and led his teammates to a second consecutive silver medal behind Great Britain. The dressage team slipped back to eighth, while the jumping team experienced the frustration of missing the bronze medal by the smallest possible margin —¼ fault. In the individual competition, however, now a separate competition for the first time, I was lucky enough to grab the proverbial brass ring when Snowbound carted me around two huge courses with only four faults, even though he had to jump the last two fences on three legs after injuring a tendon. I can remember reflecting on how long the United States had been chasing that elusive individual Olympic gold medal, and what a tremendous amount of effort, sacrifice, generosity, and support from such a huge number of people had been involved. The realization makes you feel somewhat more like an instrument of destiny than any great world-beater yourself.

No U.S. team was sent to the 1971 Pan American Games in Cali, Colombia, because of an epidemic of Venezuelan Equine Encephalitis, but even without this very useful Games experience, the team we sent to Munich for the 1972 Olympics was probably the best prepared of any up to that time. Jack Le Goff, coach of the fourth-place French three-day team in 1968, joined the USET, and had a crackerjack group of riders to work with even though perennial mainstay Mike Page was now devoting himself to national competition and a family business. In his absence, Kevin Freeman led the way for our riders, missing the bronze individual medal only by an unlucky rail on the last day, but sharing in a fine team silver medal behind the British. The jumping team had started the year with a really outstanding group of horses, but soundness problems forced them to take a

The gold medal dressage team from the 1975 Pan American Games in Mexico City: Hilda Gurney with Keen, also the individual silver medalist; John W. Winnett with Leopardi; and Dorothy Morkis with Monaco, also the individual bronze medalist. PHOTO COURTESY OF WILLIAM STEINKRAUS

patchwork of substitutes to the Games. Having lost a medal in 1968 by only ¼ fault, this time we were to miss tying the German team for the gold by the same margin, though the team silver was still a good consolation. Missing a team gold by such a narrow margin was a bitter disappointment to me personally, but I was pleased that Main Spring, my ride in what I had announced would be my last Olympics, turned in the best individual score of the day.

With the continued growth of equestrian sport in the world, World Championships had now been established in each of the Olympic disciplines. The show jumping championship had commenced as an annual event in 1953, but financial considerations restricted it to little more than a European championship with little or no outside participation. Then after 1956 the FEI decided to hold it only every four years—I had been a finalist with Ksar d'Esprit in 1960—and when this seemed too much emphasis on the Olympic year, the Federation decided to hold World Championships in the same four-year rotation as the Olympics, but two years later, starting in 1966. We were not represented at all that year, the costs of sending separate teams to Buenos Aires (jumping), Bern (dressage), and Burghley (three-day) in a non-Olympic year being more than the budget could stand. Four years later, however, a jumping team did represent us at La Baule, France, where Frank Chapot and I finished sixth and ninth, respectively. Only a single competitor carried the American flag at Punchestown, Ireland, in the World Three-Day Championships, but it was solid representation, for Jimmy Wofford and Kilkenny, who had been sixth in the Olympics two years earlier (and could easily have won, but for an unlucky fall on the flat in the stadium jumping), showed their class again and brought home an individual bronze medal.

*Enjoying a victory gallop after their triumph in the 1974 World Three-Day Eventing
Championships at Burghley, England, are: Don Sachey (Plain Sailing); Denny Emerson (Victor
Dakin); individual gold medalist Bruce Davidson (Irish Cap); and J. Michael Plumb (Good
Mixture).* USET PHOTO BY ALIX COLEMAN

By 1974, the World Championships were a priority for the USET, and Jack Le Goff was
directing, thanks to the generosity of Forrester (Tim) Clark, a full-time three-day training
center at South Hamilton, Massachusetts. Now Le Goff took aim on the Burghley World
Championships, and deadeye that he is, hit the center of the target. Bruce Davidson and
Mike Plumb finished first and second individually, and with all four riders finishing well
up, the Team was a handy winner over Great Britain for team honors. The same year,
Frank Chapot and Main Spring were equal third in the jumping World Championships at
Hickstead, England (where there was still no provision for a team classification), and with
a whole new generation of brilliant young jumping riders coming along, we were clearly
well situated for the 1975–76 Pan American and Olympic Games.

The Pan American Games returned to Mexico City after a twenty-year hiatus, and
results reflected how far the USET had come in that period. Where we earlier had won
only two medals from a smaller field, this time we chalked up a record nine, including all
three team golds, the silver and bronze individual medals in both dressage (Hilda Gurney
and Dorothy Morkis) and jumping (Buddy Brown and Michael Matz), and to top it all
off, the individual gold and silver in eventing (Tad Coffin and Bruce Davidson).

It was on this high note of a record Pan American Games that the USET's first quarter-
century ended, and even better, the Team was also on the threshold of its best Olympic
performance to date. As related elsewhere in this volume, the Team was to bring back
four medals from Montreal in 1976, including the first dressage medal in nearly three
decades (a team bronze) and almost a clean sweep of the three-day medals (the team
gold, and the individual gold for Tad Coffin and silver for Mike Plumb.

The progress the USET had made in its first quarter-century was very much like the achievement of the army teams between 1912 and 1936. At first, both organizations more or less improvised their teams, perhaps not completely recognizing how much importance many European nations attached to their equestrian representation, or how much time, effort, and money they were willing to expend on it. Both the army and the civilian teams soon found it necessary to develop a much greater continuity of training and competition before they could reach and sustain the standard of performance required to succeed internationally.

More recently, however, it seems to me that the relationship between what the USET does today and what both the Army and the USET used to do has grown somewhat more tenuous. Originally, we both thought ourselves to be involved with and dedicated to sport—three very demanding disciplines that were totally unrelated to the business of making money. But today, that distinction seems to have eroded, and the business aspects of the Olympic Games, with their billions of dollars of preparatory costs and their billions of revenues on the other end seem almost to have swallowed up the sporting aspects. These days the USET must be prepared to raise and spend several million dollars a year (as contrasted with the less than $150,000 annual budget for our first three years). And in the absence of any form of federal support (such as is enjoyed by many of the nations with which we compete), we must attempt to wring dry not only the general sports-loving and horse-loving public, but also certain susceptible corporate sponsors.

Somehow the new, money-intensive Games, with career professionals competing in many sports, seem to have become so much a matter of high-tech support teams fighting to increase their athletes' endorsement potential that what I always thought of as the quintessential Olympic spirit seems to be increasingly obscured. I frankly must admit that I find many of these developments very disturbing, and understood much better the hopes and concerns of the era I have been writing about in this introduction.* But wherever our sport goes from here, I hope to follow it and support it, and to cheer on our equestrian athletes for as long as I can draw breath. I know for certain that I will prize my own experiences with the USET and with horses just that long, and fervently hope that the words "Riding for America" will never lose their magic for all those who love our country and cherish the horse.

---

*The emphasis on Pan American and Olympic Games in the preceding summary should not mislead the reader into thinking that the USET engaged in no other important competitions in these years. As their sports expanded, our dressage and three-day riders competed both nationally and internationally with increasing regularity and success, and jumping riders most of all, because of the nature and popularity of their discipline. (Between the annual North American international fall circuit and more than a dozen trips to Europe, our jumpers had won almost every major Nations' Cup and Grand Prix in Europe, some of them several times, had won the FEI President's Cup twice, and had come to dominate the fall circuit on virtually an annual basis prior to the Montreal Olympics.)

JUMPING

Buddy Brown rides Sandsablaze at La Baule, France, in 1974, on their first overseas trip with the USET. USET PHOTO BY C. DELCOURT

Many good horses have won for Buddy Brown, including Aramis, Sugar Ray, Felton, and Tolade. But he is most often identified with Sandsablaze, who carried him from the equitation ranks to two team gold medals in the Pan American Games and a fourth-place team finish in the Olympics—certainly a unique achievement. Sandsablaze's last effort for Buddy reflected the special character of this horse, who broke his leg while winning the 1979 Garden State Grand Prix.

While he is among the most stylish riders on the circuit, Buddy is also one of the most aggressive. Testimony to determination is his record in the grueling International Jumping Derby, which he won three times on different horses from 1983 to 1989.

Buddy and his wife, Donna, are the parents of a daughter, Neile, who (not surprisingly) started competing in leadline at an early age. They live on Long Island.

Hunting for Gold in Mexico

Buddy Brown

By the age of seventeen, I had reached some of the goals usually set by ambitious junior riders. I was champion twice in the junior hunter division at the National Horse Show in Madison Square Garden. In 1973, I also won the AHSA Medal Finals riding Sandsablaze.

This flashy chestnut gelding, known as Pappy around the barn, was bought to be my second junior hunter in 1971. He was very rideable, had a great attitude, and was afraid of nothing, so he became a logical choice for the equitation division. In an effort to give Pappy and myself more mileage over technical courses and brightly colored jumps, we entered some small jumper classes.

The Westchester County, New York area, where I grew up, was also home to many jumper riders, including Barney Ward and Anthony D'Ambrosio, Jr. So much of the time, these "small" jumper classes weren't so small. Being young and foolishly fearless, I entered them anyway. We took our bumps and bruises, but kept coming back for more.

The critics kept telling me I was crazy. They claimed Pappy didn't have that kind of ability, and the equitation division was all he should try. I liked my taste of the jumper ring, though, and wouldn't take no for an answer. In 1972, I got the opportunity to train with George Morris and show his horse, Big Line, in the junior jumpers. With the experience I was getting from riding a made jumper, I was becoming more effective and able to eliminate some of the problems that Pappy and I had experienced, so we progressed rapidly.

Head up, Sandsablaze clears a big oxer at Aachen in 1976. USET PHOTO BY UDO SCHMIDT

We were competing successfully in the preliminary and junior jumper division in 1973 and capped off the year by getting invited to train with the USET for two weeks.

We won the AHSA Medal after that, and by the end of the 1974 Florida circuit, Pappy and I were competing in the intermediate jumpers with some success. This was a year in which the USET was cultivating some young riders and planning a trip to Europe. The Team would be headed by Frank Chapot and Rodney Jenkins to compete in the World Championships at Hickstead, England. I got an invitation to be part of the younger squad on the tour and train at Gladstone for a month to prepare.

Here I was, just eighteen, still eligible to compete as a junior rider, and I had the chance to ride for our country in Europe.

In addition to Pappy, I took along Aries, a preliminary horse I owned that I had shown in Florida, and A Little Bit, a six-year-old gelding off the racetrack. My family had purchased him for my sister, Leslie, but he turned out to be more horse than she could handle. I had shown him three times: once as a green hunter, once as a schooling jumper, and once in April as a preliminary jumper. He wasn't supposed to be going on the trip, but I got permission to bring him to the training session in May, where we schooled under the direction of the jumping coach, Bert de Némethy.

Michael Matz, Robert Ridland, Dennis Murphy, and myself were schooled, polished, educated, and drilled into a young but promising squad to represent the United States internationally. Due to a few injuries to other horses, all of mine got to make the trip.

We started off on a good note with A Little Bit and Aries placing in the speed classes, while Pappy finished fourth in the Grand Prix of Wiesbaden, Germany. We went on to Lucerne, Switzerland, and then La Baule, France, where Frank Chapot joined us. Then we were off to England, where Rodney was on hand for the World Championships. Only two people from each country competed at that time, but there were other classes for the rest of us. I'll never forget just being there and seeing all the really big stars of the sport (whom I had only read about previously). This was certainly the biggest event I had ever witnessed.

Buddy Brown and Sandsablaze in training at Langenfeld, Germany, in 1976, during a European tour with the USET. USET PHOTO

In training at Gladstone with coach Bertalan de Némethy (third from right) are: Robert Ridland, Michael Matz, Kathy Kusner, Buddy Brown, and Dennis Murphy. USET PHOTO

The jumps were huge and the caliber of horses and riders was incredible. Frank Chapot made it to the final four, which was exciting for those of us close to the situation.

In Dublin, it was my turn for glory. Only two went clean in the second round of the grand prix, Britain's Peter Robeson and me. In the jump-off, Peter had four faults, while Sandsablaze and I were clear. That made me the youngest rider ever to win this class. It meant instant recognition. While I stood on line for the movies two days later, people came up wanting my autograph. It was a real turning point in terms of confidence for Sandsablaze and me.

On the indoor circuit after that, I won a jump-off class at Madison Square Garden on Pappy. The following year was successful as well. Pappy and I won at Cleveland, and I was picked for the Pan American Games squad.

Fernando Senderos of Mexico had just purchased Jet Run, and that really boosted his squad's stock on their home turf, the site of the Games.

Our team consisted of myself with Pappy and A Little Bit, Joe Fargis with Caesar, Michael Matz with Grande, and Dennis Murphy with Do Right. We were there for quite a while to adjust to the altitude and became friendly with the Mexican and Canadian teams.

It was fun getting to know each other before competing, but the mental pressure and preparation were difficult. There were no preliminary competitions to keep us sharp—and this was my first Olympic-style event. Bert worried about us needing to ride more during the six weeks we were there without having to overdo it with our own horses, so he rented us school horses on which to practice, which was a big help. We all trained at the same center except the Mexican team, which didn't arrive until later.

We practiced in the "Friendly Competition," which was just one round over a moderate-size course, and it appeared we were as ready as anybody. In the last couple of days, A Little Bit had been going so well that we used him for the individual competition, which proved to be a good decision. He and Jet Run with Fernando were the only clears after the first round over a big, tough course. My horse jumped really well, but I knew it had taken a lot out of him. In the second round, we had a foot in the water and a rail down. My heart sank as the crowd started chanting, "Mexico, Mexico."

I ended up with eight faults. With the crowd cheering him on, Fernando went on to win the gold medal. I got the silver.

Even though A Little Bit did well in the individual, we stuck to our plan and used Sandsablaze in the Nations' Cup. Because he was a predictable horse and this was a stadium situation, he was the better choice.

Once again, we faced a really tough course. After the first round, it was close between the United States, Canada, and Mexico. I was the fourth rider for our team in the second round, and when I got handed the ball, there had been only two clear rounds. Sandsablaze was known as a terrible water jumper, the water stretched a wide sixteen feet, and I had to go with a score of four faults or less. And the water came up as the second-to-last jump on the course.

The schooling area was outside the stadium, and you had to walk through a tunnel under the seats to get up on the field. As I was coming out, a Mexican had just jumped a four-fault round to give them the lead over Canada.

"Mexico, Mexico," chanted the crowd, so loudly I couldn't even hear my name being announced. Luckily, I did hear the bell that signaled me to start my round. I pushed my hat down tight, gave Pappy a little pat, and squeezed my leg against him.

This was my chance for revenge, I thought, riding every inch of that round. One, two, three, four and five were clear. Despite a slight rub at the triple we were still clean as I raced down to the water. Sure enough, Pappy stepped on the tape. I pulled him together after we landed, sinking in deep and hollering at him, "There's one more."

Bert said afterwards that that little horse did everything he could not to touch the last jump. As I landed, I knew we were clear and the gold was ours. I took my reins in one hand and shook my fist in victory toward the crowd, then gave a thumbs-up to my teammates along the side.

Everyone had said Sandsablaze had no scope. But they soon learned that he had a heart of gold.

*Melanie Smith and Calypso on their way to winning the Volvo World Cup in 1982, Göteborg,
Sweden.* USET PHOTO BY FINDLAY DAVIDSON

Armed with determination, Melanie Smith came from her family's Tennessee farm to New
Jersey in the early 1970s to learn from trainer George Morris.

After success in the amateur-owner ranks, she graduated to the grand prix. In 1978, she
became the first American Grandprix Association Rider of the Year, and took Val de Loire to
the Horse of the Year title.

But her greatest triumphs were to come with Calypso, the horse she discovered in Holland
and trained to become one of the greatest in the world.

At the 1980 "Alternate Olympics," they earned the bronze individual medal, and finished
second the same year in the World Cup finals. The World Cup title became theirs two years
later, and an Olympic team gold medal two years after that.

Melanie no longer shows, but has remained a familiar face through her television commentary,
highlighted by her work at the 1988 Olympics. She still judges and designs courses, but has
stayed closer to home in Tennessee since marrying polo player Lee Taylor in 1989.

LUCK WITH A LUCKY BOY

Melanie Smith Taylor

I was lucky enough to have a fantastic son of the Dutch stallion Lucky Boy. I've ridden some great horses in my career, but none as great as that one, Calypso.

Each time I rode a really special horse, like Jet Run or Val de Loire, I thought I would never sit on a better one. And yet I got more and more fortunate.

Historically, I have found my best horses when I have had the most difficulty getting to a place, or almost didn't go at all. As fate would have it, I tried Calypso late one stormy night after a treacherous drive through Holland. A small, thin, four-year-old with an upside-down neck (caused by a too-tight running martingale on a young, sensitive horse) was led out of the stable.

My first impression was negative, but I decided to give the little guy a chance. I removed the martingale and loved the way he enjoyed his freedom and immediately tried to change for the better. That showed me he had heart and determination. Though he hadn't really come to his form yet, the power and spring were there.

In trying to assess Calypso's many qualities, his try and brilliant mind stand far above his meager 16 hands and ½ inch. He never lost his cool in competition. In fact, the harder I pressed him, the higher he jumped and the harder he tried. His ground-covering stride and catlike spring gave him the ability to win over all types of jump-off courses. I always felt that with a little luck, we could beat anybody in the world on any route if it were our day.

Calypso, whose nickname is "Lyps," was one of the first warmbloods to be imported as a young jumper prospect. I believe we helped start the trend of skipping over the hunter division to gain early experience instead in the schooling and preliminary jumper divisions.

I knew early that Calypso's career was worth planning in a very special way. He was truly destined to be world class. He won consistently in the preliminary and intermediate jumper divisions. Although showing moderately and without a solid plan, he moved up to intermediate his first year of showing as a five-year-old.

As a six-year-old, Calypso won his first grand prix—the challenging American Jumping Derby. I can remember planning to check how he felt at the halfway mark of the long course, and to pull up if he were the least bit tired. But to my surprise, he was bucking at that point, so we merrily continued to a clear performance and a remarkable win for such a youngster.

As Calypso's career unfolded, the even-numbered years were our most successful. Fortunately, the Olympics also fall in even years.

The year 1980 brought us highs and lows. Calypso was second in his first World Cup appearance in Baltimore. But for a last-minute change in the way the scores were to be tallied, we would have won.

Then I was selected for the Olympic team, but the Games in Moscow were boycotted. In lieu of the Games, the USET made a tour of Europe, culminating with the "Alternate Olympics" in Rotterdam. Calypso's reputation as the best young horse in the world preceded him. He won a class at every show on the tour. Among his victories were the Grand Prix of Paris and the Horse and Hound Cup at Wembley. He also anchored the team when we won the Aga Khan Trophy for the Nations' Cup at Dublin.

I finished the tour as the individual bronze medalist at the Alternate Olympics, and probably easily could have won there, had not a rookie groom stuck Lyps in the mouth with a pitchfork on the morning of the individual event. I was able to ride him with a halter only until the time I went into the ring. We were the first of three to jump-off for the gold medal. One of the other competitors was caught illegally poling his horse in the woods and I was held up at the starting gate for twenty minutes while the matter was investigated. The jury decided one witness was not enough to disqualify the competitor, and I was asked to proceed without returning to the schooling area after my lengthy wait. Consequently, Calypso uncharacteristically had the first fence down and we settled for the bronze.

We began 1982 with a plan to peak at the World Championships. We had not even tried to be in the running for the World Cup, but a victory in the American Invitational put us on the list of qualifiers and I had a big decision to make. Would it take too much out of Calypso to travel to Europe in April for the World Cup and then again in June for the World Championships? This was a definite deviation from my original plan, but I decided the World Cup was too important to miss in Calypso's current form.

Calypso won the World Cup in Sweden without a rail down in the entire competition. I also was proud of the fact that he received no medication whatsoever through the week. We did no poling, nor any preparation other than basic flat work. He always was a sound and naturally careful horse. I believe the odds work in your favor if horses are kept physically fit and mentally fresh.

On the USET's 1982 tour of Europe, Melanie and Calypso jump at Hickstead in England, where they prepared for the World Championships. PHOTO BY FINDLAY DAVIDSON

My long-term plan went slightly astray as Calypso peaked at the World Cup instead of the World Championships. "Four-faultitis" seemed to strike our entire team at the championships in Dublin. Calypso finished in the top ten and was the leading American horse, but not as outstanding as hoped. I think I subconsciously jinxed us, as I was worried about someone else riding Calypso if we made the final four, where each of the competitors takes the others' horses over the course. So for that, I was relieved and able to rationalize a less-than-brilliant performance.

The year ended with wins in the Nations' Cups at the indoor shows and Calypso and myself becoming the first winners of the Triple Crown of Show Jumping, with victories in the American Invitational, the Jumping Derby, and the Gold Cup in our career to date. We still are the only horse-rider team to have won all three of those events.

The culmination of a lifelong dream came in 1984, not only competing in the Olympics, but winning there. It was not an easy road, but well worth the effort.

My long-term goal with Calypso always had been the Olympics, but it took a lot of short-term planning to get there. Our focus at the beginning of the year was to do consistently well in the Olympic trials while preparing to peak at the Games. Complicating this was the fact that Calypso had been injured for the first time in his career at Calgary

At the Los Angeles Olympics in 1984, Melanie and Calypso log a clean trip in the first round of the Nations' Cup. The U.S. lead was so wide that Calypso, the anchor for America, did not even have to jump in the second round. PHOTO BY TISH QUIRK

in September 1983 while winning the Nations' Cup. We detected a slight strain in his check ligament following the competition and rested him for the remainder of the year. Usually, tendon problems of any sort take at least six months to heal. But with careful conditioning, we felt ready to begin our road to Los Angeles at the 1984 American Invitational, the first of the Olympic trials. As it turned out, we weren't ready, but we did manage a crucial win at the Ox Ridge, Connecticut, selection trials, coming from behind to earn a spot on the Olympic team. Yet the real test of dedication and determination had just begun.

Calypso was shod the day before we all flew to Los Angeles. When we arrived at Santa Anita Park, scene of the equestrian events, he was on three legs. A close nail had caused an abscess and the need for immediate attention and medication. Lyps had a reaction to the latter, however, which dropped his blood count to a very low level. We had to tack his shoe on each morning to keep him in work, then pull it each afternoon to soak the wound. Fortunately, we had arrived in Los Angeles two weeks before the competition, giving his foot the time nature needed to heal it and help him regain his normal strength.

Five of us were competing for the four spots on the squad for the team competition. The need for Calypso to come back to peak form was of the essence as far as my chances of competing in these Games were concerned. He gradually got better as the days went by with the excellent and untiring help of his groom, veterinarian, and farrier.

August 4 was the "Friendly Competition" when the final decision was made on which horses and riders would represent the United States in the team event. Our clear round tied us for first place and helped assure us of a spot.

August 7 was a day I will remember always. Calypso put in the round of his life on sheer heart and determination. We anchored the team with a clear performance in the first round, which brought us from the back to the front of the pack going into the second round. Then brilliant rides from my teammates kept us from needing to ride again. We already had won the gold medal. I was silently relieved. I had known my horse would give his all once more, but how much did he have left? I didn't want to find out that way.

My goal always had been to win the team gold medal over the individual gold. Though the individual event was very important to me, my dream had been realized in the team phase of the 1984 Olympics. Standing on the raised podium with my teammates and listening to our national anthem was a feeling I can't explain. I usually get tears in my eyes when I hear our anthem, but this time, I could only beam and revel in our glory! As my clear round replayed in my head, I thought about all the people who had shared in the effort to reach this goal. I could only hope they felt this moment belonged to them, as well as to me and Calypso.

His final grand prix win was the 1985 U.S. Cup, the world's richest show-jumping event, which he won twice in a row. He helped the United States win nearly twenty Nations' Cups and numerous individual and international events throughout his career.

Calypso is retired now, turned out in a big field where he swats flies and rubs shoulders with a bunch of two-year-olds. I often wonder if they know just who he is.

As for me, I was very fortunate to have been a part of Calypso's life. We were special friends. I was the only person to school or show Calypso for ten very competitive years, thereby creating a unique relationship. He had tremendous talent and we were a great combination. Time after time, his big heart and brilliant mind carried us to the winner's circle.

He was a Lucky Boy—and I was a lucky girl.

George Morris and Night Owl show their style as they pair up for the USET in Aachen, where they won the Grand Prix in 1960. USET PHOTO BY BUDD

Katie Monahan Prudent, Buddy Brown, Melanie Smith Taylor, Anne Kursinski—these are but a few of the many USET riders who have trained with George Morris, one of the best-known coaches in the world.

A star in the equitation division, who won both the ASPCA Maclay and the AHSA Medal at fifteen, and a member of the silver medal team at the 1960 Rome Olympics when he was twenty-two, Morris spent a long period concentrating more on training others at his Hunterdon Inc. in New Jersey than on riding himself.

But he took up grand prix again with determination in the early 1980s. Though he characterizes himself as a "hobby rider" these days, that is a bit of an understatement. In 1988, George won the world's richest grand prix, the du Maurier, on Jane Clark's Rio.

MOVING UP FROM THE MACLAY

George H. Morris

The Medal/Maclay classes go back now almost sixty years. And what an inspiration these equitation classes and finals have been to young riders, teachers, trainers, and parents! Without this division, which judges riders up to their eighteenth birthday on seat, hands, guidance, and control of their horse, our standard of horsemanship, both at home and abroad, would certainly not be at all what it is today—the best in the world.

Not only is it important that a young Medal/Maclay rider be concerned with his or her riding prowess, but he or she must also be involved with the horse's care, maintenance, and turn-out. The animal must be sound, in show condition, and beautifully presented. All of these things are taken into account by the judges and, therefore, necessitate that young riders become better all-around horsemen and horsewomen.

In the beginning—the 1930s and 1940s—doing well in the Medal/Maclay finals certainly was a ticket toward getting better rides in the hunter division. To be asked by a wealthy hunter owner to ride in the ladies', gentlemen's, or amateur appointment stake class was the ultimate compliment offered a successful Medal/Maclay rider. Remember that in those days, the jumper division was a stepchild. Hunter classes were the centerpiece for the horse show and as a rule, the "scruffy professional" with the "unruly horse" participated in the jumper ring.

With the advent of the USET in the early 1950s, this situation changed overnight. All of a sudden, riding with "the Team" was possible for the civilian, not just for cavalry officers. And believe me, the possibility of riding with the Team was on many people's minds, if not their lips. In those days, many a boy's parents and teachers thought often about the Team. This is as true today as it was then, except that now the girls have taken their equal share.

The finals of the Medal/Maclay—then held at Madison Square Garden—were really the showcase for the future. All the reigning powers were sure to watch the winner and those others close to the top. Succeeding at the Garden became a natural stepping-stone to the Team's doorstep; the winner of one or both finals was almost considered a crown prince, with his rightful inheritance a chance at the Team. Among the early finals winners who later rose to USET prominence were William Steinkraus, Frank Chapot, Michael Plumb, Michael Page, and myself. Of course many, many others came out of the following decades, and the Hunter Seat Equitation division continues to be the spawning ground for young Team riders. It is a great system, unique in the world, and we mustn't ever lose it. One grade must lead into another, and one good school into another to insure continuity of excellence.

Luckily my early mentor, Gordon Wright, was very Team-minded. While he is most famous as a teacher of equitation winners, a hunter rider, and an author, his real love was the open horse and he inspired his more talented students to ride jumpers. This teaching approach not only got me on the Team but also, and what is more important, correctly molded me for my teaching career. Never did I (nor did he) train someone to win the Maclay or Medal finals as an end in itself. Success in the equitation division, while important, simply meant that one was riding and jumping well enough to move on, hopefully toward the Team. I could never imagine teaching someone for the upcoming

High Noon and George Morris competing in London in 1967. USET PHOTO BY MONTY

George Morris with Game Cock after taking the ASPCA Maclay finals at Madison Square Garden in 1952, when at fifteen, he became the youngest rider ever to win.
PHOTO COURTESY OF GEORGE MORRIS

weekend. To win an equitation class on Saturday was never really the point. It was what lay beyond that mattered.

After I won the Medal and Maclay, I was asked to ride hunters for Eleonora Sears and Mrs. John Farrell, as well as quite a few of Gordon Wright's clients. Because I won the finals at fourteen, I was in no-man's-land. If you won both finals, spiritually you were out of the division, though I competed for another six months to retire some nice challenge trophies on which I already had two legs. Now people who win the Medal and/or Maclay finals can go on to the USET finals.

When I was fifteen and sixteen, however, things were difficult for me after I finished in equitation. There were very few junior jumper classes at the time, so when I bought a horse named The Gigolo from Otto Heuckeroth and Roger Young, I started showing in green jumpers.

I remember winning a Junior Olympics class on the polo field at Fairfield in 1953 or '54. It was a course comparable in size to the USET class today, and a very big deal. But it wouldn't remotely suggest the intricacies and subtleties of courses today, where sophisticated distances and options require an educated rider.

In 1956, I participated in the trials for the Stockholm Olympics. I had The Gigolo and War Bride; Mrs. Joshua Barney loaned me both Magnify and a green horse named Master William. I was really well armed. I should have been put on the Team, but I was only eighteen. The selection committee wisely sent Warren Wofford in my place.

I was very upset—I was ambitious and aggressive. But I got to spend the whole summer in Mexico with General Humberto Mariles. Then I entered school at the University of Virginia. Bert de Némethy—who showed the United States (and the world) how ladies

The American Horse Shows Association Hunt Seat Medal final became part of a double for George Morris at the National Horse Show in 1952 at Madison Square Garden, where he also won the Maclay. Here he is aboard Shady Pete. PHOTO COURTESY OF GEORGE MORRIS

and gentlemen could and should ride beautifully schooled open jumpers—was nearby at Whitney Stone's farm, Morven, so I had a chance to start riding very quietly with him. In the summer of 1957, Bert let me ride in the national shows with the Team. In 1958, I was selected for a summer tour with the Team, and Billy Steinkraus gave me Night Owl. He and I got along very well, and we went on to win the Grand Prix of Aachen. All that equitation training had paid off.

Moving up from the Medal/Maclay ranks was relatively easy thirty years ago. If one had some good hunter mileage and perhaps a little exposure to national jumper classes, the transition was possible. With the help of Bert de Némethy, a youngster could move from Madison Square Garden through an intensive winter-spring training session to Europe—lo and behold, an international rider! Of course, Bert is retired now, things are more competitive, and that just doesn't happen anymore. For another thing, the "reservoir" contains many more potential Team candidates today. Now one must almost invariably cross the plank of the USET equitation class, junior and/or amateur jumpers, intermediate and open jumpers, and eventually ride grand prix successfully at home even to be considered.

One of the great links in this chain, the USET equitation class, has been going on for about twenty years. This class was brought into existence to facilitate the transition to advanced classes, which was becoming more and more difficult due to the sophistication of the sport. The USET class goes beyond the Medal/Maclay in that it demands more dressage work on the flat, cavalletti and gymnastics, and a modified jumper-type course. It is a decisive step for the equitation rider. Those who cannot handle this competition easily know early on that jumper riding is not for them. It saves a lot of time, money, and heartache. This class has proved a great addition.

The junior and amateur jumper classes and courses are much better than before. First of all, the variety is tremendous—often the rider encounters the same type of competition and rules that will apply later on. This needed experience can only be gained in the show ring itself. Sometimes the shows offer both lower and higher amateur divisions, so even the greener rider and horse can build confidence. Most riders in these low jumper divisions have experienced the nuances and subtleties of similar courses many times before if they have competed in the equitation division. Our courses in the United States are the trickiest and most technically challenging in the world:

The final step in moving up from equitation classes to the USET is jumping big jumps. There is no substitute, and it is a unique riding experience to graduate from the junior/amateur jumper ranks and prove oneself in the intermediate and open divisions. Of course, the grand prix is the primary goal. The wonderful thing about our step-by-step, systematic approach toward teaching and showing is that all the riding problems encountered over the biggest courses have been encountered many times before, only in miniature. All the solutions are learned. The only difference is the size of the fences. In my experience, it is most important at this stage of learning for the student to be with someone "who has been there before." Of course there are exceptions, but confidence through knowledge and experience is so important at the grand prix level.

In short, the move up from the Medal/Maclay level of riding into the world of grand prix and the Team is now quite lengthy and detailed. Very little is left to chance. Fortunately, in America today there are many good teachers and trainers for every grade. And it is best to be with an instructor who does excel at his level. Few can (or know how to) work with an Olympic rider as well as a beginner. Once a person has qualified for the Maclay and has successfully ridden in the finals, it is assumed his basics are secure. It is not known, though, how strong and flexible a rider he or she may be. The ability to handle varied and difficult problems as they arise with the feeling (and often courage) of a true horseman must be learned and usually taught. At this point the "nice" riders are left behind and the true team riders emerge.

I hope, when all is said and done, to be remembered for the people I've taught who have gone on and contributed to the success of the USET. That is what has always mattered most to me.

Conrad Homfeld with Balbuco, the gritty South American Thoroughbred whom he rode to a World Cup title in 1980 and two consecutive American Grand Prix Association Horse and Rider of the Year titles in 1979 and 1980. USET PHOTO BY SUE MAYNARD

Another successful graduate of the equitation division, having won both the Maclay and Medal finals, Conrad Homfeld started training with the USET as a teenager.

The native of Texas was a natural who began making his mark, both domestically and internationally, in a big way almost as soon as he went on the grand prix tour.

Twice American Grandprix Association Rider of the Year, Conrad took the silver individual medal on Abdullah in the 1984 Olympics, where he also rode on the gold medal team. The gold-silver combination repeated itself for him at the World Championships in Aachen two years later, where he was aboard Abdullah again.

Since then, Homfeld, a two-time World Cup champion, has put riding aside to concentrate on teaching, judging, and course designing.

PUTTING IT TOGETHER

Conrad Homfeld

PUTTING IT TOGETHER

Bit by bit, putting it together
Piece by piece, only way to make a work of art.
Every moment makes a contribution,
Every little detail plays a part.
Having just the vision's no solution,
Everything depends on execution:
Putting it together,
That's what counts.
Ounce by ounce, putting it together . . .
Small amounts adding up to make a work of art.
First of all, you need a good foundation,
Otherwise it's risky from the start.
Takes a little cocktail conversation,
But without the proper preparation,
Having just the vision's no solution.
Everything depends on execution.
The art of making art
Is putting it together . . .

In the early 1980s, *Sunday in the Park with George*, by Stephen Sondheim and James Lapine, played on Broadway. The musical is about the French Neo-Impressionist painter Georges Seurat (1859–91) and is a celebration of his masterpiece, *A Sunday Afternoon on the Island of La Grande Jatte*. In this show, the song "Putting It Together" describes the joys and frustrations of making a work of art and addresses the constant struggle between art and commerce.

With their usual confidence, Conrad Homfeld and Balbuco clear an oxer. USET PHOTO BY SUE MAYNARD

When I first heard this song, it struck me that Sondheim's lyrics could just as easily describe a rider trying to get to the World Championships or Olympic Games, or just wanting to be the best. As with any artist, many elements ultimately determine the rider's success.

The first ingredient is the talent of the horse, not the talent of the rider. It always amazes me how many riders say they are going to try out for a major event, even without the proper mount. Only good manners prohibit the obvious question: "Did you get a new horse?"

A very common word when horse people are talking about riders is "genius." They say, "Little so-and-so is a genius!" The word gets knocked around like a Ping-Pong ball, and riders start believing hyperbole. I would hate to go to an Olympics armed only with my puny portion of genius. I pride myself on always having had the good sense to attempt these things over-mounted. I do attach some importance to a talented rider, but they are like pretty faces—a dime a dozen.

When playing with the best, however, it is more important that a talented rider become an accomplished horseman or horsewoman. The top riders are able to establish realistic long-term goals, like the Olympic Games, as well as short-term goals, such as the Olympic trials. Once these long- and short-term goals are established, every detail or decision concerning horse and rider should serve the long-term goal. Good riders are also able to adjust to changes, such as problems with the horse's health, and keep advancing toward their long-term goal. No detail or decision is too minor. Top riders are able to set the stage to get a winning performance out of a gifted horse and an adequate one out of a lesser horse.

Now knowledge, training, and experience come into play. These are priceless tools to both horse and rider. When I rode Balbuco, I wasn't accomplished enough to live up to his talent, but what he taught me helped me maximize the talent of Abdullah. The necessary tools are those that allow you to put yourself behind the eyes of your horse. Since horses weren't born wanting to do what we ask of them, it has always helped me to ask myself, "What would it take to get me to jump willingly and obediently over a pile of wood without touching it if I had the personality of the horse in question?" The answers might include more longeing/less longeing, more flat work/less flat work, more poling/less poling, more medication/less medication, and on and on. With luck, I can use my talent, knowledge, and experience to choose the right tools to develop the talent of my horse fully, and to produce a healthy, happy, serviceably sound, experienced, winning competitor ultimately. The combination of all these ingredients by horse and rider is the

Conrad Homfeld up on the Trakehner stallion Abdullah at the 1984 Olympics, where they were part of the U.S. gold medal team and won the individual silver medal. USET PHOTO

Conrad Homfeld takes a break from the course-designing duties that occupy much of his time these days. USET PHOTO

very foundation of putting it together. Without it, you may have your moment but that will be it.

Having now covered the basics for a world-class combination, money—who you know and how you are promoted—enters the picture. How do you get to know the people who either will select or reject you from a team you are trying to make? Since there are many riders out there as good as you are, how do you get the money to finance your ambitions?

If you are poor and haven't any plans of marrying money, your work is cut out for you. I always have disliked this part and have been very bad at it, but like it or not, you constantly have to get out there and sell yourself to the people who can give you work. No matter how talented, successful, or rich you are, self-promotion is essential to a career that not only is competitively satisfying, but feeds you as well.

I believe results are your best advertisement, but many riders can produce results. You must place yourself among the people with any combination of money, interest, power, and talent, so you can promote yourself as the person to get the job. It can get very discouraging when you have to deal with the wrong owners, horse dealers or equestrian journalists in an attempt to get your work noticed.

Once in a while, though, you do come across a great owner, teacher, or horse (or one of them comes across you). Such an experience lifts you to new heights, and you realize it was well worth the wait.

So now you have the gifted horse, and you are a talented and educated rider. You have a wealthy, nice owner and the best trainer. You are selected for a major event. Your horse is healthy, sound, and oh-so-sharpened for your moment. You seemingly have put it together.

Then everything goes wrong and you get last place. How do you live through it? Resilience and perseverance count very much at a time like that. You just pull yourself out of the mire, put a smile on your face, and plod along. It's so easy to be gracious and accept responsibility for the outcome when it goes right; not so easy when it goes in the other direction.

When Balbuco and I were no longer winners, the horse community had sort of written me off. In other words, I didn't have so many friends. I continued to be involved with horses but in different areas, and often I would wonder where on earth my next good horse would come from. I tried to have one purchased for me, but that fell through, and I just couldn't make it happen.

But in December 1983, a call came from Terry and Sue Williams asking me if I would consider riding Abdullah. As it turned out, a mutual friend recommended they call me when the word was out they needed a rider. Just by staying in the line of fire and having a good connection, I was back in business. In that year, I produced some results, qualified for the World Cup finals, fell off Abdullah twice there, and finished last. Then I came home and produced some results in the Olympic trials, went to the Olympics, almost won a gold medal, and most of my long-lost friends came back. The point is you must have the ability to rebound from brutal disappointments and performances, and persevere with your ambitions.

Your ambitions must also demand that you be the winner. There are people who say placing doesn't matter as long as you did the best you could: "The fun and satisfaction is in the participation." That's great if you're a millionaire. Otherwise, where you place does mean a lot. Take it from me, I have two of the best silver medals in the business. All the cameras, the best opportunities, and most of the bucks are aimed at the people with individual gold medals hanging around their necks.

Finally, a good sense of humor comes in handy. Few riders have this quality, but most of the very best are able to use humor to lighten up the inevitable explosive situations during a major event. They are also able to use humor to relieve the anticipation and anxiety that come with the territory, enabling them to bring a relaxed concentration to their work, which is when, I think, you make your best efforts.

A sense of humor helps lend perspective to what you do and reminds you of the insignificance of show jumping in a galactic sense. To look at most riders you would think that the grand prix on Sunday is the hub of the universe. Without a sense of humor, how could I survive losing the two biggest classes in the world to Joe Fargis and Gail Greenough? A sense of humor and proportion allows you to be self-effacing and generous when it goes right, and to go on living happily when it goes wrong.

In show jumping, when both horse and rider successfully put all of these elements together, they are truly state of the art.

A strong combination: Frank Chapot on Viscount at the 1976 Olympics, where they finished fifth individually. USET PHOTO BY GAMECOCK

Six-time Olympian Frank Chapot, who has ridden on more winning Nations' Cup teams than anyone else in the world, is a master at rising to the big occasion.

When the USET was in need of a clear performance to win a Nations' Cup or clinch an Olympic medal, Frank was always the man to count on, whether aboard Trail Guide, San Lucas, Main Spring, or the sure and speedy Good Twist.

Though he had not ridden in grand prix for more than a decade, Frank won a 1989 master's class in Germany, beating Olympic gold medalists Hans Günter Winkler of West Germany, Pierre Jonqùeres d'Oriola of France, and Jan Kowalczyk of Poland.

These days, his forte is course designing, training, and guiding international teams to glory. The USET's vice president for jumping was the chef d'équipe of the 1984 Olympic gold medal team, the 1986 World Championships gold medal team, and the 1988 Olympic silver medal team.

He and his wife, former USET rider Mary Mairs, live in New Jersey at Chado Farms. Their daughters, Wendy and Laura, are carrying on the family tradition by being outstanding riders themselves. Gem Twist, a horse bred by the Chapots, won two silver medals at the 1988 Olympics under the guidance of Greg Best, who is coached by Frank Chapot.

Rising to the Big Occasion

Frank Chapot

Nothing compares with winning the big one—the Derby, the Super Bowl, the Olympic medal. And in every sport, certain competitors seem to have a flair for the big occasion.

When the time comes, your attention focuses on these individuals. And when it's all over, their names are in the headlines. How do they do it? What separates superstars from those of equal talent who look unbeatable at lower levels, but somehow always seem to come up a little short on the big day?

I can't tell you about other sports, but I've got a pretty good idea when it comes to show jumping.

Back in the Dark Ages, before I was on the team, one of my greatest heroes was Joe Green. Joe was a great rider and a big gambler. He would bet that he could win a particular class at a special horse show, and he usually did it. In those days, most classes were judged on rubs and there was no drug testing, so some of his methods were a little rough. But even though we wouldn't use the same tools today, we still want the same results—a sharp and brave horse that we can "spot" to win a big class.

After I made the team and went to Europe, I was influenced by Hans Günter Winkler and his ability to win the big classes. Hans used his great mare, Halla, and other horses that were better than anyone else's. He specialized in winning the important competitions.

Frank Chapot on Viscount in the team competition at the 1976 Olympics in Montreal, where they led the team to a fourth-place finish. The USET missed the bronze medal there by one fault. USET PHOTO BY SUE MAYNARD

Hans would skip the early "mandatory" German Olympic trials, then win the final trials to make the team. His horses were always fresh, sound, brave, and able to jump the big fences at the Games and the Championships. Hans rode in six Olympics, winning four team gold medals and one individual gold, numerous German Championships, and so many grand prix that one loses track. Hans could always get himself and his horses up for the "big" competitions.

I believe Bill Steinkraus was also influenced by Hans Winkler's methods. Bill brought Snowbound along slowly and carefully, so that he peaked in Mexico in 1968 to win the individual Olympic gold medal.

In my early years, off and on the team, I always wanted to win. My mistake was that I wanted to win all the classes. "You can't win all the classes if you don't win the first one" was my motto. I had some luck along the way, but probably shortened the career of some horses trying to win too often. If you want to win the big class, you can't try to win them all.

In this era, courses have become very technical with many distance problems and perfectly milled rails on shallow cups that can't take much of a hit. This is a step in the right direction, as it keeps courses smaller. Course designers can build lower courses without super-wide oxers and still get the results they want. Hopefully, we won't wear our horses out jumping the mountains we used to. But there are far too many big-money competitions to try for; it is difficult to keep your horse at his peak all the time. Every year, there seems to be one big competition—or more: the World Cup Finals, Pan American Games, Olympic Games, or grand prix with escalating purses. We all have to be better horsemen than ever before to win the big competitions.

It is tempting to try winning everything in sight, but that can mean having nothing left for the Games or Championships.

I've trained Gem Twist since he was a baby. When he was young, he would overjump, especially the oxers. His rider, Greg Best, and I worked on this problem by jumping a lot of wide fences. Sometimes we used a tight distance (forty-five feet or fifty-seven feet) to a low, but very wide, oxer. We jumped an oxer more than seven feet wide, but only three and a half feet high. This gave Gem the confidence to jump width without running at it.

Of course, I don't advise you to try this with just any horse. Gem Twist is a special animal and he still gets too high over the wide oxers. But with exercises like this, we kept him brave without his losing a natural desire to be careful.

All horses are not born the same. Some horses are more careful than others; and some are braver than others. A horseman must know how to mix "chicken" (not liking to hit

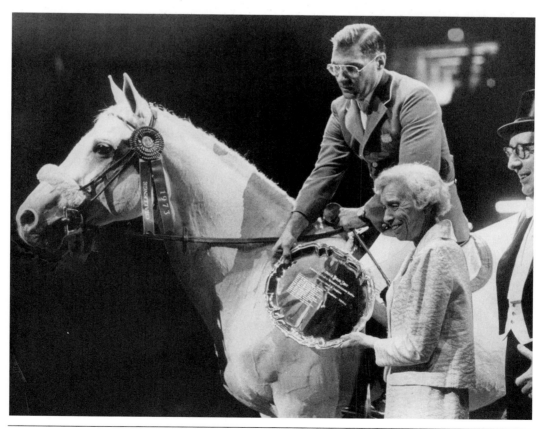

Aboard Good Twist, one of his most successful mounts, Frank Chapot accepts the Frederick D. Mackay Memorial Trophy at the 1973 National Horse Show. USET PHOTO

At Aachen in 1967, Frank Chapot and San Lucas, who would go on to finish fourth individually in the 1968 Olympics. USET PHOTO BY CONRAD HORSTER

the jumps) and bravery to produce the willingness to jump fences consistently. Too much chicken and the horse will stop; too much bravery and the horse knocks down jumps. Knowing the proper mixture for your particular horse is what it's all about.

I think the answer to winning the big competition comes from the lessons we learned long ago. Keeping your horse sharp, brave, and fresh are the principles that Joe Green, Hans Winkler, and Bill Steinkraus used to apply. Don't get primed for every competition or you won't have any horse left for the important one. If you get too careful, you might lose the bravery necessary for the challenging courses with the tricky jumps and liverpools used today. If you get a horse careful too often, you will lose the effectiveness of your tools.

I believe that the success of our best riders is not just their riding ability, but their skills as horsemen and horsewomen. They have the ability to find the right horses and train them to be able to compete with the best in the world. When they reach this level, it is important that the horses are not asked to peak too often. Save something and peak at the big competition.

On their way to a team gold and an individual bronze, Michael Matz rides Chef at the 1983 Pan American Games in Caracas. USET PHOTO

Starting to ride seriously in his late teens after taking up the sport for pleasure a few years earlier, Michael Matz rapidly became one of the country's most successful grand prix competitors.

He has won practically every major competition in America with a fabulous string of horses including Grande, Jet Run, and Chef.

Internationally, his credits include a victory in the 1981 World Cup on Jet Run, Pan American team and individual gold medals, a team gold medal in the 1986 World Championships, a team and individual bronze in the 1978 World Championships and a fourth-place team finish in the 1976 Olympics. Michael, who has ridden on more than thirty Nations Cup teams, twice has taken the American Grandprix Association's Rider of the Year title. He has diversified at his Pennsylvania farm by becoming involved with racehorses as well as jumpers.

GROUNDWORK FOR THE JUMPER

Michael Matz

Preparing a horse for major competition begins long before the actual event. Show jumping, particularly at the grand prix level, requires a horse with more than sheer athletic ability. The horse must be conditioned correctly so that he can withstand the physical demands of today's challenging courses. Proper flat work and common sense in a horse's daily training routine can facilitate the rider's task on course while simultaneously conditioning the horse's muscles and mind for the show ring. I have found that the majority of good performances derive from a proper foundation on the flat.

While each horse is an individual, certain goals in care and conditioning are similar for all horses. Setting a routine in training, stable care, and the right feed is vital to proper conditioning for the show ring at all levels. A horse that is well fed (not overfed or underfed), shod correctly, groomed vigorously, and kept on a regular veterinary program of worming and vaccinations is much easier to condition than a horse lacking adequate stable care. Conditioning begins on the inside of a horse, and the rewards are often felt in the competition arena.

Flat work simulates situations found in the show ring, without the fences. When done properly, flat work not only helps make a horse easier to ride, it also helps to condition a horse's muscles and respiratory system. The back muscles, in particular, need to be extremely strong in a grand prix horse. Suppleness throughout the horse's muscular system also is paramount to a good performance in the show ring. If a horse is conditioned

*The flat work includes a victory gallop for Michael Matz and Chef after winning the
1983 Garden State Grand Prix.* USET PHOTO

properly for the ring, his job is made much easier and a great deal of physical and mental
stress can be avoided.

Whenever I ride a horse on the flat, I concentrate on keeping it as round as possible.
The term "round" defines the ideal position of the horse's overall carriage. A round horse's
back is up, beneath the rider's seat, rather than hollow. His head should be lowered with
the neck muscles flexed, not evading the bit by throwing his head up or over-flexing. The
hind end should be beneath the horse, where it can act as the motor, not drifting out
behind him.

In order to get a horse round and work his muscles effectively, the horse must be ridden
forward from the hind to the front end. I personally feel a fat snaffle is the best bit in
which to work a horse, so the animal can remain comfortable while being ridden forward
onto the bit. Ultimately, I like to ride a horse that can be controlled essentially from the
leg and seat, rather than the hand.

Jet Run was certainly the best horse I've ever ridden in the ring. While nervous around other horses in the practice arena, he was a real performer on course. Besides being an exceptional athlete, he was light and a pleasure to ride in the ring. Outside the ring, however, Jet was difficult to train. He had a very strong personality and it was difficult to keep his attention. Furthermore, he was somewhat hollow-backed naturally, so I constantly had to work on strengthening his back muscles.

I always concentrated on keeping Jet very round during our daily flat work. I would use a bend to correct him if he started to hollow his back. I also used a bend or turning exercises to help keep him supple. When bending a horse, it is very important to make sure he bends through his back and rib cage, not just through his neck. If a horse only bends through the neck, he is probably not following properly with his hind end. The hind end must be beneath the horse so that the energy it generates can be utilized effectively. Jet's power came from behind, so the bending and turning exercises we practiced helped make him an exceptional horse in twisty-turny jump-offs.

In order to establish a sense of discipline in such a willful horse, I was forced to be creative in our daily flat work. It was difficult to keep Jet's attention, so with the suppling exercises, I also did a number of transitions. The transitions helped focus Jet's attention on my aids, while enhancing his naturally good balance. While constantly concentrating on keeping Jet round, I also concentrated on keeping him as straight as possible. A horse that is straight, with his hind end engaged, has a lot more power than a horse that is constantly bent. By varying the exercises I did with Jet, yet still concentrating on the basic principles of a round, straight, balanced, and supple horse, I was able to condition Jet effectively for the ring. I was never able to ride Jet as forward outside the ring as I ultimately would have liked, but some concessions must be made with all horses. Training any horse requires a very fine partnership of give-and-take.

I think Jet's conscientious care and properly maintained physical fitness added years to his career. He was an exceptionally brilliant performer, but the fact that he successfully jumped in grand prix competition for more than ten years is amazing. While Jet Run required a great deal of discipline and had a difficult temperament, I'd certainly love to have another horse like him.

Toward the end of Jet's career, I found a promising young horse. Chef was a very different type from Jet, but he was an extremely athletic young animal. While Jet was lanky with a very long stride, Chef was rather short and stocky. He also was extremely sensitive and tended to get excited in the ring. It took me a year and a half to gain Chef's confidence and realize his potential in the show ring. His early training in Germany had produced a highly sensitive hot horse, and it took a great deal of time to adapt Chef to the American style of riding.

The first thing I had to work on was levelling out his stride. When he became nervous in the ring, he would begin to bounce up and down and then make one big bid at the fence. By levelling his stride, I could optimize its length and place him more effectively at the fence. I did a lot of forward work with Chef, concentrating on keeping him relaxed and level. I rode him at the same pace as I would in the ring and worked to keep him responding to my aids rather than trying to escape them by running away or bouncing. Eventually, I gained Chef's confidence enough to be able to collect him intermittently

F. Eugene Dixon, Jr.'s Jet Run, perhaps Michael Matz's most famous mount, here takes him to double gold at the 1979 Pan American Games in Puerto Rico. USET PHOTO

during a workout. I would, in a way, be simulating the forward and collected rhythms one would find on course.

Another problem I had with Chef was his spooky nature. While he was very brave at the fence, he would often spook at something on the ground or around the ring. Again trying to ride him forward and keep him level, I generally ignored his spooks, thinking that if I didn't make it an issue, he would eventually tire of it. He did stop spooking to a certain extent as he became more confident and less nervous. I always kept in mind, however, that he was a sensitive horse and could spook without warning. While some riders might view Chef's spookiness as a negative characteristic, I tried to make it work for me. In many ways, the "spook" in Chef made him a more alert and careful horse at the fence and a brilliant performer on course.

Working with a horse's particular personality without sacrificing discipline is an intricate aspect of flat work. It is important to avoid boring both horse and rider by varying the routine. By using cavalletti, the rider can add interest to the routine and help regulate the horse's rhythm. Cavalletti are also useful to teach a horse to place himself at an obstacle. For young horses, they are especially useful, as the rider can lengthen or shorten the horse's stride; and eventually, a horse learns to judge the striding on his own. For older horses, cavalletti help add variety to the routine, while reinforcing the rider's rhythm. A horse should learn to follow the rhythm of the rider's seat and legs, thus lessening his dependence on the rider's hands. I often use cavalletti with Bon Retour, as he tends to get bored easily and becomes less attentive to my leg.

Other exercises that help keep a horse alert and attentive to the rider's leg are the turn on the haunches and the two-track. I frequently practice the turn on the haunches, as it helps balance a horse and bring him together. It also helps prepare the horse for the tight turns he will be required to execute in a jump-off. The horse learns to respect the rider's leg and understand the leg aid as a lateral command, not just a forward command.

The two-track is useful in teaching the horse to follow the rider's leg and seat. The seat keeps the horse moving forward, through his back, while the leg moves the horse laterally. This exercise helps strengthen a horse's muscles while keeping him supple. I often begin the two-track by walking forward and doing a nice turn-back. After I have turned, I ask the horse to two-track back to the long wall. Once a horse has learned to two-track at the walk, he can then progress to the trot and finally the canter. When two-tracking at the canter, the horse must be collected and balanced. With my more advanced horses, I'll two-track at the canter back to the long wall, and then have them execute a flying change at the corner. After they have done it, I'll collect them more and do a tight turn-back, almost a pirouette, and continue the two-track exercise. This can only be done with horses that are fairly advanced, as it requires strong muscles in the horse's back and hind end. It can be done in lesser degrees, however, and gradually build the horse's strength through his back and haunches. This exercise is excellent for teaching a horse to follow the rider's leg and seat and preparing the animal for today's tricky courses.

While lateral and collected work can help strengthen a horse's muscles, long trots and gallops help build a horse's wind. With all of my horses that have shown at the International Jumping Derby or over other long courses, I concentrate on building up their wind. By trotting forward and then galloping, either around a track or cross-country, a horse's respiratory system can be strengthened. Frequently, I'd alternate between a day of flat work and a day of galloping. With some horses, however, I'd simply add a little gallop to the latter part of their flat work.

Certain horses, like people, attain fitness faster than others. Some horses also are capable of retaining their level of fitness more easily than others. It is important to be aware of each horse's particular needs. While I recommend some sort of exercise every day for all horses in competition, some horses require less work than others. The trainer must decide just how much and what type of work a horse needs. Does he need much work on the flat every day to maintain his level of performance, or should he go out on the trail one or two days a week?

Only the rider or trainer who sees the horse every day can decide what is right for that particular horse. Like human athletes, show jumpers are individuals and have different needs and requirements to reach their peak.

Common sense is probably the most important aspect of training a horse. While it is vital to have a grand prix horse broken properly on the flat, it is equally important to pinpoint in exactly what areas a horse needs work. All my horses have had certain flaws, so I am constantly seeking to correct these imperfections. By recognizing each horse's strengths and weaknesses, and working with them, I've been able to get a lot out of my horses. By making sure they are properly cared for and staying in tune with any problems that may arise, I have been able to keep my horses competing successfully for long periods. Attention, recognition, and common sense are the basic traits upon which my care and conditioning are founded.

On his way to winning the 1983 FEI Volvo World Cup in Vienna, Norman Dello Joio sails over a fence with I Love You. USET PHOTO BY FINDLAY DAVIDSON

A member of the 1980 team that went to the Alternate Olympics, Norman has been a consistent competitor with the likes of Johnny's Pocket, Allegro, Aga Khan, and I Love You.

It was aboard the latter, a French stallion he trained himself, that he won the World Cup in 1983.

Another banner year for Norman was 1979, when he was third in the World Cup finals and a member of the gold medal Pan American Games team, both on Allegro.

Norman, his wife, Jeannie, and their daughter live in Bedford, N.Y.

LOVE CONQUERS ALL

Norman Dello Joio

My wife, Jeannie, and I sat silently in the stands before the last round of the 1983 Volvo World Cup Finals in Vienna, both of us trying to remain calm. I attempted to concentrate on the course as the other horses went around, and I pictured myself executing it well. Still, I must have looked rather nervous, because our chef d'équipe, Frank Chapot, kept asking me if I was all set. The group we were sitting with consisted of friends from home and other American riders. Earlier in the week, we had all yelled encouragement to each other, but before this last round, everyone kept turning away from me and avoiding eye contact. I felt as if I were about to be executed, and thought I would be quite glad when it was over.

The chain of events that brought me to that moment had started two years earlier, when I was riding on the USET during the North American fall circuit.

The French team was over here competing. Having shown in France and shopped around for horses there, I knew a few of the French riders. At the last indoor show in Toronto, where I finished the circuit as leading rider, I went to say good-bye to everyone. The acting French chef d'équipe, Phillipe Jouyet, congratulated me on a good fall circuit and I kiddingly mentioned that if they ever got tired of Galoubet, my favorite horse at the time, to give me a call. That was a little bit like asking for the Eiffel Tower or the Arc de Triomphe, but Phillipe did mention that he knew of another stallion in France that was very special and by the same sire as Galoubet. He said he didn't know if the owner

Norman Dello Joio proudly accepts the World Cup trophy atop I Love You. PHOTO BY TISH QUIRK

was interested in selling him right away, so I promptly forgot about it and went home to prepare for the Florida circuit.

Then came a call from George Morris, who was giving clinics in Europe. He told me he had heard of (but not seen) a very special Almé stallion named I Love You. It was the same horse Phillipe had mentioned. Both the owner and rider of I Love You had participated in George's clinic in France on other horses—not with I Love You. (Other professionals often use their clinics as a means of testing horses to buy, rather than focusing on teaching and training. Not knowing George very well, the Europeans didn't want this particular horse to be considered for sale.) I asked George to keep me posted and arranged with the horse's owner to come to France to see him.

In the meantime, I mentioned to one of my clients, George Lindemann, Sr., that I had heard of a top young horse in France. Although I had no definite price for him as yet I was sure he was expensive. Mr. Lindemann basically said, "Nothing ventured, nothing gained," and added that, if I had the time, I should have a look. Just after the first grand prix in Palm Beach, my friend, Judy Richter, and I caught a plane to Paris.

My first impression of I Love You was of a unique-looking individual. He had one of the strongest backs I had ever seen, but a very ponylike expression. There was nothing ponyish about his supple way of moving, though. While he didn't have a very educated mouth, his balance galloping was wonderful. Just riding him on the flat made me want to buy him, not a very safe practice, but something I don't mind admitting now.

I played with him over a few rails on the ground and low jumps, immediately realizing what a great natural desire he had to jump clean. I finished trying him over a few big fences, and although he jumped each a little differently, he had wonderful use of his body.

I had never ridden a horse who was so careful. Although his tendency to become nervous put him in some difficult situations, his ability to jump out of them really impressed me. I felt that, if I could harness his nervous energy and teach him to accept my aids a bit more, there wasn't anything he couldn't jump.

When I spoke to Mr. Lindemann the next day, I explained that the horse was a little green, a little difficult, and way too much money, but I had a very good feeling about him. He said he would think about it. The next evening at a horse show party, he called me over to his table. While lighting a cigar, he leaned over and said, "Go ahead and buy him." I was surprised enough to be at a momentary loss for words, but I think the grin on my face indicated some sort of thank you.

The first day I Love You was released from his three-month quarantine in Maryland was very eventful. We were showing at the Ox Ridge Horse Show in Darien, Connecticut, about twenty minutes from Coker farm in Bedford, New York, where I kept my horses. I had been to the barn about 6 A.M. to check on our new arrival and we were all very pleased with his condition. We put him in the biggest stall in the barn (though he stood only 16 hands) and opened the top of his Dutch door so he could look out all day.

Back at the show, I was just coming off course on a preliminary horse when I saw Jeannie gesturing wildly at the in gate. She told me in about three seconds that our barn manager had called to say someone had turned out a mare in a paddock facing I Love You's stall. He had broken down his four-inch-thick oak door and was running wildly around the farm. I threw the reins of the poor horse I was riding at whoever was standing next to me and drove to the farm in record time.

When I arrived, our barn manager was holding him in the middle of the driveway. I Love You had a huge gash in his side. Apparently in his enthusiasm to get to the mare, he had jumped over a manure spreader and cut himself on the back of it. As it turned out, this was to be the only injury he had during his career with us and it kept him out of work for just a few weeks.

Our first show with I Love You was Lake Placid, New York, a little later that summer. I entered him in schooling jumpers, with fences about three feet nine inches. Those were the days when schooling and preliminary jumpers got to show in the main ring once in a while and he was obviously very impressed. He literally jumped a foot over each jump in all three classes.

As the year progressed, it became more and more clear to me that this was not only the most special horse I had ever ridden but also one who needed a tremendous amount of basics and confidence. When I started to move him into the intermediate and open divisions, his great desire to be careful was at first a hindrance. He was in such a hurry to get to the fences and jump them clean that he would put himself at distances that scared him and, because he was so careful, forced him to stop rather than hit a fence. A lot of people started to think he really didn't have enough heart to jump in a major grand prix, but I always felt that if he even met me halfway in rideability, it would be good enough.

In combinations especially he had no judgment or "eye" of his own and sometimes felt like he just wanted to swallow the whole thing whether it was a double or triple. Through repetition and ring experience, most horses learn to judge whether a distance is short or long and sooner or later they develop their own timing or eye for a distance. I Love You had absolutely no judgment of his own inside a combination. He could canter slowly and softly to a thirty-six-foot in-and-out and just out of nowhere jump it in one stride. On the other hand, he could gallop at a medium pace to a twenty-five-foot combination and chip in two strides. Although he always somehow would find a way to make it without knocking it down, he would scare himself into not wanting to listen at all. The thing I really had to keep in mind was that this problem stemmed from being almost too conscientious and wanting so badly not to touch the jumps. It had to be dealt with more as a confidence problem than a disobedience problem if he stopped or made a mistake. For months, we worked only through combinations of various distances but by keeping the fences low, height or width never became the main issue.

By fall, we started speaking the same language, and although I lost about half the control I had gained at home when I went to a show, I learned to compromise with him a bit. All of the single jumps were consistently good and he at least let me dictate enough to him in combinations so that we always arrived at a place where he could jump comfortably and not scare himself.

In jump-offs, I could make up a lot of time jumping single fences, but whenever I approached a combination, I really took time and made sure we got there as balanced and calmly as possible. This whole training experience made me a big believer in not taking advantage of a horse's ability and talent before he has fully digested the basics. A lot of talented young horses are ruined because they can launch themselves into the air over big fences but get confused when jumping related lines and distances.

During the fall circuit, the repetition of schooling over rails on the ground or low jumps in the morning and competing at night made me feel that we were over the hump.

But the first show in Florida after the break proved to be a disaster. Since my last show had gone so well, I had lightened up on my training with "Bruno," as we now called him. The combination of the breeding season, the big grass fields in Palm Beach, and not enough work made me feel like maybe this wasn't going to succeed after all. Fortunately, as the Florida circuit progressed, his attitude improved, and we finished at least on a confident, if not spectacular, note.

In 1983, I qualified for the World Cup as the next-to-last rider in our league. The points I had earned to qualify were on three or four different mounts, so they were all eligible for the finals.

I remember thinking that taking I Love You to Vienna was perhaps a gamble at this stage, but on the other hand, if I could keep his mind together and confident, he had a better chance of jumping more clean rounds than anything else I was riding at the time.

Before the World Cup, I went down to hunter rider Dave Kelley's barn in Southern Pines, North Carolina. There I had a chance to do the flat work that invariably is skipped during intense competition. What works for a pre-green hunter can work just as well for a grand prix jumper (and vice versa). Just watching Dave work reinforced my conviction that good horsemanship and plain old common sense go hand in hand. So much can be learned from watching others—sometimes just by understanding a feeling, rather than stiffly trying to do what you're told, without even realizing why you should do it. So many of our young riders, even the top ones, work hours to put horses in a "frame" only

Norman Dello Joio riding I Love You at the Spruce Meadows show in Canada.
USET PHOTO

because their trainers tell them that it looks better or that the judge likes it. The hardest thing to get in riding is feeling, but that's what riding is all about. After a certain point, our sport really is 90 percent horse and how you can learn to adapt to that horse.

When we arrived in Vienna, the thing that struck me most was the beauty of the city. The horse show had a tremendous amount of atmosphere and the facilities for the horses were fine with the exception of a small warm-up area, which only allowed a rider to jump in one direction and walk back. It was a little like being in a chute, which in the beginning wasn't all bad for Bruno, since it held his attention.

Bruno was so impressed with the ring that he was jumping extra carefully over a few small jumps. Nick Skelton, a friend of mine and a terrific rider from England, was watching and asked why I had tuned the horse up so early in the week. I tried to explain to Nick that the last thing I needed was a "tune-up," which was why I was jumping so many low and easy fences before a big competition. He just looked at me suspiciously.

The warm-up class worried me a lot when I walked the course because the triple combination lay off a very short turn and was a vertical followed by two others, both with long distances between them. I remember thinking that if this was just the warm-up, maybe I had brought too green a horse to this competition after all. Bruno handled everything well, however, and on the advice of Frank Chapot, we skipped the jump-off and waited for the first leg of the World Cup the following night. We went in about the middle of the class, and watching the other riders helped me understand all the options of this long and trappy speed course.

The year before he won the World Cup, Norman Dello Joio competed in the event in Sweden on Allegro. USET PHOTO BY FINDLAY DAVIDSON

I had never really gone for time all-out with Bruno and I didn't want this class to be the test case. On the other hand, if I were slow and clear, I wouldn't help my case a bit, as this leg was judged by converting faults into seconds. The course basically made my decisions for me and I attacked the early portion, which was all single fences, and ended up a little careful toward the end, which included two large combinations. After I finished, we were in the lead but I was so pleased with Bruno that I honestly didn't care where we ended up.

As it turned out, Hugo Simon of Austria, the 1979 World Cup winner, had a great round with Gladstone. He left out strides to the combinations where I had added them and West Germany's Paul Schockemöhle had a go-for-broke round with Deister to win the first leg. Gladstone was second and Bruno third. That night, all the Americans and their wives, husbands, or friends went to a small pub just down the road from the show, where we ate a little and drank a lot to each other's good luck. Hugo was in a drinking contest with the German and Austrian riders, and they tried to get me in on it. After each toast, one of the riders would bite his glass, chew it, and at least give the impression of swallowing it. There was absolutely no way I was going to keep up with that, so Jeannie and I went back to the hotel.

The next morning, Bruno worked really well but I could tell he was starting to get a little bored and frustrated being inside so much. I had his groom graze him all afternoon so he could be outside.

That night was a timed second jump-off class in which only clean rounds advanced to the first and second jump-off. Seven horses, including Gladstone, survived the two rounds. Paul's horse, Deister, had problems and finished pretty low on the list in the first round. Michael Matz and Jet Run went early in the second jump-off, were really in form that night, and ended up winning the second leg. Because I had earned a high placing the night before, I opted for a slower clean round and finished third again, just in front of Hugo, who was fourth. With my two thirds and Hugo's second and fourth, we were tied for points and the lead going into the last leg.

When I went out to ride on the morning before the final segment, Bruno had a lot more on his mind than jumping fences. Some ponies were on hand to give an exhibition and he became more than a little infatuated with a few of them. I gave him an extra hard work on the flat, getting him to concentrate a little, but not happily. It began to worry me that he was going to come unglued. The third and final leg was just two rounds with no jump-off. Points in the earlier rounds were converted into faults, with Hugo going last. I was next-to-last.

In the warm-up area, Bruno was prancing around, trying to inch his way closer to an exhibition pony standing along the wall. Even so, we were clear in the first round and I watched as Hugo had a bad-luck, four-fault round immediately after. Now the pressure was really on. I had to go last and, if both Hugo and I were clear, I would win. A four-fault round by me would force I Love You and Gladstone into a jump-off, and if I had more than four faults, Hugo would win.

I had no idea what to do about Bruno's concentration, which was deteriorating rapidly. I began to resign myself to the fact that I should be pleased to have gotten that far. It was my job to finish riding well and not let the rest of it affect me. On the way down to the warm-up area, George Morris and Leslie Lenehan, who were there as spectators, both wished me luck. Barney Ward gave me what he thought was a light pat on the back—it just about knocked me over.

About three rounds before I was to go, Frank came down and set up a huge vertical and told me to get a rub. My main problem wasn't getting a rub but getting to the fence at all, for to do so we had to pass a line of ponies who were already preparing for the ribbon presentations. I finally managed to get him there and he jumped it too well, without touching it.

I could tell Bruno was seriously longing for those ponies and I really didn't want a war at that moment. I watched Hugo jump a clean round from the in gate and the Austrian crowd went a little crazy for him, which didn't help me.

The main thing I remember about that last round was that the rub I should have gotten in the schooling area came at the third fence. Somehow the rail stayed up. After that, I could feel Bruno sharpen up and pay attention. Halfway around, I knew we were clear and it took a little discipline not to start celebrating too early and lose my concentration. After I jumped the last fence, I looked up to see the whole American contingent standing and cheering. It felt pretty good.

USET Executive Vice President John Fritz and Team Chairman William Steinkraus present Leslie Burr Lenehan and McLain with the USET jumping championship trophy in 1986. USET PHOTO

Drive and determination have been the hallmarks of Leslie Burr Lenehan's riding career from her days in the junior ranks, when she won the ASPCA Maclay Hunt Seat Horsemanship Championship at Madison Square Garden, to grand prix.

The daughter of actors, she decided in her teens to concentrate on riding rather than pursue a life in the theater. Success followed in the hunter ranks and then the jumpers. She has been the American Grandprix Association Rider of the Year, was a member of the 1984 Olympic gold medal team, and won the World Cup two years later.

Married to horseman Brian Lenehan, she operates out of the Fairfield Hunt Club in Connecticut, where she is sought after as a trainer as well as a rider.

THE AMERICAN WORLD CUP PHENOMENON

Leslie Burr Lenehan

Why do the Americans win the World Cup so often? I know the Europeans would like the answer to that, since they took the first Cup in 1979 and then were winless for the next decade.

The first major difference is the fact that we're coming from an outdoor circuit to an indoor competition. This has a great sharpening effect on our horses. Having just completed two months of showing in Florida or Arizona, the sudden closeness of the jumps indoors leaves our horses (and riders) a bit in awe. There is nothing like a little uncertainty to make horse and rider try a little harder.

Change in climate also makes a difference. A sudden drop in temperature will make any horse brighter. The Europeans, however, are coming to the World Cup off a winter indoor circuit. There is no change in climate or "atmosphere," encouraging boredom and dullness in the performance of horse and rider.

Another variable to be considered is the system under which both groups qualify. In America, there are three qualifiers for the East Coast league in Florida in the months of February and March, while in Europe, there are six.

Obviously, a horse that has been asked to peak six times, as opposed to three, is going to lack brilliance by comparison.

Team spirit is another factor. It has been said that the World Cup is a competition of America versus the world, and in many ways, that philosophy cannot be denied. And

Leslie Burr and Albany compete at the 1984 Olympics in Los Angeles, where they were part of the gold medal team. USET PHOTO

Canada and the United States are so close that in essence they compete as one. We help each other, cheer for each other—even share the same veterinarian. In contrast, the Europeans seem to maintain their individuality. A German would seldom cheer for an Italian, nor would an Englishman root for a Frenchman.

My last reason just boils down to the fact that the average American rides better than his European counterpart. That is not to say that Joe Fargis rides better than Nick Skelton, because there you are dealing with elite super-talents.

But the teaching system in America has made a big difference in general. Teachers in Europe are the exception and not the rule. Unlike our system, where horsemanship plays a major role in the development of young riders, equitation classes in Europe are virtually nonexistent.

In every sport, anyone can win on any day, but in terms of consistency, I feel the Americans will continue to dominate until the Europeans develop a better educational system for their young riders.

Two accomplishments in my life make me very proud: the team gold medal at the 1984 Olympics and the 1986 World Cup. As much of a thrill as the gold medal gave me, the World Cup was more of a personal victory. At the Olympics, I was part of a team. My horse went well, but I wasn't responsible for jumping the double-clear. I certainly felt I held my own, but it was the other people on the team who won the gold medal. In the World Cup, I earned the win myself.

The World Cup has always been a funny event for me. I've finished in last place, twice in the middle, three times in the top ten—and won it once. The years I finished low, I had entered feeling as confident as anyone. The year I won, I had entered feeling, "Well, why not go?" That year, I didn't even qualify. I was fourteenth in the standings, and got to go only by default when some other people dropped out.

A goal for me in every World Cup is to finish in the top ten. If you're consistently finishing among the top ten, sooner or later you're going to win the thing, with any luck. Look at how many years Canada's Ian Millar finished in the top five, and then he won it two years in a row, in 1988 and 1989. That shows you something about consistency and a good partnership with a horse.

Finishing fourth on the first day of competition at Göteborg, Sweden, in 1986 put me in contention, and winning the second phase put me nicely into the lead. It also, however,

Just one fence away from winning the 1986 Volvo World Cup in Göteborg, Sweden, Leslie Burr Lenehan is all smiles on McLain. USET PHOTO

Leslie Burr Lenehan competes at the 1986 Volvo World Cup in Sweden, where she was the winner on McLain. USET PHOTO

left me with the memory of two years earlier, when I was standing second and blew it. My thoughts this time were: "So now you're here again. Are you going to blow it or figure it out?"

McLain was as nice a horse as there is, but I think he was underrated. By the time I started riding him, he was fourteen years old. In the two-year period I had him, he won five grand prix—a lot for any horse. When I was fourth after the first day of the World Cup in Göteborg, Sweden, I knew the horse was capable of winning. He had never proven himself to be that big a winner, but I always had faith in him. If you don't believe it can happen, why bother being there? And if you know you're in contention, just keep kicking. After that first night, I felt I might not win, but that I had a shot.

On the afternoon of the final competition, we knew the course in the Scandinavium Arena suited the horse. It was probably the scopiest course I've ever ridden. The last line was an oxer with an option of three or four strides to a tall plank vertical; then another option, two or three strides to a very wide oxer, which was buried right in the corner.

A horse without scope couldn't survive, because if he took three strides to the last jump, he lost so much impulsion by adding the third stride that he couldn't clear the back of the fence. Many horses wound up swimming through it. On the other hand, the horses that took two strides had the impulsion but often were too far away from the front rail to make it to the back, so they had the same result.

Added to that, the next-to-last jump was a very careful tall plank obstacle, so it wasn't as if you could come barreling down there if you wanted to do the two strides. You had to jump the plank with a great deal of balance and steadiness and then go ahead and get the two. I did the two, and that's where McLain's long stride and being such a scopey jumper helped him clear the jump—he didn't need a running start at it.

I was relaxed going into the last round. It was sort of like walking in the gate at the Olympic Games. I was there already; what was going to happen at that point was going to happen. The hardest part of a World Cup or Olympics is qualifying. Once you're there, you know what you have to do, and you do it.

McLain jumped the first three-quarters of the last course clean and the closest person to me was Ian Millar, who was three rails away. As I was turning the corner to that last line, I thought: "There are the three jumps. If I clear the first one, I've won the World Cup."

So I jumped the first oxer, and I could tell when he left the ground that he was going to jump it clean. A big smile came over my face. Then suddenly I thought to myself: "Honey, you better stop smiling, because you could fall off at the next jump and it will be all over."

But the smile came back for good after we cleared that last oxer. It had been a long week.

Course designer Bertalan de Némethy at work with the tools of his trade. PHOTO
COURTESY OF BERTALAN DE NÉMETHY

*In his quarter-century as the USET's show jumping coach, Bert paved the way for America's
domination of the sport in the mid-1980s.*

*After his "retirement," he went on to show his talent in another area, course designing. His
routes for the 1984 Los Angeles Olympics received universal praise, as did his layout for the
1989 World Cup finals.*

*Although Bert and his wife, Emily, live just a short hack from the USET Training Center,
he's not home much. Between course designing, giving clinics all over the world, writing books,
and serving as a technical delegate, Bert has to search for time to visit the Team.*

MODERN COURSE DESIGN

Bertalan de Némethy

Before we discuss the subject of designing jumper courses, I believe it would be interesting to remember the evolution of the equestrian sport, and try to explain the reasons why this subject is important for trainers, riders, and others.

We all know the art of riding has a long history, a tradition going back many centuries.

Because of its beauty, the entertainment value to participants and spectators, and the thrill of competition, the equestrian art has developed its own literature. Great individual personalities, often after a lifetime of experience, published their views and came to agree upon the basic principles of the art of riding that still are accepted in our time. In all those books, they described the proper way to train horses and riders, how to establish the relationship between man and animal and how to make the equestrian art even more enjoyable and attractive.

Historically, however, there has been little written about jumping, or training riders and horses to jump.

Jumping is a natural ability and instinct of the horse, and our predecessors jumped as a necessity. In general, an average horse is capable of jumping obstacles approximately three feet eight inches (1.10 meters) high and about ten feet (3 meters) wide. In ancient times, people hunted for every sort of animal with the horse and used it as transportation in the armies. So of course, they could not avoid the necessity of getting over natural obstacles such as walls, banks, ditches, and streams.

Bert de Némethy in a familiar pose as he gives a clinic. PHOTO COURTESY OF
BERTALAN DE NÉMETHY

Certainly, hunting contributed to the development of steeplechasing, but even before
that, racing was practiced in England. There is record of a race in Yorkshire in A.D. 210.
After flat racing came the even more challenging race, the steeplechase. Perhaps we can
assume this was the beginning of the jumping competition as we know it today.

At the beginning of the century, riders still leaned backwards over a fence, jerking the
mouth of the horse in the process, but still they managed to jump natural obstacles.

The revolutionary change in the concept of style of the rider and horse over jumps is attributed to the Italian Captain Federico Caprilli. The invention of his "Natural Method" proved that he had found a way in which horses were able to jump better, more safely and higher, as well as wider. There is much written about his system of training horses and riders by his followers, but very little by himself.

Unlike most other equestrian activities described and explained in the literature, nothing of historical significance has been found about designing courses for jumping or about jumping competitions. We can read only about the types of obstacles and lines for racing and steeplechasing—which were either straight or slightly curved. Although Caprilli revolutionized equitation in most of Europe, riders still jumped traditionally in England, where the fences were usually vertical obstacles and time was not a factor.

We cannot separate the development of modern jumping courses from the success of Caprilli's "Natural Method." Jumping higher and wider, the delight of harmony between rider and horse, got more interest from onlookers, and the evolution continued. There were jumping competitions (Concours Hippiques) from 1866 to 1912 in many capitals in Europe as well as in New York, Toronto, and Ottawa. Certainly the composition of the courses was simplistic compared to those of today. On the other hand, high jump competitions with vertical obstacles over six feet seven inches (2 meters) or more were cleared several times.

A record height was set at eight feet four inches (2.45 meters) in Vittel, France, in 1912 and the FEI went on to recognize the record of eight feet ten inches (2.47 meters), cleared in Santiago, Chile, in 1949. The long jump record, twenty-seven feet, six and three-quarter inches (8.40 meters) was established in 1975 in Johannesburg, South Africa. Subsequent high jumping records were achieved only by centimeters, so it became obvious that there was a limit to the jumping ability of the horse, just as there is a limit for humans. A need had arisen to change the concept of show jumping and, instead of higher and wider fences, to encourage a more sophisticated course design.

Stadium jumping first appeared at the Olympic Games in Stockholm in 1912. As jumping competitions increased in number and popularity, more regulations were needed. Speed requirements became mandatory and the dimensions of the obstacles were regulated and limited according to the various types of competitions.

The objective of modern course design is that the more experienced rider's judgment and the better trained and controlled horse should have the advantage. Naturally, there are many different ways to achieve this goal. A great attribute in a course designer is a background of competing at a high level—knowing from his own experience what is difficult and what is easy, as well as what is unfair or dangerous.

It is essential for the course designer to realize the level of the rider's experience and the horse's training when he devises a test. The type of competition must naturally be taken into consideration, as well as the conditions of the jumping area, the composition of the footing, and the character of the surface.

Before making the plan, there are also other important considerations, such as the position of the sun, the jury box, and the location of important supporters of the organization. The highlights of every course are the double and triple combinations. Of course, a prominent position should be selected for them.

The sense of horsemanship requires that courses start in an easy way and the more demanding fences should be introduced gradually. The horse and rider deserve a chance

*Bert de Némethy with technical delegate Arno Gego and Prince Philip, then FEI president, at the
1984 Los Angeles Olympics.* PHOTO COURTESY OF BERTALAN DE NÉMETHY

to start with confidence, establishing balance and control. The so-called riders'
problems—obstacles related to each other by distances that require more experienced
judgment and control of the rhythm of the horse—must be invented with utmost care
and knowledge, so as not to disturb the confidence of horse and rider. Many times, course
designers without sufficient experience or knowledge are too ambitious to create riders'
problems, ruining lots of good young horses in the process.

The spectators should be entertained in attractive surroundings. Tasteful decoration
of the competition site and the obstacles creates a pleasant atmosphere. The course designer
should have the imagination to do this, but there also should be a limit. Overdoing the
decoration could disturb the concentration of horse and rider. Obstacles ought to have
a natural, rather than a theatrical, appearance. Artificiality should be avoided. The evolution of stadium jumping began with hunting and steeplechasing, and it should remain
a natural sport with its connection to the countryside. This principle must be preserved
in modern course design.

The line of the course makes the competition interesting for the riders, as well as the
spectators, so it should take the competitors everywhere in the arena. All spectators like
to see the horse and rider from a close distance as much as possible.

As show jumping became more popular, horses and riders by necessity grew more skilled,
the level of their training improved, and the quality of the horses became better and
better.

Through the news media and television, the general public became more informed,
more supportive, and more interested. This happy development makes it imperative to

attempt to make it as safe as possible for rider and horse to compete over demanding jumping courses. Accidents can always happen, and for all kinds of reasons. But there should be a chance for rider and horse to escape serious injury. Construction of the obstacles is the responsibility of the course designer. Practical knowledge, common sense, and imagination are requisite to design safe and attractive fences. Competitors must have confidence that the fences they will jump are fair and safe. Avoidable accidents are not good advertisements.

It is a regrettable observation that the sound philosophy of modern course design is still not understood by many course designers and not at all by a number of show managers. A lot of confusion and misunderstanding remains.

It should be acknowledged that not all courses are for the World Championships, Olympics, or World Cup finals. Even the grand prix with six-figure money prizes should not be confused with the aforementioned special events.

The tests used in such highlights of the competitive calendar should gradually improve the performance of participants as the meet progresses, testing the rider's skill, knowledge, and judgment; the training level of the horse; and how they function as a combination.

Katie Monahan with The Jones Boy, her first top grand prix mount, at the Chagrin, Ohio, show in 1978. USET PHOTO BY SUE MAYNARD

From the very beginning, Katie Monahan Prudent was a winner. She took both the AHSA Medal and ASPCA Maclay horsemanship championships at the age of sixteen, setting the tone for a brilliant career.

A rider before she could read, Katie was always goal-oriented. Though she has been successful in the hunter ranks with such standouts as Whadyasay! and Tindle, her greatest fame has come with jumpers.

She was the first person to win the American Grandprix Association Horse and Rider of the Year title three times. Her efforts for the USET have been equally stellar. She has ridden on numerous winning Nations' Cup teams, was selected for the 1980 Olympic team that couldn't go to Moscow but went to the Alternate Games, and was part of the 1986 World Championships gold medal effort.

She and her husband, Henri, live at Plain Bay Farm in Virginia with their son, Adam, and have an operation in France as well.

ON TOP OF THE WORLD

Katie Monahan Prudent

I'm often asked if it's hard to keep going in this sport, pushing to be at the top of my game year after year. After all, grand prix show jumping has the longest season of any sport, starting in Florida in February and going through the American Grandprix Association Championships in late autumn. It also is a sport where one can't reach the top on an amateur or weekend basis. In my opinion, to be a really great rider you have to participate in every phase of this business, which means riding different types of horses and lots of them, teaching students, developing young horses, buying and selling, running a stable, conditioning and keeping horses sound.

Showing in America is a job that takes seven days a week and sometimes twelve to fourteen hours a day. So to answer the question: Yes, it does get hard; the show schedule is grueling, and the days are long. There are times when it's one hundred degrees and I've already ridden ten horses and it's five o'clock and I still have a few more to ride, maybe a lesson or two to give, and I'd really rather go inside, have a drink, and soak in a hot tub like a normal person! But I've never, ever thought of giving it up, because ever since I was a little girl, I wanted to be a really great rider and, to be honest, I've never felt that I was good enough. I've always wanted to do what I do . . . but better. And I still feel that way. When I achieve a goal I've set for myself it makes me happy, but I usually already have another goal on the horizon.

When I was a junior rider, my goal was to win the Medal and Maclay finals, but beyond that, my main interest even then was to ride jumpers. My first year in the big division was 1972. A good friend from my home state of Michigan had a horse that everyone thought would make a good jumper and I needed a jumper—so the mount was given to me. I have to say that one of the main factors contributing to my early success was pure good fortune. Many good people helped me out along the way, starting with my family. Even though we didn't have a lot of money, my dad managed to send me wherever I needed to go with a car, a two-horse trailer, and my old Quarter Horse junior hunter, Miltown.

Talk about luck, when my parents bought Milt we knew nothing about horses. It just sounded like a good idea to buy a three-year-old horse for their eight-year-old daughter! Can you imagine? As it turned out, Milt was a fabulous jumper with a perfect temperament and went on to be one of the best junior hunters of his day.

Because of my success with Milt, I was spotted by a number of Midwestern professionals, and over the years they asked me to catch ride many different horses on a regular basis. Because of this, I was very confident riding different horses, so in 1972 when I was "given" my first jumper, the thought never crossed my mind that we couldn't go all the way to the grand prix. Hallelujah was a big Thoroughbred who was a powerful jumper and very brave. He had years of mileage in the working hunter division so he was ready to go on quickly—and go on we did.

For several years my coach had been George Morris. As he does with all his students, George had instilled in me a trust in everything he said. At the beginning of the Florida circuit, Hallelujah and I started in the preliminary jumper division and even managed to win a class or two. By the middle of Florida we were in intermediate, and by the end of the circuit we had moved up to the open division. When George said that he thought Hal and I were ready for the American Invitational (at that time it was the Gold Cup) I thought, "Why of course we are." I was so excited I couldn't wait to go! After all, doesn't every green jumper rider on a green horse go from preliminary to the Invitational in four shows? I was so confident at the time (in retrospect *stupid* is a better word) that I even thought I could win! Well, I didn't win but I did survive. Hal and I finished ninth in Tampa Stadium.

Unfortunately, Hallelujah looked so impressive carrying me around that several people wanted to buy him. He was sold shortly after Florida and I was temporarily devastated. The sale of Hallelujah was, however, the first of several painful lessons that eventually led to one of the major decisions in my life.

Over the next few years, I continued to luck out with some lovely catch rides, including Judy Richter's wonderful young Thoroughbred, Johnny's Pocket. I had some great moments with Johnny, but as I look back, I realize how little I knew about anything to do with training a jumper. My goals were sincere: I wanted to ride in grand prix and win! But I was disorganized, emotional and without much of a system of my own.

I rode every jump-off like a wild woman, always seconds ahead of everyone else, but rarely clean. I remember one grand prix jump-off on Johnny's Pocket where I was so clever in angling the first fence sharper than everyone else, I totally missed the starting timers. What a genius!

Shortly thereafter, Johnny's Pocket developed a very severe crack in one hoof. It became so bad that he had to be laid up for more than a year. Being the catch rider that I was,

On her way to a team gold medal, Katie Monahan rode Amadia at the 1986 World Championships in Aachen, West Germany. USET PHOTO BY TISH QUIRK

and not involved with the care of the horse in any way, I always met Johnny and his groom at the ring. When Johnny went lame I felt very bad and blamed myself for not being wiser and more "on top of" his physical problems.

If I had been more aware, possibly the injury would not have gotten as bad as it did. With another painful lesson and my loss of a great horse, I was really beginning to wonder if I'd ever be good enough or smart enough to win a grand prix. It was time to rethink my goals. I had been riding in grand prix, and of course I wanted to win, but just how was I going to do that?

By the late 1970s, I had three grand prix horses that George Morris had found: The Jones Boy owned by George, and Pantheon and The Roofer owned by Mrs. David Clark. Jones Boy was stabled with George in New Jersey, and Pantheon and The Roofer were at Mrs. Clark's in North Carolina. I was splitting my time between north and south, still the catch rider, hopping on to have a school or go in the show ring, still not in control of what went on with the horses in between times. All of these horses were well schooled and well cared for, but I was becoming increasingly frustrated with my mistakes in the show ring and found myself saying, "If only I had schooled a little differently" or "Is this groom really taking care of that leg?" I was reaching the point where I wanted to be in total control of the horses I rode: how they were trained, how they were cared for, when they were bought and sold. I remember saying to my family, "If I'm going to make mistakes, I want them to be my mistakes. I want no one to blame but myself."

So, in 1979, with borrowed tack room curtains and equipment, Plain Bay Farm was started. I had a few customers already, since I'd been teaching for years and had many students. By the end of 1979, Plain Bay was thriving with three or four hunter customers, but no jumpers.

It had been a year that was both good and bad for my jumper riding. Jones Boy and I had qualified for the World Cup finals in Sweden and finished second overall, definitely the biggest thrill in my life to that point.

On the way home from Sweden, however, Jonesy contracted a rare sickness called purpura, which is almost always fatal. He went into the clinic in April 1979 and didn't come out again until mid-1981. It was a big loss for me, but as usual, my mentor and friend, George Morris, came to the rescue. (All during those early years George was not only a fabulous instructor but someone who opened my eyes—and many doors—inspired me, and gave me opportunities that I never would have had on my own. I'll never be able to thank him enough.)

After Jones Boy fell ill, George arranged for me to ride a talented young jumper named Silver Exchange. Silver and I did well and were chosen for the 1980 Moscow Olympics. Even though we didn't go to Moscow, the team had an incredible tour in Europe doing the shows in Paris, Hickstead, Dublin, and Rotterdam. Other than the World Cup finals the year before, I had never shown in Europe, so the 1980 summer tour was a fantastic experience for me.

Silver and I finished second in the Grand Prix at Hickstead and second in the Grand Prix of Dublin (still no grand prix wins) so I came home sitting on top of the world.

What goes up, must come down! George had arranged with the owners of Silver Exchange for me to use the horse for 1980. As per his agreement with the owners, Silver was sold when I returned at the end of the summer. No jumper for indoors (Pantheon and Roofer were out of the picture, too), no security, no control. Bad times but good lessons!

By 1981, Plain Bay Farm was in full swing. I had gotten my own equipment, truck, grooms, etc., and the help of a very capable young barn manager, John Madden. We had some great customers, great students, but no grand prix horses. By the middle of 1981, I knew that if I were ever going to "make it" as a grand prix rider, I had to do it on my own. My new goal was to find and develop a string of grand prix jumpers.

First, I needed some investors, so I went to the fathers of two junior riders I was instructing at the time, Paul Inman (father of Paula) and Adam Sanford (father of Shanna). I made a deal that if I would put up a certain amount of money, they would match it, and we would go into a partnership (with me being the general partner, of course) on the new, great jumper I would find. They went for the deal! And I went off to Europe to find my wonder horse. At the end of 1981 I came home with Noren, who wasn't exactly a wonder horse at the time. But I loved his great jumping ability and, more important, he was one of the few horses I liked in our price range.

One of the most rewarding years of my life turned out to be 1982. The best thing is that I was lucky enough to hire Poncho Lopez as my barn manager. For years Poncho was considered the best in the business, and with him overseeing the care of my horses, I knew they were getting the best care of any horses in the world. With the addition of Poncho to Plain Bay, I felt we were really becoming a top barn.

I was bringing Noren into the grand prix, Jones Boy miraculously had come back, and I had acquired a third grand prix jumper, the gentle giant Jethro. My whole attitude changed; I no longer had this burning desire to win grand prix. With Noren especially, I just wanted to prove to my partners (and to myself) that I had made a good investment for them, that I really did know what I was doing. It wasn't always easy to make Noren look good, because even though he had great jumping ability, he was sometimes a head-tossing, wild maniac to ride. I learned early that in jump-offs I could never, "put the pedal to the metal," as had been my habit, or I would be totally out of control.

Interestingly, my first major grand prix win came in Tampa that year on the noble Jones Boy. He had come back from a horrifying ordeal of years of skin transplants and needles. His neck was lumpy and hard from all the transfusions, and his back legs looked like a patchwork quilt. But he was sound, and even in his condition, had more ability than most grand prix horses. In the Tampa Grand Prix, only four were clean in the first round. I remember thinking, "Poor old Jonesy, I'm not going to run him off his feet. I'll just make neat turns and be smooth." But when the class was over we had won. Not by our usual five-second margin with a rail down, but by a few tenths, *clean!* The vets who had kept Jonesy alive, George Morris, the grooms, all came into the ring for the award. We all cried. Great old Jonesy. If any horse deserved to win, he did.

Jonesy didn't do much after that; Tampa was kind of his final fling, but he had taken me over the hump of winning a grand prix and made me realize that I could be fast without pushing so hard. By mid-1982, Noren was winning grand prix (still never going what I considered to be fast in a jump-off) and Jethro was always hanging in there as a great backup horse. The American Grandprix Association Horse and Rider of the Year titles came down to the final two shows, Washington and New York. I was leading going in and could clinch it at Washington if I could win the President's Cup. Melanie Smith and Calypso, the next closest contender for the title, went early in the jump-off, clean and fast. She was still leading when I came in, last to go. Noren was especially wild that night as we flew over the first fence. Turning to the second, he did his thing, head straight up in the air, racking, trotting, leaving off one leg for a huge oxer. I closed my eyes thinking, "How in the world did he make that fence?" At that instant I decided, "Slow down, smooth it out, go for second or third, there's no way to go this fast and stay in control." When we went through the finish line, we had won! I couldn't believe it. If I learned one lesson in 1982, it was to stay calm and cool no matter what. Don't get excited, don't get emotional, don't push too hard.

Over the next few years, I continued to search for more owners. In 1984, when Noren went lame during the selection trials for the Olympics, I decided that never again would I be dependent on one horse. My new goal was to have many owners and many horses, never to have all my eggs in one basket, so to speak.

By the time of the 1986 World Championships, I had three winning grand prix horses: Amadia, owned by Mr. and Mrs. Paul Inman; Harry Gill's Bean Bag; and Mrs. W. Averell Harriman's The Governor. At the same time, I had three younger jumper prospects coming along: two more owned by Mrs. Harriman, Special Envoy and The Empress, and Mr. and Mrs. Adam Sanford's Make My Day. At the end of the selection trials I was chosen for the team . . . but which horse? The Governor wasn't jumping well toward the end, Bean Bag didn't like water, so Amadia was the one.

Even though I was considered a seasoned competitor in America in 1986, I still didn't believe that I had enough international experience. I was feeling comfortable and confident competing at home, but Europe was a different ball game. Doing well in the trials and

*Wearing the leading international rider sash, Katie Monahan Prudent receives another trophy at the
1987 National Horse Show aboard Special Envoy.* USET PHOTO BY FRED NEWMAN

getting selected for the team had been my main concern for months. Now that I was on
the team, could I win?

The World Championships were in Aachen, West Germany—one of the biggest, most
impressive shows in the world, famous for its massive stadium-type arena, natural derby
obstacles (lake, double liverpools, devil's dike, hedges, etc.) and attendance by more than
fifty thousand people.

Showing there was incredible. I was on a fabulous team made up of some great riders
and some great horses. Conrad Homfeld and Abdullah, Michael Matz and Chef, Katharine
Burdsall and The Natural, and one of the strongest and most supportive chefs d'equipe
that we have, Frank Chapot.

Team competition day was our day, and we won the gold. Being a member of that
team is an honor I'll cherish forever. But most important, showing on the World Championship team in 1986 was a tremendous learning experience. My performance was not
as good as I wanted and I didn't make the final cut for the individual title. Even though
I left Aachen with a gold medal, I was determined that the next time I competed in a
World Championships or Olympics, I would do better.

I learned two important things that year. I felt that I had gained a much better understanding of the type of horse it takes to stand up to the pressure of day after day of competition. I also felt that to ride my best, I needed European experience.

Now I had another set of goals: to find a horse that I considered to be an Olympic or World Championship type—brave, dependable and careful, with a lot of scope and tremendous stamina. While the grand prix horses I had at home were good, and they were winners, they each had something lacking in one of the necessary areas. Finding a horse with no holes is a very difficult task indeed.

Second, I wanted to show more in Europe so I could familiarize myself with different course designers, different terrain, and various shows.

At the end of 1986, even though I again was Rider of the Year on the American Grandprix Association (AGA) circuit, leading rider on the U.S. Grand Prix League circuit, and winner of a team gold medal at the World Championships, I still felt, more than ever, that I wanted to do better on an international level.

At the end of 1986, I had one other fabulous thing happen to me—I married Henri Prudent. This is one of the few areas of my life that I don't want to make better. My goal: to keep it forever as good as it is now.

It seemed 1987 flew by, and although Henri and I searched the world for horses, the good ones were getting harder and harder to find and the prices were getting crazy. As we went into 1988, I had a good group of grand prix horses, but still not one I could say was an Olympic horse. Special Envoy was my best hope that year, but we didn't perform well enough in the trials to be selected. He did come into form at the end of the summer, however, and we would end up as AGA Horse and Rider of the Year respectively.

In January 1989, after searching for years, Henri and I found a new, exciting eight-year-old jumper prospect who had competed up to intermediate level in Europe. We bought Nordic Venture in England for new owners Mr. and Mrs. Bertram Firestone and we had the horse shipped immediately to Florida for the beginning of the 1989 circuit.

As Florida progressed, I became increasingly excited about this horse. He seemed to be the type I had been looking for: no holes! He was brave and careful. He was easy to ride and scopey, sound and strong. The only thing Nordic Venture lacked at the beginning of 1989 was experience. In order to pursue the goals I had set for myself, I had already planned to spend most of the summer competing in Europe.

I organized a schedule for myself to include many of the biggest shows in Europe: Rome, Aachen, Dinard, and finally Stockholm, where the 1990 World Championships would be held. By the end of the Florida circuit, I felt that Nordic Venture definitely was ready for the European tour and would greatly benefit from it. My judgment luckily proved correct.

Even though Nordic was green, he faced the big courses in Europe with ease. He even finished second in the Grand Prix of Aachen, which was amazing considering my whole philosophy with Nordic in 1989 was not to win, just to go slowly and get mileage. I returned home at the end of the summer finally feeling comfortable showing in Europe.

In 1982, Anne Kursinski rode Livius at the Göteborg, Sweden, World Cup show. USET PHOTO BY
FINDLAY DAVIDSON

*After winning regularly on the grand prix circuit in her native California, Anne Kursinski
headed east in the early 1980s to try her luck. But luck had nothing to do with her success,
which was fueled by talent and determination.*

*With Livius, she took the 1983 Pan Am Games individual gold medal and was the alternate
for the Olympics in 1984, the year she was honored by the Women's Sports Foundation with
its "Up and Coming Athlete" award. By the time the 1988 Olympics came around, she was
a starter with Starman, contributing to a team silver medal and finishing in a tie for fourth
individually.*

*Anne, who started riding with Jimmy Williams, began working steadily with George Morris
after her move. She now teaches out of his Hunterdon Inc. establishment in New Jersey, and
enjoys helping members of the three-day event squad with their show jumping.*

NO CAKEWALK IN CARACAS

Anne Kursinski

The 1983 Pan American Games in Caracas, Venezuela, were my first Games experience with the USET. It was not just another Nations' Cup at an international horse show, though that is no small thing in itself.

In a Games situation, there are no extra classes or extra horses to ride. To get there, one must go through an observation and selection process before being named to the squad, as four of us had been for Caracas.

Once we were chosen, we became part of the Pan American Games team, composed of numerous athletes in every sport. The novelty is heightened because like the Olympics, the Pan Ams come only once every four years.

Livius, my Pan Am mount, was a wonderful, bighearted chestnut gelding purchased for me by a partnership of members from the Flintridge Riding Club in California, where my riding career began. The horse was found by my trainer, George Morris, who felt Livius would be ideal for me for both the Pan Ams and the 1984 Olympics. George was right!

Our U.S. show-jumping squad also included Michael Matz riding Chef, Leslie Burr (Boing), and Donald Cheska (Southside). Frank Chapot, a six-time Olympian, was our chef d'equipe, while Chrystine Jones served as our manger.

The experience was not a new one for Frank and Michael, but for the rest of us riders, it was an adventure, and we had a good team spirit.

At the 1983 Pan American Games, Anne Kursinski takes Livius over an oxer on the way to two gold medals. PHOTO COURTESY OF ANNE KURSINSKI

I will never forget arriving in the Caracas airport, to be greeted by soldiers with machine guns. All over the equestrian facility, young boys in their military uniforms marched with their ever-present guns, something I never got used to.

The show grounds were beautiful, with permanent stalls landscaped with tropical foliage. The sand arena was large with great footing. There was plenty of room to school and prepare for both dressage horses and jumpers.

The atmosphere was alive with the sense of serious competition. Press people were everywhere, doing interviews and taking photos, while other sports were on television continuously. All over the city, billboards advertised the Games.

Because the equestrian facility was so far from the athletes' village, we stayed in a not so nearby hotel. In the mornings, before it got too hot in the strong sun, we would work our horses and observe the competition. Many teams looked quite tough. Canada had veterans Jim Elder and Ian Millar riding for them. Alberto Rivera and Jamie Azcarraga rode for Mexico. In contrast, our team was relatively young, and the only one with two women.

George Morris came along to help Livius and me. This event was what we had been working toward since 1981, when I began competing in the East. George was a tremendous positive influence for me in my first Games. He is a master at knowing when to give you confidence, or make you work a bit harder.

Everything was going along well until Livius developed some filling in a front leg. This put a new twist in my plans. He was sound, but the team veterinarian, Dr. Dan Marks, suggested I not use him in the warm-up class, and I felt confident enough to save my horse until it really counted.

Since Honest Tom had come along as the team's reserve horse, I used him in the warm-up class. But as I was getting him ready to go in the ring, I questioned why I had been invited to ride for the United States at all. Even though I had ridden on Nations' Cup teams since 1978, I felt like a novice.

The warm-up area was surrounded by press and spectators who came to see the Americans train. George didn't say much. Michael Matz was Honest Tom's regular rider, and he gave me a lesson while I warmed up. Frank tried to help me with his comments. Former USET jumping coach Bertalan de Némethy was the technical delegate, so as I made my way to the arena, he had a bit more advice for me.

The course was rather inviting and straightforward, thank goodness. Honest Tom and I had a comfortable clear round, and it felt good to get that under my belt and see how happy all my coaches were.

Though I was concerned about Livius's leg, Dr. Marks felt the horse would be fine in competition. We were there, after all, as part of the U.S. team. This wasn't just another horse show, and there are chances you must take in a team situation. Livius looked fine jogging in hand and felt ready to perform under saddle. Our time was now or never.

The initial round of the Pan Am games was scored against the clock. Speed classes never were my strong suit, but Livius and I were prepared to give it a go.

Galloping around the course at the 1983 Pan American Games, Anne and Livius are intent on their job. PHOTO COURTESY OF ANNE KURSINSKI

*On the highest level of the podium, Anne Kursinski accepts her individual gold
medal for the 1983 Pan American Games. The silver went to James Elder of
Canada (right), the bronze to Anne's teammate Michael Matz (left).* PHOTO
COURTESY OF ANNE KURSINSKI

Our team walked the beautiful course designed by West Germany's Arno Gego, known
for doing the routes at his country's famed Aachen show. The jumps and foliage were
tropical with a Latin-American flavor. The fences were not too high, but required a careful
ride if they were to stay up. After walking the course with Frank, and then with George,
I felt confident about our plan.

The press and onlookers in the warm-up area had become distracting. I began to tighten
up, but Livius seemed happy.

Once in the arena, however, I rode "backwards" to the first fence instead of flowing
forward freely. The rest of the course was slow and stiff, and Livius finally knocked down
a fence as old, bad habits I had tried to correct surfaced in the tension.

George spoke strongly to me, telling me how poorly I had ridden. I felt I had let down
everyone—Livius, his owners, my teammates, George, and the USET. How could I have
ridden so badly? I was seventeenth in the individual standings, and figured I would never
qualify to ride in the individual event the final day.

I tried to get control over my mind. Chrystine Jones had organized a sports psychology
seminar just prior to the Games. I tried to put into use all that the speaker, Dr. Robert
Rotella, had said about concentration, shutting things out of my mind and focusing. From
now on, I would think "let go" and "relax." Some people may not believe in sports
psychology, but it helped turn things around for me during that week in Caracas.

The second leg of the Games is the team competition. That meant my scores would affect the whole team and I had to ride well. My teammates were great in the speed class, all finishing in the top placings. I just hoped I wouldn't let them down.

This course was very difficult, with huge fences, but the sizable jumps were in Livius' best interest. He could jump anything if I rode him right.

Frank put me in first of the American riders. George always felt I rode best in that position. We had our plan of attack and I stuck to it. Livius and I were on the money that day. He jumped two effortless clear rounds and I redeemed myself. What a thrilling moment it was when I stood on top of the podium with Leslie, Donald, and Michael to receive our gold medals.

Only three riders per country were allowed to compete for the individual medals, and my double-clear had earned me the right to take a shot at them. There seemed no hope of getting an individual medal, but I was excited about the chance of competing again anyway.

My main concern was whether Livius was physically up to one more grueling day of jumping. His leg was not perfect to look at, but he didn't seem to notice the problem. Somehow, he knew how important this competition was.

Going into the final event I was not thinking about winning. I just wanted to ride well and make a good showing. Perhaps with a bit of luck I could move up in the placings, but a medal appeared totally impossible.

The course for the individual test was enormous, very European in its dimensions, scopey combinations and tall verticals. This was right up Livius's alley. George and I had discussed how to ride each line and I was confident about our strategy.

As I watched the other riders have rails down and problems at the water, I focused more on my route. George kept our warm-up calm and simple, trusting Livius and me. This gave me tremendous confidence. We walked into the stadium with a goal of jumping a clear round and we did, just as planned.

This moved us way up in the standings. Suddenly an individual medal was in sight. I could not let myself think about that, however. If I did, I would be certain to stiffen up.

In the final round, more horses had trouble. Though many were tired from so many large courses, Livius felt ready to show his strength. I just tried to stay with him, loose and relaxed. It was the correct strategy, as we scored another faultless round. The only trouble I had was believing it.

There were still great riders closer to a medal that had to jump after I did. I couldn't watch, but listened to the crowd as rails fell. When the final rider, Canadian Jim Elder, completed his round, I was walking in front of the grandstand toward the in gate. The crowd cheered wildly as I passed, but I wasn't sure if they were cheering for Jimmy or me.

As I neared the in gate, I learned the answer. Everyone congratulated me. Livius had outjumped them all to capture the individual gold medal for me.

Standing on the podium between two such accomplished horsemen as Jim Elder, who had taken the silver, and Michael Matz, who won the bronze, it all seemed like a Walt Disney story come true.

A partnership of friends bought Livius for me to compete with. From the first day in Caracas, beginning in seventeenth place with no chance for an individual placing, we had come all the way to the gold medal. It seemed a fairy tale, but it was true.

The crowd watches in rapt silence as Touch of Class curls over a vertical at the Los Angeles Olympic Games. USET PHOTO

With a style that is envied around the world, Joe Fargis is among an elite group at the pinnacle of show jumping, having two Olympic gold medals to his credit.

He rode Touch of Class to the team and individual golds at the Los Angeles Games in 1984. Four years later in Seoul, he was aboard Mill Pearl, an Irishbred mare he trained from the ground up, to ride on the silver medal squad.

As good a teacher and trainer as he is a rider, Joe has been competing for the team since 1970 and has performed well with a variety of horses, including Pueblo, Caesar, Abdullah, Bonte II, and Old English, in addition to his two famous mares.

CLASS WILL TELL

Joe Fargis

From the beginning, Touch of Class was a winner. She had many riders, and all of us who rode her—Debbie Connor, Jamie Mann, my business partner Conrad Homfeld, myself—won with her.

Touch of Class came to us as a preliminary jumper when Janet Nonni owned her and Debbie Connor was the rider. It was apparent that Touch of Class was a nice horse. You didn't have to be a genius to discover her. She was easy to take care of, she was a good shipper, and she could be ridden by anybody. The mare had good fundamentals and she had been with a lot of good people.

I started riding her at the intermediate level. Debbie, who rode her to the intermediate championship at the Washington International Horse Show, had stopped working for Janet, so I took over.

Certainly, I wasn't thinking Olympics at that time. The Games were a long way off and my immediate goals are usually day-to-day things. Besides, it was a post-Olympic year, which made it a relatively uneventful season in terms of international show jumping.

Our first attempt at the open division was the Upperville Grand Prix in 1981, where she was fifth. Touch of Class went on that year to win classes at Harrisburg, Washington, and New York.

Meanwhile, Janet Nonni had said the mare was for sale, and we wanted her in our barn. So in January 1982 Mr. and Mrs. Patrick Butler, Mr. and Mrs. Brownlee Currey,

Pam Hall, Earle Mack, and Sandron (the business Conrad and I own and operate) bought the mare. (Just before the Olympics, Pam had to sell out, so she missed having her name there; but she was with us in spirit, for sure.)

The next big thing was trying out for the World Championships at Dublin in 1982, and we made that team. We went to Hickstead, England, for a warm-up show, and I broke my leg after falling from the first horse in the first class over the first fence at the first Hickstead meeting of the year. I was extremely disappointed—for me, it seemed like the end of the world.

It took more than six months for my leg to heal. So Conrad rode Touch of Class for the rest of 1982. Needless to say, the two were brilliant. With Conrad in the saddle, she was in good hands. A high point was her victory in the Grand Prix of Southampton. They also qualified that fall for the World Cup finals in Vienna the following spring, where they finished fourth.

I was a bad patient, horrible to be around, because I just wanted to be riding. Looking back, however, I benefitted from watching Conrad ride the horse. It helped me improve my performance when I began riding again.

With her characteristic poise, Touch of Class takes Joe Fargis across an oxer at the Los Angeles Olympic Games in 1984, where he won two gold medals. USET PHOTO

When I finally returned in 1983 in Florida, I rode all the horses too cautiously, subconsciously worrying about another fall. But time overcame that.

I took Touch of Class to Rome and Calgary, where she was on both winning Nations' Cup teams. Then the thought of the Olympics entered my mind. We were jumping in serious international competition, and it was working.

In 1984, the Olympic year, the first trial for the Games was the American Invitational. The week before, Touch of Class had won the Grand Prix of Tampa. In the Invitational, however, she had sixteen faults. I felt as if we had levelled the course. The horse went poorly; there were no excuses. I didn't change her work at that point, but I had to calm myself. I kept telling myself that I had to rely on the quality of the animal.

Four weeks later, she started to feel good again. She had four faults at the next trial, Valley Forge, Pennsylvania, in early May. Later that month came Old Salem, in North Salem, New York—a clear round and a four-fault round. Then in Darien, Connecticut, at Ox Ridge, she had two clear rounds, she was second, and she was great, as good as ever.

Touch of Class was starting to be precocious and bold, like her old self. I felt if I could just hold it together through the last trial at Lake Placid, New York, there was a good chance of making the team. That was a two-rounder, and she had four faults and a clear. Although she was being quite consistent and reliable, I still had my doubts about being selected, because one is never really sure of making any team. It was a very close call for the selection that year, with eight to ten horse-rider combinations in contention.

When we found out that both Conrad and I had made the squad for Los Angeles, we stopped showing in order to concentrate on the Olympics. During that time, I tried not to change one thing in Touch of Class's program. I didn't get inventive, keeping the routine as basic as possible.

Making the team was the thrill of a lifetime. The trials had been hard, and most of the time in our game, it doesn't work out. So I was happy to have made it that far.

But the first day I got on her at Santa Anita Park, where the show jumping would be held, my mood took a giant swing. The exercise area was on the racetrack, and Touch of Class did what any Thoroughbred might do under the circumstances—she remembered her racing days. She had started in just seven races, probably within a year's time, and she obviously had not forgotten what it was all about. She was in a lather within a minute, and any control I had over her was gone.

I always imagine things to be a lot worse than they are. I questioned what I was doing there, and thought, well, let's just see what tomorrow brings. It took at least a week for the horse to come back to a semblance of her former self. At that point, I started getting her out several times a day—never hard work, just lots and lots of walks.

Veteran California trainer Jimmy Williams said that if he were in my position, he'd keep her away from the racetrack. I took his advice and we went to the farthest corner of the park to do our work. And as the Olympics came closer, the track began to lose its look a little bit. When they started building the stands, the arena began to take shape. There no longer was a homestretch you had to walk by, and she started to calm down.

Things finally started taking a good direction. First came the warm-up class, where she had a clean round. I don't like to give horses human qualities, and I'm sure this horse didn't know it was a big occasion. But she became a very reliable, steady animal that started doing what she had been trained to do. All her reactions were very straightforward.

Joe Fargis competes at Aachen in 1985 on Touch of Class. USET PHOTO BY FINDLAY DAVIDSON

In a sense, the warm-up class had served as another trial. Four out of five of us were going to ride, and I was one of the lucky ones. In the Nations' Cup for the team medals, I was the first of our team to go. I watched the first two horses in the competition, and the rounds were not good at all. Again, in my typical fashion, I kept thinking, "What am I doing here?" I was worried.

The minute the warm-up started, though, things became quite settled in my mind, because the horse was again responding beautifully to the years of training. And by the time we walked through the gate, I believed the preparation for that moment was as solid as it could be. Once she jumped the first fence, I felt it was not going to be a disaster. As she continued, the horse was in a great gear, a great humor, responding perfectly. I became very comfortable mentally and physically, and started to have a good time with the course. The class and quality of the horse helped me have the peace of mind to ride well.

When I finished the round, I was as happy as a person could be. The team was off to a great start and I had done my part.

As the day progressed, we took a commanding lead and were starting to have fun with it a little bit—confidence breeds confidence. I had relaxed and the horse had relaxed in the stadium. I was breathing the second time I went.

The class of the horse *did* tell in Los Angeles. She had the stamina to do the two rounds and jump them clear. She is a Thoroughbred, and I'm sure the breeding helped, because the European warmbloods may have had a hard time in the California heat.

It is unusual for me to be elated, but I was just "up" as we received our medals. It was a happy moment for everyone—the riders, the owners, the grooms, everybody. We were in Los Angeles, and the fans were thrilled to see the Americans win. On that team were four fabulous horses. It would be hard to duplicate that team for any country in any Olympics. Among Touch of Class, Abdullah, Calypso, and Albany, it was class all the way. Every foot of every horse was solid. At their best, they were all as brilliant as anything there was in the world. And on that day, they were at their best.

Everybody took a deep breath. There was a big load off our backs because we'd won the Nations' Cup. But then the tension returned with the question of who would be picked for the individual medal contest. There were five of us there and two people were going to be left out. I had my doubts about my chances even after having done well.

But I was selected again. On Saturday, the day before the competition, we schooled normally over an oxer-vertical combination. I was totally relaxed. How could I duplicate my previous performance? I was grateful for what had happened so far, and anything that occurred that day would have been fine. Not that I wasn't going to try, but I was prepared for the worst, and if it came, nothing could keep me from being happy.

The course for the first round of the individual was approximately the same dimensions as it had been for the Nations' Cup, and we rode clean again. But when it came to the second round, I really had some questions. Touch of Class had never jumped anything that big and I knew it would be the hardest test the horse had ever faced.

Again she rallied and did everything asked of her. We had four faults in the second round as we knocked down the last jump, a vertical, which was excusable. After all these clear efforts on her part, it wasn't even a serious fault. She had just touched it and it came down, tying Conrad and me for the lead.

I remember Conrad and me before the jump-off jumping over the same jumps and having a good time with it. We were the winners for sure, one gold medal and one silver. It was just a question of who would get which.

He had the bad draw and had to go first, winding up with two rails down as he pushed for speed. I opted not to go so fast and tried to finish clear. Touch of Class cooperated. All I could think was "thank God."

It never crossed my mind that I might win two gold medals. I went in with the objective of doing the best I could. None of us had any idea how the Olympics would take shape; none of us had any idea it would be so successful.

But it all came about as the result of having four horses that were bursting with class, and as we learned in Los Angeles, class will tell.

Gem Twist always makes the oxers look easy. USET PHOTO BY KARL LECK

Though Greg Best's rise in the grand prix ranks was meteoric, taking him from rookie to Olympian in eighteen months, he labored in the equestrian vineyards for years before that to gain the foundation that would serve him well internationally.

The New Jersey resident started riding under the guidance of his mother, Maxine, a professional horsewoman who specializes in ponies and hunters.

When her son was fifteen, Mrs. Best brought him to six-time Olympian Frank Chapot for training. Chapot's back trouble was being aggravated by the energetic jumping style of Gem Twist, a gray homebred son of his favorite speed mount, Good Twist, out of a Thoroughbred mare named Coldly Noble.

Greg and the young jumper prospect clicked, eventually winning the Rolex/USET Talent Derby before breaking into the grand prix ranks. In 1987, his first year on the American Grandprix Association circuit, Greg was Rookie of the Year and Gem Twist (also a rookie) was Horse of the Year, an unusual combination and an unparalleled one.

Chapot was the chef d'équipe at the 1988 Seoul Olympics, where Greg and Gem took two silver medals, making it a special triumph for everyone involved.

SILVER IN SEOUL

Greg Best

Every little boy has a dream. Some dream of pitching in the World Series, some of playing in the Super Bowl. My dream was to ride in the Olympic Games.

I started riding and showing at the age of four and got my first taste of success in the leadline class at the Hamburg Fair Horse Show. Although I don't really remember being struck with Olympic fever right away, I'm sure that the possibilities seemed endless after parading around with a fourth-place ribbon on my coat pocket.

Over the next fifteen years or so, my riding career progressed naturally. I met with considerable success during my early years in the walk-trot and short-stirrup divisions. And I began to dream of Olympic stardom. I would imagine my pony, Trinket, and me galloping over those huge fences and racing home to victory. The picture is still vivid in my mind: Trinket, with her long pinto coat, pink pom-poms in her meatball-size braids, and me in my little red, white, and blue plaid jacket with a blue clip-on bow tie, soaring effortlessly over the course. Eventually, of course, Trinket was retired and I dreamed of new Olympic mounts.

Looking back on my short career, I consider the pony years to be among the most influential. It was then that I first received recognition as a good rider. I was given some great ponies to ride and show (as well as some not-so-great ponies), and I gained the confidence that it takes to be a winner. I got to meet and know such famous riders as

Greg Best on Gem Twist at the 1988 Olympic trials at Lake Placid. USET PHOTO
BY FRED NEWMAN

Melanie Smith, Joe Fargis, and Leslie Burr. But most important, I had the opportunity to
tell people about my dream of riding for the USET.

When I graduated from the University of Pennsylvania in May 1986, I made my first
real commitment to riding. All through grade school and high school, as I moved from
ponies to junior hunters and jumpers, my studies were my first priority. If I felt that my
riding was interfering with my education, I backed off the riding. Finally, when I finished
college, I could make riding my main objective. One of the decisive influences on me was
Michael Golden's Gem Twist, a super young preliminary, soon-to-be-intermediate, horse
that I had been showing. And, if I were ever going to put to rest this dream of mine, now
was the time to do it.

Early in 1987, I rode in my first grand prix. Four weeks later, I won back-to-back grand
prix in Tampa. Later that summer, I was on the USET for the first time at the Pan American
Games. Having never ridden for the Team before, I did not really know what to expect.
What a shock! It's a little bit different riding for your country than it is riding for yourself.
I knew it would be, but there is no substitute for experience and I just hoped that the

experience I got wouldn't hurt my chances for making future teams. After all, the next year was a big one.

By the end of the '87 season Gem and I were a lot wiser. Some even said we might make the Olympic team. All through the summer and fall, I still thought of myself as too inexperienced to be considered in 1988, even though I knew that Gem could do it. Then in December, we returned to Tampa (where we had had success early in the year) for the AGA Championships. Winning the event was my greatest achievement; for the first time, I believed I had ridden consistently well in a pressure situation. And for the first time, I believed that a lifelong dream had a chance to become reality.

But going into the Olympic trials, I still felt that I had something to prove: to the selection committee, that I was good enough to be an Olympian; and to myself, that I wouldn't be fooling the selection committee.

Old Salem was the first official trial, and Gem was great. By winning that day, I knew that we were going to be among the leading candidates for the team.

At Ox Ridge and Lake Placid we got ribbons in the grand prix, and after winning the final phase of the trials at Southampton, I thought that they had to take me. And so they did.

Soon after the class, it came time for me to begin my duties as an Olympian, and first on the list was the mandatory urine sample. I will spare you the details, but after a nerve-wracking day of showing and several trips to the rest room, the well tends to run a bit dry. But at some point during the ensuing wait I realized that my dream had become reality.

Over the next couple of weeks, time seemed to move very slowly. I was reluctant to ride too many horses; I wouldn't play any sports. Frankly, I was afraid to do much of anything because I certainly didn't want to get hurt. By the time we left for Korea, I was ready to go, and I think everyone was glad to get rid of me.

The trip to Seoul was a long one. On the way, we stopped in Los Angles for "processing." In L.A., we received everything from language lessons to a hair dryer. "Processing" began with a lecture on the anti-American protests, terrorism, and how not to look like an American athlete. Next we moved on to a physical exam, and other than finding out I was a little bit flat-footed, everything checked out fine. Then came the fun part—we got uniforms, shirts, socks, shoes, shampoo, athlete's foot powder, cameras, sunglasses, hats, luggage, and even underwear. I did not know why I bothered to bring anything of my own. The only thing that I couldn't figure out was how we were supposed to look inconspicuous wearing this stuff; it was all red, white, and blue, and had USA written everywhere. So I ended up sending most of it home, figuring I'd be patriotic later and, for now, worry about staying alive.

When we finally arrived in Seoul, the organizers didn't seem to share in our enthusiasm. I'm not sure what I expected (maybe a small drum-and-bugle corps), but our hosts looked exhausted. As it turned out, we had been just about the last group to come in, and it was midnight. On arriving at the athletes' village I noticed a striking resemblance to a prison camp: barbed-wire fence, guards, guns, the whole works. At first, it felt intimidating, but as time passed, this security became comforting.

My roommate for the first couple of weeks was Joe Fargis. After the first day or so, we were right at home with each other, and I still consider some of our experiences as the funniest I can remember. For about the first week, Joe and I were waking up at 3 or 4

A.M. because of the vast time difference between Seoul and home. We would eat breakfast, go to the gym and then to the practice track to watch the track-and-field people work out. All of these activities were short-lived, except for breakfast. Joe is a very realistic and modest person, and he had a great way of putting everything in perspective. We think of ourselves as being the ideal physical specimens for our sport, but when we would watch those track-and-field athletes go through their routines, it was truly a humbling experience.

For the next week, things were relatively quiet. The horses were all being good and we anxiously waited for things to get started.

The opening ceremonies were inspiring. I rode over on the bus next to John Thompson, the U.S. basketball coach. I did most of the talking, and finally, he asked what I was doing there. (I don't think he really cared, but it was kind of him to ask.) I told him that I rode horses. He said, "Oh, you're one of those equitarians." I just smiled and nodded my head and figured that my knowledge of basketball was about as good as his knowledge of the equestrian world.

We milled around on the field at the ceremonies, talking with Carl Lewis, Edwin Moses, and Chris Evert. But after the lighting of the torch, the novelty wore off, and pretty soon I was searching for a cool cup of water and a spot of shade.

With opening ceremonies behind us, we still had another week before starting to compete. I spent most of this time sick on my back in bed with a bug that struck hard intestinally. The closer we got to showing, the worse I felt, and the doctors couldn't do much for me because so many medications were banned for athletes. The first two days of showing came and went without any disasters, however. Gem was behaving well and I was okay, too. But the next two days before the Nations' Cup were miserable.

Because I wasn't feeling well, I watched a lot of the events on TV. I knew things were getting pretty bad when I moved the television out of the living room and into the bathroom.

I can't ever remember feeling as bad as I did on the day of the Nations' Cup. This was the moment I had waited for my whole life, and all I could think of was whether I could wait until finishing my round before finding a bathroom. Between rounds, I took a nice little nap and felt a bit better afterwards. This was a heck of a way to keep myself from getting nervous, but I guess it worked.

What we jumped at home in the trials was probably every bit as difficult as what we jumped in Korea in the team competition. Because the jumping was spread out over so many days with different warm-ups and individual qualifiers, course designer Olaf Petersen couldn't set as big a route as he could have for a one-shot grand prix, since doing so would have created a test of endurance for the horses.

The jumps, reflecting the artistic and historical heritage of Korea, were beautiful. They made quite an impression on me the first time I saw them. But we were more concerned with their dimensions—whether they were wide or solid or airy—than with how they looked, because the colors and structures were not a big deal to Gem.

It was as much of a competition with myself as with the jumps, feeling the Olympic pressure and the chaos involved with the Games. There was also the turbulent political situation in the country and the threat of terrorist activity at the time.

Anyway, we finished up the day with four faults in each round and I had an Olympic team silver medal to show for it. On the way back to the room, I kept feeling worse and worse. The bus trip wasn't easy.

. . .

I didn't ride the next two days before the final individual qualifier. I knew that all I had to do was complete the course, and that was about all I did. I had only four faults, but it really was worse than it sounds. That was the day of the famous "chip;" the one jump that I almost chewed up and spit out was the one jump that they showed on television every time they talked about the equestrian events. Gem came into the jump so close that he went almost straight up and down to clear it.

Two days later was the last day of competition, the day of the closing ceremonies, and, most important, of the individual finals. And finally I felt great!

We had to get up early to go over to the main stadium. Arriving before the sun had risen, we saw the torch softly lighting the field. As the sun came up and the mist started to lift, the course became visible. It was quite a sight.

Jumping through the Kwachon Gate, one of the signature fences of the Seoul Olympics, Greg Best and Gem Twist compete in the Prix de Nations. USET PHOTO BY TISH QUIRK

Left to right on podium: *1988 Olympic show-jumping silver medalists Joe Fargis, Lisa Jacquin, Greg Best (who went on to take the individual silver), and Anne Kursinski.* USET PHOTO BY TISH QUIRK

Gem just kept getting better the whole time we were in Korea. That's very typical of him; he settles into a groove and once he starts to relax, he really jumps, because he is less distracted and easier to control. The fact that we had moved our activity to the stadium in Seoul from the Olympic equestrian center about forty minutes away was a factor in brightening him up.

There is no doubt that he understood the last day was really special. He made a very special effort, despite the fact that he was tired after all the jumping he already had done at the Games. He knew he was on stage and this was his big moment.

The course was extremely large and difficult. It rode differently for the two rounds, the distances were very complicated, and the horses were tired anyway.

After a jump-off with West Germany's Karsten Huck on Nepomuk (who had the advantage of not participating in the team competition), I went on to win the silver medal behind Pierre Durand of France with Jappeloup. I will remember it as the greatest day of my life.

When we finished up with everything after the class, there was no way that I was going to make it to the closing ceremonies, so I met a couple of friends. We went to a bar to order a round of celebratory drinks, and as I sat there watching the closing ceremonies on television, I thought to myself, yes, it was real. The dream I had lived with for so long finally had come true.

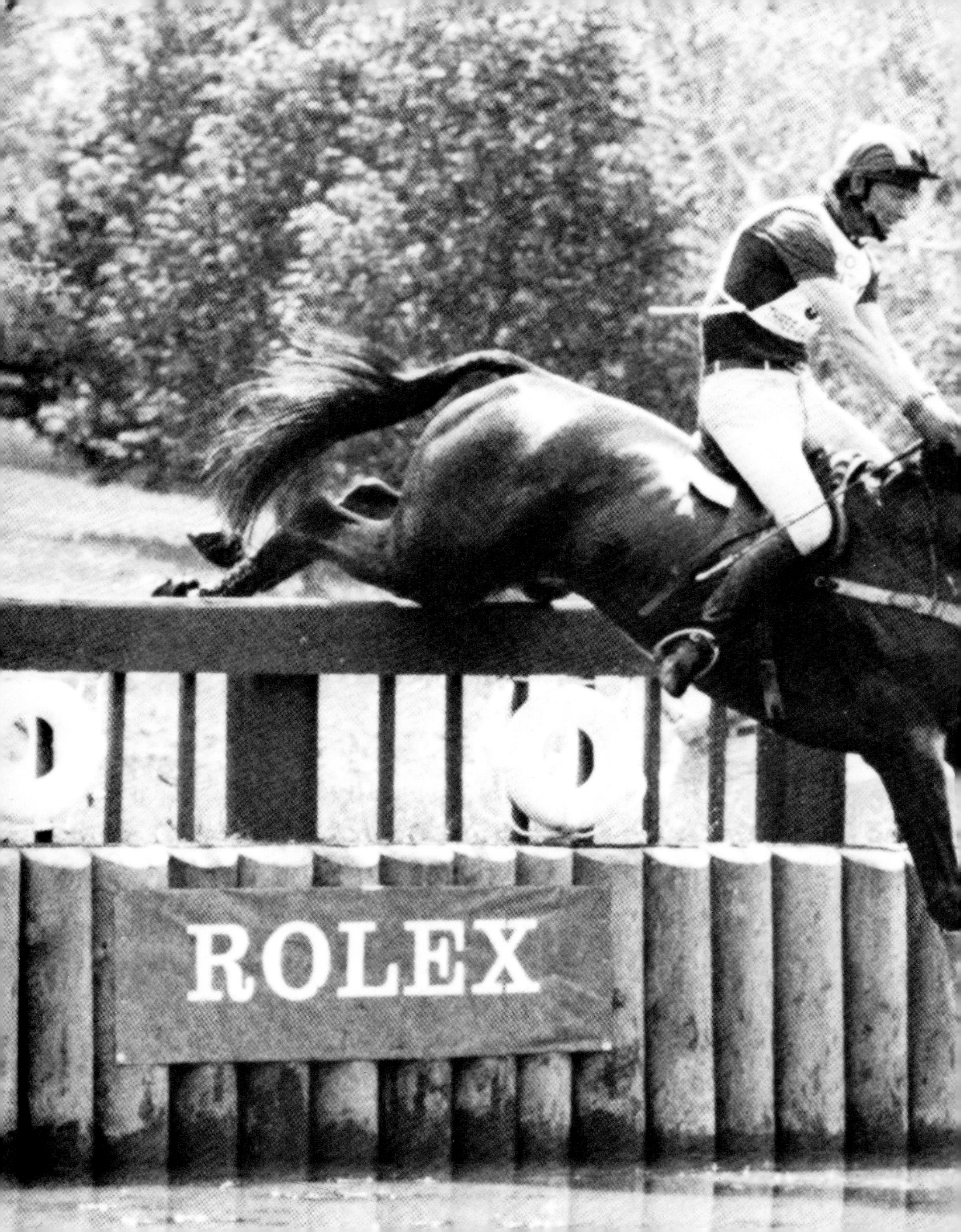
ROLEX

EVENTING

The USET gold medal team at Burghley, England, in 1978: Mike Plumb on Good Mixture, Bruce Davidson on Irish Cap, Denny Emerson on Victor Dakin, and Don Sachey on Plain Sailing. USET PHOTO

Both national and international distinctions have come to Denny Emerson, a member of the gold medal team at the 1974 World Championships and the reserve for the 1976 Olympics aboard Victor Dakin, the mount on which he won the 1976 U.S. National Three-Day Event Championship.

Three years later, Emerson took the same title with York and received the Markham Trophy for leading amateur rider in U.S. open competition. It was his third year to take top national honors—in 1972, he had won the AHSA national championship and the U.S. Combined Training Association's national leading rider title.

The Dartmouth College graduate went on to head the USCTA for three years and become an eloquent spokesman for his sport. A successful coach and trainer, he lives with his family in Vermont.

THE EVOLUTION OF MODERN EVENTING

Edward Emerson

When I began eventing in 1962, there were not many opportunities to learn how to ride correctly, nor were there many events in America, or even many competitors. There was, of course, the USET, which sponsored major international competition, but at that time fewer than twenty people benefitted from the instruction or support it provided.

There was also a fledging U.S. Combined Training Association, which had been founded to support and popularize eventing at the grass-roots level, but it had no office, no newsletter, no real organization, and few members.

By contrast, twenty-seven years later, the USET teams are among the world's leaders, the USCTA has over eight thousand members, there are hundreds of horse trials all across America, and the sport is thriving and growing. There are dozens of local combined training associations, there are numerous event-oriented centers of instruction, and no event rider in America is without access to at least part-time orthodox instruction.

What were the forces and circumstances and who were the people who effected this dramatic and rapid turnaround? What had been the history of the sport prior to 1962, and who were the key historical figures in eventing's American development?

Eventing first appeared as an Olympic sport in the 1912 Games in Stockholm. The sport had been designed by cavalry officers to simulate the kinds of athletic feats that a trained army horse might be expected to perform under actual battlefield conditions.

From 1912 until 1948, all the Olympic three-day event teams that represented the United States were army teams comprised of officers. When the U.S. Army finally phased out the horse cavalry after World War II, the sport lost its primary source of funding as well as its primary source of horses and riders. General Jonathan Burton states in his excellent history of eventing, "The Military in Mufti," in *The USET Book of Riding*:

> The postwar transition from an Army equestrian team to a civilian one was not as smooth and easy as one would have liked, but that was probably unavoidable. Several former Army horsemen assisted in the transition and helped in various ways to diminish the trauma. Of equal importance was the fact that the horses used by the Army team in Europe from 1946 to 1950 were made available to the infant USET, to provide a cadre for the first civilian attempt to prepare an Olympic equestrian team, and the training facilities at Fort Riley were made available.

The fifties were probably a low ebb for U.S. eventing; for the military was no longer officially involved and there was little civilian involvement either. Luckily, however, such men as General Burton, General John Tupper Cole, Brigadier General F. F. Wing, and Colonel John W. Wofford were determined that the sport would not die here. In England, simultaneously, a development was occurring that would have the most profound impact on the future of the sport. This was the liaison between former British Olympic riders (also army men) and the avid foxhunter, the Duke of Beaufort, master of the Beaufort Hunt, and owner of the magnificent country estate, Badminton House. The duke, persuaded by the former Olympians that eventing was made to order for the foxhunting fraternity, instituted the world-famous Badminton Three-Day Event in 1949. He was fortunate to be able to acquire the services of the exceptionally capable Colonel Frank Weldon to become Badminton's director, and for the past forty years, that event has been the standard against which all other events have been measured. In fact, it is difficult to speculate in what state eventing would exist today if Badminton, with its magical aura of challenge, enthusiasm, and excitement, had never existed.

If the military and the foxhunters formed a special relationship to save eventing in England, it seems to me that a similar relationship developed here in America. In fact, when I started eventing, many of the leaders of our sport were people who were primarily identified with foxhunting. These included Alexander Mackay-Smith, Master of Foxhounds and editor of *The Chronicle of the Horse*, and Philip Hofmann, who was the first president of the USCTA. The alliance between the military and foxhunters, along with a few dressage people like H.L.M. Van Schaik, had the unenviable task of attempting to pull eventing up by its bootstraps.

Eventing in the 1960s was infinitely less available than it is today. Except for the events at the Green Mountain Horse Association, at the Winthrops' Groton House Farm, at Edward Harris's Hideaway Farm in Geneseo, New York, and a few scattered smaller trials, eventing scarcely existed in the Northeast. There were pockets of strength in California, a strong but low-level series of trials in Virginia, and at the USET headquarters in Gladstone, New Jersey. But if you were then a young aspirant looking for coaching and guidance, it scarcely existed unless you were a USET member under Major Stefan von Visy, the USET coach at Gladstone. True, there were clinics at such places as the GMHA each summer with instructors including Stuart Treviranus and Captain John Fritz, but plentiful and easy availability of correct coaching just didn't exist here in America.

Poised and ready to go at Radnor in 1985 are Denny Emerson and For Pete's Sake,
who went on to become the rider's advanced horse at the end of the 1980s. PHOTO
COURTESY OF DENNY EMERSON

Sometimes, like the proverbial U.S. cavalry, the right person appears at just the right time to save the day. So it had been in England in 1949 with the Duke of Beaufort, and so it would be in the United States with the appearance of Neil Ayer. He was the master of the Myopia Hunt in Hamilton, Massachusetts, and had gotten interested in eventing at Groton House. He succeeded Gibson Semmes as president of the USCTA in the early 1970s, and immediately, the force of his vigorous and innovative personality began to transform the sport in America as never before—or since. He hired Eileen Thomas from the British Horse Society in England to run the national headquarters, a move that finally meant records would be kept, letters answered, organizers encouraged, and all the details and logistics of the sport would have a competent administrator. Neil also was involved with USET Chairman Whitney Stone in hiring Jack Le Goff from France to be the three-day team coach. In addition, Neil instituted the Ledyard Farm Horse Trials, which in 1973 would grow into the first modern major international three-day event to be held in America.

The USCTA and the USET have for years enjoyed a symbiotic relationship, and it seems to me that the real successes of the USET's international teams have come as direct results of two converging forces that had been growing during the 1960s but coalesced during the early 1970s. The first of these was the grass-roots strength provided by the USCTA. That included a marked increase in the number of events, number of competitors, and quality of competition. These events provided the training ground for horses and riders as well as a pool from which new talent could be drawn. At the same time, the USET teams under von Visy, Major Joseph Lynch, and Jack Le Goff had won team silver medals at the Olympic Games in 1964, 1968, and 1972. Also, with the arrival of Jack Le Goff, the three-day team acquired its own headquarters in South Hamilton, Massachusetts. This move not only provided the team with enhanced facilities, much better footing, and access to the superb cross-country facilities at Ledyard Farm, Flying Horse Farm, and Groton House Farm, but it provided a meaningful psychological boost as well. When I first became interested in Olympic level competition, if you heard the phrase "the Team," it basically referred to the USET show-jumping squad. That squad was literally on the

Denny Emerson on his 1978 World Championship gold medal mount, Victor Dakin. USET PHOTO
BY SUE MAYNARD

first floor of the Gladstone facility and the three-day squad literally in the cellar. With a new coach and a new headquarters, however, combined with a healthy level of sport in the country, we were poised for new and amazingly dramatic results.

The real breakthrough was the USET's double gold medal victory over the British at the Burghley, England, World Championships in 1974, when we won the team gold and Bruce Davidson and Irish Cap won the individual gold. This victory was followed two years later by another double gold medal effort at the Montreal Olympics, with the USET winning the team gold, and Tad Coffin and Bally Cor winning the individual gold. Since then, we have won another Olympic Team gold at Los Angeles in 1984, and an individual World Championship gold in 1978 at Lexington, Kentucky, as well as numerous other international medals.

Thus eventing in America from 1974 onward had well in place the two main ingredients for growth. These were a solid grass-roots organization, the USCTA, and a highly visible top level, the gold medal–winning USET. The publicity that always surrounds a winner inspires others to become involved. The USCTA provided the structure and the lower-level competitions for these new converts to get into eventing at the entry level. It seems to me that this is a most crucial difference between "old eventing" and "new eventing."

"Old eventing" with the U.S. Army teams was very successful, but it was tightly limited to adult male army officers. Under that structure, children, women, and nonmilitary men had no chance of aspiring to Olympic competition. Thus there was no real reason for any grass-roots organization to exist.

During the middle period, roughly from 1948 to 1970, we were, as General Burton has pointed out, in a difficult transition. Several factors eased this passage. The most crucial of these was the opening of Olympic eventing to women in 1964. The USET's Lana du Pont, atop Mr. Wister, rode at Tokyo to become the very first woman competitor in Olympic competition. That opened the floodgates, to the extent that in the most successful eventing countries like England and the United States, women now comprise about 50 percent of the teams. That they do not in other countries is probably only because those countries have a male-oriented ethic. Imagine, for example, a competition between Great Britain and the United States that excluded such winning international riders as England's Virginia Leng, Lucinda Green, and Karen Straker, or America's Karen Stives, Torrance Watkins, Karen Lende, Ann Hardaway, and Nancy Guyotte. It would be a pointless competition, because on any given day, any one of those riders can beat any man anywhere in the world.

Another key growth factor has been the emphasis the USCTA placed on involving junior riders, helping them acquire correct instruction, and providing them with their own competitive divisions in horse trials and three-day events. The AHSA sponsors the Peters Trophy, which is a highly coveted young rider championship at a USCTA three-day event. For years, it was held at the Radnor Three-Day Event in the autumn, and became a mecca for the best young riders in the country. We also have had Canadian-American young rider team championships every summer. These have provided excellent training opportunities for hundreds of aspiring youngsters and given them team riding experience.

Virtually all of the younger riders over the years who have won spots on USET squads have been products of these various junior programs, thus proving how critical they were to USET success.

York, Denny Emerson's U.S. Combined Training Association Horse of the Year in 1979, as he won the U.S. National Three-Day Championship. PHOTO COURTESY OF DENNY EMERSON

An often-overlooked but equally crucial ingredient in the American story is that the USCTA provides five levels of competition, beginning with a very easy novice level. This has allowed very amateur adults to become active competitors. These adults, more than anyone else, provide the vast foundation of financial support and volunteer help that make eventing function as a broad-based sport.

Probably the most significant difference between the early 1960s and the mid-1980s, however, has to do with the horses themselves. Twenty-five years ago, the prevailing wisdom seemed to be that an event horse was one that didn't use his knees well enough to be a hunter, lacked the scope to be a jumper, or was too poor a mover to be a dressage horse. Event horses were inexpensive and generally of mediocre quality. Today, at the major American events, there are literally hundreds of absolutely lovely high-quality horses from everywhere on earth.

Just over the past few years, my barn has housed horses from England, Australia, New Zealand, Chile, Argentina, Germany, France, Sweden, Canada, Ireland, and Holland. People scour the globe seeking the ultimate athlete. Prices have risen dramatically in response to this demand, though event horses are still much less expensive than show jumpers.

These equine athletes need to be excellent jumpers and gallopers, because today's cross-country courses have become highly technical. Cross-country course designers have used so many related distances and multiple obstacles that noted international course designer Mark Phillips recently commented to me that it is difficult to do anything truly innovative anymore.

If eventing has had three major phases over the past seventy-seven years—the military years, the transitional phase, and the current quite technical and sophisticated phase—where then is the sport heading as we approach the twenty-first century? It is obvious to most observers that the horse, as an athlete, has some pretty definite outer physical limits. Every few years, some major competition has unusually adverse conditions, and numerous horses are either injured or exhausted. The 1978 World Championships had excessive heat and humidity; the 1986 Gawler, Australia, World Championships had rain on a clay base, which caused exceedingly slippery footing. These are examples of natural adversity; sometimes an overambitious course designer has built a track that is simply too testing for all but about the best ten or fifteen horses in the world. That modern phenomenon, television, brings these top competitions into the living rooms of the world. This is a built-in safety factor, for while people will tolerate the most appalling carnage to other people, they will not permit injury to animals. Several countries, including Holland and Sweden, have such powerful animal protection lobbies that the very sport of eventing is on tenuous footing.

It has been suggested by some experts that the dressage and show-jumping phases be made more difficult and the cross-country phase be made less so. This would, they say, reduce the stress level and reward the true all-around athlete. Other equally knowledgeable horsemen feel that with technical safeguards, it is possible to have safe competitions with very difficult cross-country courses, and to do less would cut the heart out of the sport. These proponents of Badminton-type cross-country courses (basically ultimate tests), feel that the elite event horse must possess sanity, soundness, courage, stamina, and athleticism to a profound degree. Only the most taxing tests, they say, allow the truly great horse to prevail. Perhaps in this controversy, we can see vestiges of the old military tradition of battlefield testing being juxtaposed against the more modern concept of eventing as the all-around test, or *concours complet*, as the French call it. Right now, I believe, we are on a seesaw. Sometimes eventing becomes too severe; then there is an international reaction, which causes a lessened difficulty. Then, because "higher, farther, faster" is an innate human longing (which we impose in turn on our equine companions), the difficulty again begins to escalate. I personally believe that if we do not regulate our own sport, some unwanted governing body will be happy to impose strictures upon us. To prevent horse abuse and governmental meddling, all the vested interests such as the FEI, USET, and the AHSA must, through vigilance, keep the courses within sane limits. Battlefield testing was once appropriate; but those days are gone. There will be continuing evolution of this sport, of course, but I hope that the real heart of it, the cross-country, remains the essential ingredient. The three-day event is a test of soundness and stamina, speed and courage. Only if we test for those qualities can we really determine who are the ultimate equine athletes.

Aggressiveness was one of Jimmy Wofford's trademarks when going cross-country. USET PHOTO

A member of the USET's three-day event squad for two decades, Jimmy Wofford was named to four Olympic teams and won two team silver medals in the Games.

The four-time national championships winner still operates a stable in Upperville, Virginia, but generally confines his riding to hobby status these days.

He comes from a long Olympic and Team tradition. The son of the USET's first president, Colonel John Wofford, who competed in the 1932 Olympics, Jimmy has a brother and a sister-in-law who also took part in the Games.

Wofford is a director of the Team and has taken a leadership role in the U.S. Combined Training Association. Elected president of the American Horse Shows Association in 1988, he is married to a horsewoman, Gail Williams, and their two daughters also ride.

THREE-DAY TRADITIONS AND CHALLENGES

James C. Wofford

A few years ago, I gave an interview in which I referred to sport as a crucible. My point was that if things are done correctly, the heat and pressure generated within the crucible of competition should burn away all that is base and false, leaving only the pure and true.

I suppose this is as good a vantage point as any to peer into that crucible and see what we can find. The first and most obvious change in the sport over the last decade is the quality of the horses and riders competing. I would yield to no one in my delight in telling you war stories about the good old days, but let me say something here. These kids today are good; they are really good. The average modern international competitor can solve problems of a degree and complexity that would have baffled most of the riders of the last generation. They do this with a consummate ease that evokes awe more in the eye of the knowledgeable onlooker than it does in the view of the average spectator.

There are several reasons for this dramatic improvement in performance at the international level. Obviously, there are more international competitions than even a decade ago. The ease and frequency with which horses can fly around the world continues to astonish me.

Certainly, the coaching that riders receive surpasses in every area that which was available to young team riders of twenty-five years ago.

*After winning the USET open event at Myopia on Kilkenny in 1967, Jimmy
Wofford receives the challenge trophy presented in memory of his father, Colonel John
Wofford, the USET's first president. Making the presentation are Henry Cabot Lodge
and Iris Winthrop.* USET PHOTO BY McCLARY

Finally, and probably most important, course designers are becoming increasingly sophisticated in their demands. They are now very clever about the distances they use
between fences, the proximity of those fences, their placement in terrain and their appearance. Yet our competitors handle those problems with ease.

"To jump huge fences with invisible aids," as George Morris often says, is commonplace
for today's rider and certainly a tribute to the beneficial effects of competition.

Every benefit to mankind seems to have a darker side, though, and certainly we should
be aware of it at this juncture. The pressures that are generated these days are not confined
to jumping clear rounds, producing a brilliant extension or going fast. These days, we
have pressures from sponsors, owners, and organizers that were unheard of a few years
ago. The reason is simple—money. The level of investment required by all of these new
support groups has risen dramatically and shows no sign of slowing down. These pressures
were unheard of not long ago.

In 1967, I purchased my Olympic horse, Kilkenny, for $7,500. By that time, he already
had been around Badminton, had competed in the Tokyo Olympics, and had been on
the gold medal team at the first World Championships at Burghley in 1966.

Kilkenny carried me to two Olympic team silver medals in the 1968 and 1972 Olympics, one individual bronze medal at the 1970 World Championships in Ireland, a team gold and a fourth-place finish in the 1987 Pan American Games. That is not to mention one national championship and innumerable placings at other events, both here and abroad. I had the fastest round of the day at the 1967 Pan Am Games, 1968 Olympics, and 1970 World Championships. Not bad for $7,500!

I could not afford to buy a horse like that these days; but if I owned him, I would not be able to sell him. It is hard to describe the bond that grows between horse and rider at that level, but it truly surpasses our normal understanding of mankind's relationship with animals.

These days, escalating costs of horses and competition mean few people can afford to own or campaign horses of Kilkenny's caliber with their own financial resources. But sponsors now want to support riders who are proven international stars. This means the rich get richer and the poor get poorer.

Organizers seek horse-and-rider combinations that are winning at the highest levels. At the same time, owners are becoming increasingly aware of the importance of prize

Jimmy Wofford on Touch and Go at Ledyard in 1975. USET PHOTO BY ALIX COLEMAN

Jimmy Wofford (on Kilkenny) salutes the judges at the 1972 Olympic Games in Munich. USET
PHOTO BY ELSIE WISE

money in reducing the staggering costs of maintaining a horse on the circuit. All of these serve to pressure a rider into asking more of a horse than he can or should produce. Perhaps we have arrived at a point where we should ask ourselves if we are even a sport anymore.

In a world where millions will starve and die this year, it is strange that many of our best efforts are put into improving pharmacological and mechanical painkilling preparations and applications so that injured horses can continue to serve as vehicles for the human ego. The classical horseman, dedicated to creating the best possible relationship between himself and his horse, will either be driven to the sidelines by those less scrupulous or forced to join them. It seems to me that we are developing some kind of crazed Gresham's law of equine economics, under which the good horsemen get driven out by the bad.

Both Ernest Hemingway and James Michener have pointed out that a thing ceases to be a sport and becomes entertainment when the first paid spectator steps through the gate. It is clear at this point that riders can no longer consider themselves athletes. They must now recognize that they are in the entertainment business.

The USET by definition is made up of its horses and riders. Therefore, if our riders are entertainers, what does that make the team? Are we an institute for the training and perfection of equine and human athletes or are we in the entertainment business? The answer, unfortunately, is both. Mankind has always wanted to have things both ways, and we are no different in that respect. The pressures that are exerted on the riders have their parallel at the USET. It would be wonderful to have some huge international corporation increase our budget by some unheard-of number. Certainly, our programs, and hopefully our successes, would double and redouble.

What would the team's answer be when that corporation put forth a subtle but forceful hint that they wanted representatives on our selection committees? As you can see, it is not so easy. This is only one of the pressures that the team soon is going to face, and in some instances may initiate.

The answers to all of the above must lie in the unique nature of the team. From its inception, and even more so today, the team has stood for values that are literally and figuratively beyond price. The team can remain truly successful only so long as it stands for those elements in the Olympic movement that speak for the good in sport. It is only by a reaffirmation of those values that the team will continue to occupy its mystical place in the horse world. The standards of ethical behavior between and among horses and riders have not changed over the years. Only the price tag has changed. The team and its riders must continue to conduct themselves in such a fashion that we remain the standard of conduct, both in and out of the ring, for all the world.

My crystal ball gets a little cloudy at this point. I cannot predict the pressures, dangers, and pitfalls that await us as we ride into the twenty-first century, but there is one thing I can assure you. Whatever arena, in whatever part of the world, the team rides into, we will go with our heads held high and we will be there to win.

Tad Coffin and Bally Cor show their finesse in dressage. USET PHOTO BY JIM RAFTERY

After a childhood spent showing hunters, Tad moved on to show successfully in equitation and dressage on Long Island. At the age of fifteen, he started combined training through the U.S. Pony Club.

He achieved his A rating in pony club, then started training with USET coach Jack Le Goff in 1973.

The next year, he was fourth at Ledyard, his first international competition, with the fabulous mare Bally Cor. He took her to the Pan American Games in 1975, winning the team and individual gold medals.

It was to be the same story in 1976 at the Olympic Games in Canada, where he led the USET to a team gold, winning an individual gold in the process. In only two years, he had earned four gold medals—an incredible record.

Now a trainer, teacher, and clinician, Tad lives with his wife, Patti, on a Virginia farm.

LEARNING THE USET WAY

Tad Coffin

I will always remember my first trip to USET headquarters in Gladstone, New Jersey. In the mid-1960s, I had gone there for the day with my riding instructor, Raul de Leon, and some of his other students to watch Bertalan de Némethy work with members of the show-jumping team.

From the moment I stepped out of the car, I was awestruck. To a young teenager, the stables at Gladstone seemed like a castle. The massive stone-and-brick building set in a horseshoe configuration was complete with an archway entrance. Through the archway, the enormous outdoor arena was visible. Fenced with a stone wall and black iron piping, its footing was raked in perfectly straight lines. To the left were the stalls, painted in a pale green, each appointed with a polished brass door latch and brass balls set atop the corner posts. Racks held blue-and-red wool coolers, marked with the simple white letters U.S.A. The horses' hoofbeats echoed as they were led down the brick corridor.

The horses I saw that day were the most beautiful creatures I had ever laid eyes on. Many of them were legends—their names, ages, and pedigrees beautifully hand-printed in black and red on each stall door.

From somewhere deep inside the castle emerged Mr. de Némethy, slight of build and agile-looking, a gentleman who truly fitted his surroundings. He was meticulously dressed in jodhpurs and boots, welcoming us in accented English, offering a smile with a twinkle in his eye. He lent a warmth to the building.

*Over the rookery jump in the cross-country at the 1976 Montreal Olympics is
eventual double gold medalist Tad Coffin on Bally Cor.* USET PHOTO BY UNITED
PRESS INTERNATIONAL

After a short tour, we followed him to the indoor arena, where he introduced the horses
and riders that were working in each of the training sessions that day. We watched every
session from beginning to end, completely absorbed.

The exercises they were doing were surprisingly simple, consisting of longeing, basic
dressage, cavalletti work, and gymnastics—the exercises that later became the trademark
of the de Némethy method. Certainly, I had seen such horses and riders elsewhere doing
far more difficult things, but the simplicity of the work was beautiful.

An added dimension made these horses and riders look larger than life. Where those
I had seen elsewhere seemed to scurry and struggle, these were elegant and composed.
There was a sense of power and elasticity in the way the horses moved and jumped. You
just knew that what you saw in their execution of these simple exercises were glimpses
of extraordinary accomplishments yet to come.

From that day on, I was intent on becoming a rider for the USET, and I'm sure others
who shared the experience felt the same. To me, it represented the pinnacle of achievement

in the equestrian world. Being selected to train at Gladstone, to be worthy of this honor, was more important than success in any competition.

From this initial experience, the USET began to play an increasingly influential role in my development as a rider. First, it provided a goal, a source of inspiration and motivation. There was now a greater sense of purpose behind riding and stable chores, particularly on those cold, wintry afternoons. It also provided an answer for pestering school coaches and peers who always wanted me to participate in other sports and after-school activities.

The USET set standards for me by which everything in horsemanship was measured. More than just standards of riding, they included every single aspect of horse care, stable management, the maintenance of equipment and riding facilities. At home, I tried, quite unsuccessfully, to turn my small corner of our farm into a miniature Gladstone, with that same air of meticulous attention and care. I swept and I raked and I groomed. I even painted everything I owned blue and red.

The USET also played an enormous role in my education as a rider, at first in an indirect way, and then directly.

My riding instructor, Mr. de Leon, came to this country as a young man from Cuba, where he had been taught to ride by some of the finest German instructors. He had learned from them the principles of dressage and their use in preparing a horse for jumping.

Once in this country, his source of inspiration became Mr. de Némethy, and he trained his riders with the same approach. He would visit Gladstone frequently, learning everything he could. As his eleven-year-old student, I already was benefitting, in a sense, from the coaching at Gladstone.

It was an approach to riding that was not usually followed at that time in the United States, and watching Mr. de Némethy's training sessions became a crucial support for Mr. de Leon professionally and a great help to me in understanding what I was working toward.

My competitive experiences at that point were in equitation and hunter classes, and in dressage shows, which were held infrequently. Toward the end of my high school years, I also began to compete in combined training events, with some success.

I loved this sport, which was quickly gaining popularity in the United States. The USET had recently engaged Jack Le Goff as the coach for the combined training team, and he also was training riders at the Gladstone headquarters.

In the year after the Munich Olympics, I graduated from high school, and the USET designated certain combined training events as selection trials, to pick riders to train with Mr. Le Goff.

After the selection trials in which I competed, I received an impressive white envelope featuring the blue-and-red USET shield and block letters that read United States Equestrian Team Inc. Inside was a simple letter stating that I had been invited to attend a training session. It was an extraordinary moment for me and the beginning of an unusual educational experience that spanned the next four years.

The USET has always been much more than a source of inspiration for young riders. It has helped many of them to develop their skills and talents in all of the disciplines over the years, providing them with a chance to learn more.

I happened to come along during a unique period when the USET had two of the finest coaches in the world training teams at the same time and, for a while, in the same location. Mr. Le Goff and Mr. de Némethy were conducting resident young rider programs, inviting

Bally Cor's retirement ceremony at Radnor in 1978. On hand were USET three-day coach Jack Le Goff; Bally Cor's rider, Tad Coffin; groom Tasha Zabrisky; and owners J. Harden Crawford and Dr. Charles Reid. USET PHOTO BY JAMES DEUTSCHMANN

selected riders from around the country to train with them. These young riders were matched with USET horses, on the assumption that, after time and training, horse and rider would perform well enough to represent the United States successfully in international competition. This program was well established and already had produced many good pairings.

I was selected for the resident training program and, in the summer of 1973, Gladstone became my new home. I lived in the castle, upstairs above the offices with other young riders.

Two USET horses were given to me to ride: Bally Cor, the mare that would eventually be my Olympic mount, and Irish Warrior, a young horse who had yet to compete. They had arrived at the USET shortly before I did, so we began our training together.

Marshall Grey, the stable manager for the three-day squad, was responsible for teaching the young riders a whole new standard of stable management. She had her work cut out for her as we struggled inexpertly to polish and shine and clean and scrub and groom to these new specifications. We learned an enormous amount about caring for the many needs of horses that were in this demanding training.

Mr. Le Goff instructed us in the theory of riding and training, in addition to teaching us while we were mounted two or three times per day, in both group and private sessions. We had opportunities to ride older USET horses that knew more than all of us put together.

The daily work was not glamorous. Daily training of horses and riders, or any athlete for that matter, requires the repetition of many simple exercises. Mr. Le Goff worked diligently to improve our seat and our ability to coordinate our influences. We rode a lot on the flat and most of the jumping work consisted of cavalletti and gymnastics as we learned the basic principles of dressage and jumping. The horses galloped and jumped only enough to prepare for the upcoming competitions.

Our active day consisted of riding and learning, and the best possible circumstances in which to do both were provided. Our education covered every aspect of horsemanship and we were expected only to learn and improve. This was not so easy, however, and we often failed to live up to our part of the bargain.

In 1974, the three-day squad relocated to new headquarters in South Hamilton, Massachusetts, and I moved with them. I did not, however, make the group that was headed to England for the World Championships. I had to learn that being at the USET was an opportunity to improve, not a guarantee of success. It was not an easy lesson.

That fall, I was given another chance by Mr. Le Goff and returned to Hamilton for further training. Bally Cor and I were reunited and both of us were bent on redemption from our earlier failures. We succeeded the next year at the Pan American Games, winning team and individual gold medals. The following year at the Olympics, we repeated our performance.

I attribute my success to the education that I received as a young rider. So much of it was provided by the USET, which has assisted many other young riders through similar programs over the years.

While the resident young rider program no longer exists, the USET will continue its effort to provide training and education for young riders. It will have to, as the future success of American teams depends on their preparation and education.

The USET provided me with a most unusual opportunity to study every aspect of horsemanship. On behalf of all of those who have benefitted and will benefit from this organization in a similar way, I salute the leaders, the coaches, the personnel, and all the horses who have made it possible.

Bruce Davidson and Might Tango, one of the many horses he has made from scratch, take the Gladstone Trophy at the Chesterland Three-Day Event in 1978. Earlier in the year, Bruce won his second consecutive individual World Championship gold medal on the ex-racehorse. USET PHOTO BY JAMES DEUTSCHMANN

Two-time World Three-Day Eventing Champion Bruce Davidson is an all-around horseman. He competes in steeplechase races and is a dedicated foxhunter. At his Pennsylvania farm, Chesterland, he breeds horses and trains them, supervising every aspect of their care. In addition, Bruce passes his expertise along to many students.

Riding is also a passion of his wife Carol, a former eventer, and their two children, Buck and Nancy, who are often on hand with Bruce at events.

His international competition record is legendary, with two Olympic team gold medals (on Irish Cap and J.J. Babu) and one World Championship team gold (on Irish Cap) to his credit. A nine-time U.S. Combined Training Association Rider of the Year, he has won everywhere from Stockholm to Boekelo (Holland) and Rome, with top placings at Britain's prestigious Burghley and Badminton events as well.

MAKING THE EVENT HORSE FROM SCRATCH

Bruce Davidson

I t's best to start with a prospective event horse when it's really young, so you can ensure it is raised out in the open in big fields where it can get fit by nature. Most successful, high-quality racehorses are raised in places like Kentucky, where they are able to develop their natural gallop and fitness out in the open, rather than in small paddocks. I think it's important that event horses be physically tough. It's much better for a youngster to stand out on a cold night and shiver than to be inside, fat and soft.

Our youngsters don't come in to live in the stable until they're four years old, unless they get an injury. Then they have a stall for a day or two and we get them handled and tame, so to speak.

If I'm buying a young horse that is more than one or two years old, I really prefer a racing background. I lean very much toward a Thoroughbred, and I think a competitive background tells you much more about the horse in the long run. As is the case with people, if a young horse is really properly fit early in his life, it will carry him on. If he is left soft too long, it will always be more work for him than for one who did it as a juvenile.

If he has raced and is still sound, I think that's the most wonderful vetting you could ask for. It's more than we're going to ask him to do the rest of his life.

I usually don't X-ray horses that I am considering buying. What do X rays tell you? I can tell if the horse is sound or not. A perfect example is when we first vetted Irish Cap, on whom I won the individual World Championship and team gold in 1978. He was an

Great Britain's Princess Anne congratulates Bruce Davidson after his sixth-place finish on J. J. Babu at the Badminton Horse Trials in 1986. He won an award as the highest-placed competitor on a horse owned by a rider. USET PHOTO BY FINDLAY DAVIDSON

unpapered five-year-old Thoroughbred when we bought him. The vets flunked him and told me he had fractures in both front feet. But then the noted veterinarian Dr. Jacques Jenny said to me, "Has anyone ever told the horse that?" I said, "What do you mean?" and he pointed out that the horse wasn't going unsound. As long as he doesn't show any symptoms, there's no problem.

The background, age, growth, and temperament are all important in considering a young horse. But it's also vital to know what you ultimately want for the horse's life. Once you get him broken and see his temperament, how he moves and how athletically he is inclined; once you have a feeling for his soundness and so forth, you can start to say, "This horse leans toward being a wonderful family horse, or a big-time show jumper." Then you can start to head him in the direction that makes the most sense for his life—including after the end of his competitive career. Being a person who loves to deal with a horse from conception right through to the last day, I like to think about the time when Might Tango or Pilot Kid or Samuel Gwiffey or any of them will no longer be competing. I want them to be nice horses either for a young rider or a lady who will hunt or my family or somebody who will be learning dressage. If they are trained right and raised properly, they will retain this usefulness throughout their lives, and it's the best thing for them. Just as with a person, it's better for a horse to keep doing something than to be left idle.

As I'm making a young horse, I always try to keep these factors in my mind. If I know it's going to be a young rider's horse, then I try to make it with the idea that it not pull or learn to become too aggressive, because that would intimidate a young person. If I'm making it for myself because I think it's a horse that will suit me, then I make it a little bit sharper, a little bit quicker, a little bit more competitive, because those are the characteristics I like in an international horse.

That's the privilege of working with a young horse. You get to make it exactly what you want. If you don't want it to take too much of a hold, then teach it not to.

I break horses as two-year-olds and I think that's important. I have followed and watched other systems, especially the English and the Irish breaking them at the end of their three-year-old year or in their four-year-old year, and I don't agree with that. I like to break them as early as possible, and in some cases, I'd say to break them late in their yearling year is not wrong.

You do very little with them, maybe only ten-minute periods, and you put no stress on them, but you teach them their place in the world, and you teach them their place with man. They have to learn that man is not someone you walk over or strike at or kick at. Just like baby humans, they become confident and at ease when they know what's expected of them.

I turn them out after I've had them in as two-year-olds and trained them for about ten weeks so that they walk, trot, and canter, and have just a little bit of condition to their bodies. They're brought in every day from the fields to be ridden and turned out afterward during training, but immediately after the ten-week period, they get turned out to play for the rest of the year.

Their three-year-old year, we repeat the whole thing. They come in, and go through the longeing and backing process again, but it goes more quickly because they have been there before and they understand it. They do a little more work during their three-year-old year. They work forty-five minutes to an hour a day, right through the summer. If they come up about the beginning of April, when the ground and the weather are good, I like to get the Thoroughbreds a little fit. I get them to gallop two or three days a week. They'll do thirty, forty, or fifty minutes of trotting on the hills every day. They'll do a little bit of flat work once a week. In July and August, they might start jumping a few jumps, logs, and chicken coops out in the countryside, just before we let them down again. If they are going to go racing, they stay in. These days I intend to race many of the young event horses I'm raising myself before I bring them back to become event horses.

The fourth year is the first that I get quite serious with them. They come in the first of April, but I still don't give them a stall. They get their first real proper stable in autumn, when they're going to go hunting. But they do an hour's work six days a week and gallop two days a week to get properly fit. On the first of August, we start hunting them.

We hunt them very seriously. Our four-year-olds hunt one or one and a half days a week. And of course, each day's hunting is considerably more work than a preliminary three-day event.

By the end of the season, my four-year-old will probably have done thirty days' hunting, and that's a lot. He's fitter than he probably would need to be to go intermediate or advanced, because we hunt from four to five hours and cover twenty-five miles on the hills.

I don't put shoes on the horses until they're four. I think good feet are very important, and only if a horse has a foot problem will I put shoes on him. If a horse has good feet, and the ground is good, I'll go on and hunt him without shoes until Thanksgiving. It's not a big deal for a barefoot horse to do the basics of hunting and jumping three- to four-foot fences, and it's better for them to do it in the long run. You end up with a much sounder horse.

As they turn five, by March hunting is finishing and the competitions are starting. Now these horses are ready to come out and, in some cases, they compete on the training level a few times. We do the latter with a horse that has very little exposure off the farm, and probably not quite enough hunting; perhaps he didn't come to me in time or he got hurt halfway through the season. Maybe he's a little bit of a nervous animal, and the first few times off the farm I want to give him that much of an advantage.

Then there are some like those we brought out this year—five-year-olds that we brought along all the way. There wasn't time to take them training and they went preliminary straightaway.

Bruce Davidson competes cross-country with J. J. Babu at Badminton in 1986, where they finished sixth. USET PHOTO BY FINDLAY DAVIDSON

Again, I think if you are fortunate enough to live in an area where there is the countryside that we have, you can make a horse much more naturally than if you live in an area where you're mostly in the arena or on the little track where you exercise them.

If they have had a full season hunting and they've been off the farm for a hunter trial or two, then I probably will go right into preliminary with them in their five-year-old year. I have always believed that if a horse puts in one good season in preliminary horse trials, is well ridden and well exposed, and does one preliminary three-day event, I know by then whether he is of international ability, whether he has the speed or the stamina.

That exposure is his undergraduate work. With that, you know right away if you can go on into advanced or not. He's seen the ditches, he's seen the water, he's seen the coffins, he's seen the drops. If he can jump them when they're three feet seven inches, he can jump them when they're two inches higher.

As time goes on, I think we'll find that to abolish the preliminary three-day makes more sense than to keep it. Many people use the preliminary three-day as an end to itself, and a horse does so many under bad conditions where the ground is too hard or the weather's too hot that it is detrimental to his future.

I use the intermediate division purely because you have to wait for the horses to get old enough to go advanced. I take mine advanced at seven, and a lot of people say I do it too fast. But my theory is: take them preliminary as five-year-olds; as six-year-olds, let them run in as many intermediate horse trials as you can. I let them do one intermediate three-day event. At the end of the six-year-old year, let them do a small international event, whatever it is in your area. As seven-year-olds, I think it's in the trainer's hands and depends on that year's calendar. Our calendar fluctuates so much on the year of Olympic Games or World Championships that, if you're dealing with a top-notch young horse—a horse like Pirate Lion—he may step into the advanced division as a seven-year-old and be able to handle it. Of course, such horses are better as eight-, nine-, and ten-year-olds—when experience has taught them to settle in the best position—but they're competitive as seven-year-olds.

The other route is to have them come out quietly as seven-year-olds, run them again in a few intermediates, and then step them up at the end of the year. Again, that depends on the calendar, the availability of events, and the severity of those events.

Much in this schedule and routine of training horses has proven to work in my circumstances. Everyone has to adjust to his own circumstances, but horses like Might Tango, J. J. Babu, Pilot Kid, Mystic Hazzard, Mystic High, and Samuel Gwiffey have all developed through the above routine and come out on top.

The best example is J. J. Babu, my mount for the 1984 Olympics. We bought him at the end of his yearling year, broke him as a two-year-old and followed this program right on through. He would have come home and been a horse for my son Buck and my wife to enjoy after his competitive career, had he not broken a pastern. He was at the stage where Buck was riding him and getting to know him, and I was just enjoying letting him run around the horse trials. He was well and happy and still very much wanted to be part of it. He probably was going to run at Badminton in 1989 and then be retired. Unfortunately, he broke the pastern in a spring 1989 horse trials and had to be destroyed.

Another example is Dr. Peaches, who won the Kentucky CCI three times. He was raised here since he was a yearling and went right down this line. Might Tango, on whom I won

Dr. Peaches, who has made a habit of winning the Rolex-Kentucky three-day event, does it for owner Bruce Davidson for the second year in a row in 1989. USET PHOTO BY FRED NEWMAN

my second World Championships individual gold in 1978, was an ex-racehorse who came here too late to start as a two-year-old. We converted him from racing and from having a difficult temperament to being very useful. He went on to be successful with me and with others later. He ended up being my wife's horse, and Carol hunted him for four seasons, won the FEI class for dressage at Devon on him, and showed him in hunter trials. He's retired here with our broodmares.

Facilities are the other thing that's important in understanding the training of young horses or the remaking of older horses. I made reference to the area where we are lucky enough to live and have countryside and facilities that make it possible to train properly.

I think that so much of a horse's success is having the facilities available to train him. You have to be able to make him familiar with water, with hacking on hills, with galloping, with a lively routine. It's important to have a similar environment that stimulates competition if you're going to be successful. I don't think you train a competition horse by having him at a farm so private that no one is allowed to drive in or make a noise while that horse is working. No one competes in that kind of an environment; to create an atmosphere that is awake and moving and requires the horse's attention, understanding, and participation is what's ultimately going to get him into the proper routine, so he acts that way away from home.

You have to be able to understand horses from their point of view, but you need the facilities to deal with whatever problems come up.

I have gotten to the point where, the more I understand about breaking horses, the more I like to give them new experiences—putting them in a two-horse trailer, if they have never been in one, or on a hot-walker. I think that's how horses mature. It's just like sending your kid to college.

Now I hope someday to have the joy of winning on a horse that I not only made, but also bred. We're working on it.

The ultimate in the sport is to breed, train, and win, to carry the whole system right on through.

Queen Elizabeth congratulates Mike Plumb and Plain Sailing for their efforts at Badminton in 1968. USET PHOTO BY FINDLAY DAVIDSON

With six Olympics to his credit, J. Michael Plumb has earned himself recognition as the iron man of the USET. That Games record includes two team gold medals, and three team silvers, not to mention an individual silver on Better and Better at the 1976 Montreal Games.

Mike has ridden in four World Championships, garnering a team gold and two bronzes, as well as an individual silver in 1974 on Good Mixture.

The list of his honors is too long to detail, but other highlights include several U.S. Combined Training Association Rider of the Year titles and the individual gold in the 1967 Pan American Games on Plain Sailing.

While others are content to concentrate on coaching when they near the half-century mark, Mike has continued as an avid competitor as well as a sought-after trainer.

COPING WITH THE CROSS-COUNTRY

J. Michael Plumb

Cross-country is my favorite part of an event, and at the international level, it is the most important section. In a two-star or three-star CCI, it's the vehicle for moving up from a lower placing in dressage. It's where we're going to make or break our reputation.

At Burghley in the 1974 World Championships, when Good Mixture was second, my score was not competitive in the dressage—he was never a very easy horse to ride on the flat. But my cross-country ride there was the best of my life. Had I been competing as an individual, I would have chosen to go a shorter way, which would have broken my time down to even less and I probably would have won the gold medal. But since I was a part of the team, I had to finish, and I had to make a team score.

That ride reminded me of good music. It was effortless and every jump the horse met was right on. There was no interference on either one of our parts. We were a pretty good combination. We knew each other and that is what you need on the cross-country course. The minute you start to get in the horse's way and tell him where to jump and which way to go, you start to rack up the penalty points by trying to dictate strides. That is something I try not to do, although I am guilty of it occasionally. It's what causes the German riders to move down on so many weekends when they do good dressage and are not able to keep that score.

Mike Plumb and Better and Better go cross-country in perfect form at Ledyard in 1977, where they placed second. USET PHOTO BY SUE MAYNARD

When you buy a potential event horse, and you're thinking about cross-country, you must look for boldness. There can be no question that when that horse is aimed at a jump, he will jump it and be respectful of it. We can teach him the dressage. It's the desire to get on the other side of the jump, almost to the point that you have to pull him up in front of the jump because he wants to go so much, that is the most important requirement for the horse.

Free and Easy, the horse I rode in the 1972 Olympic Games, was a show hunter in Maryland and a very English type of horse—a lot of bone, good substance, a good jumper. He was a little bit coarse, but you couldn't pull him away from the jumps. That's what I like. Desire is such an important part of this game, for the horse as well as the rider.

When I went to grade school and prep school, I didn't really focus on the riding. I was a baseball, basketball, football person. I displayed a trait that would get me in trouble in sports, because I would play defensive back and every once in a while I would make a tackle a little too hard and knock myself out cold.

Once I get on a cross-country course I feel that same kind of adrenaline, and it has caused me to get in trouble there too. Sometimes you don't feel when something is not right and you just keep pressing.

For instance, at the Rolex-Kentucky Three-Day Event in 1988, I started out on an old horse, Gold Band, that I had admired for a long time and once tried to buy. I got the ride on him three weeks before Lexington. I needed another shot at Seoul—I had one, but it was not very strong—so I chose to ride him.

I knew when I started out on cross-country I was in trouble. The course got to you right from the beginning, and he was not jumping well. I should have pulled up, but I didn't. He made a mistake on the lane crossing, throwing me into a tree and separating my shoulder. But because of my desire—I don't know whether it was fueled by ignorance or stupidity—I needed to go on. So I did and he fell later, and then I had the common sense to pull up. Still, that's the sort of desire that I need to see in my students and myself to be able to come home all the time. I think my record has shown that I may have a fall or two, but I manage to get through the finish flags.

One of the most important factors in coping with the cross-country is walking the course. In the last ten years, because I have so many students, I generally walk the course with somebody else two or three times, but I try to walk it at least once by myself to put things in perspective.

By that fourth time, you really have a feeling for your way around and for the fences. The ones that concerned you early on shouldn't concern you at that point. You have developed a real plan and you have confidence, walking it that last time as if you were riding it. You have come up with all your alternatives by then. It's vital to have a real plan before you walk it the last time. If there are fifty people to go and you're fortieth, you try to get around and see as many fences as possible. But because I try to do my homework, it usually confirms what I already know.

Attention to flat work and gymnastic jumping makes a successful eventing competitor. It's the German approach to dressage, which I think is the best, and the British and New Zealand approach to cross-country. They have a lot of experience because of the number of events in which they participate. They're able to gallop over cross-country courses three and four times a week. Here, we can't event that much, so we have to train.

When it comes to show jumping, I would have to say the American approach is best because we're very strong there and it holds up pretty well in our sport on the third day.

Good basics can stand up to what needs to be done at international events. I believe in having a system to work with. A good system enables riders to make adjustments when they feel they're necessary on cross-country. You can instruct students all day long, but you can't tell them about the feeling they have, the adjustments they have to make throughout the course; that has to come through them. Some people never get a feel for the cross-country. Others, like two-time Olympic gold medalist Mark Todd of New Zealand, are instinctive. From the time they got on a horse, they made all the right decisions by themselves.

I try giving students the tools to make those adjustments. With experience they gain the feel to apply the tools and adjustments to particular needs.

Safety is an important consideration. We need to be able to stop people from competing cross-country when they have no business being there. The way I deal with it is to make it as safe as possible with attention to boring details. I think people don't have enough respect for the sport. They consider it fun and have never galloped at a jump with the

Blue Stone, Mike Plumb's mount for the 1984 Los Angeles Olympics, was, like his rider, a cross-country specialist. USET PHOTO BY MARY PHELPS

speed they finally attain once they're on the course. Then they're lost. They've gotten into it out of ignorance and they eventually pay for it.

There are too many shocking reminders that it's a serious sport. When horses go that quickly with solid jumps, and riders have no idea of what they're doing and the horses aren't ready for it, accidents are going to happen. You have got to know at what speed you're traveling, and we train ourselves and our horses in those speeds so we know them and are able to move up and bring back at that pace. To clear some of those wide oxers in the middle of a big field, you've got to be able to work at those speeds with plenty of energy. I think that's often what the inexperienced lack.

The desire to stay on is another thing that plays a big role in cross-country success, and that has to come from inside. I don't know how to teach people to stay on their horses. At Groton House in June 1989, I had a near-fall and was sideways on the horse, a Dutchbred mare named Simona. She jumped into a water complex and just kept getting too bold. I rode her too strong in because I thought she would be "looky," but she wasn't; she tripped coming out and went right to her knees. I went off to the side but managed to cling to her until I could get back in the saddle. It's not something I can explain to other people how to do, it's just instinct, and I think it has to do with being a good athlete.

Fitness of horse and rider are important cross-country, but no matter how fit you are, the time comes when you and your horse are tired. You have to be prepared to handle that.

At the 1986 World Championships in Gawler, Australia, I didn't have a lot of horse left by the time I got up the steep hill near the end of the course. All I had was a horse that would keep going. I didn't have an adjustable horse, and that's a terrible feeling, because after the top of the hill, there were a few jumps for which I would have liked to have adjusted his stride and approach. Instead, I had to just stay on and pray. Blue Stone was going to finish, but he was going to try moving the cordwood pile obstacle on the way, and I had to make it my business to stay on him. You don't want to try to adjust a tired horse, because you've got to let them do what they can do, if you feel that they're safe.

In contrast, the course for the Olympics in 1984 went pretty much as planned. We had four serious trials before that, and Blue Stone competed at three, so he was about as fit as he ever has been. Though I always worried about his fitness because he was a heavy Irish horse, he didn't really start running out of gas until the very end.

I use the cross-country as a barometer of when it is time to move up a level, as opposed to the dressage or show jumping. You can always work on the other two, but there can be no fudging with the cross-country.

Think about heading for the next level when you have repeated safe rides and when the horse continues to cope, or learns from his mistakes. When he runs and jumps with ease, it's time to move up. But remember, you have to have some genuine courses to jump. It requires some sort of standard of the same type of jumps you'll see at the advanced or international level.

I see too much overconfidence, people who have done well and sort of talked themselves into a situation where they move up without having jumped serious fences at low levels. As coaches, we too often want people to move up without the proper homework. You either have it or you don't have it, and if you program that rider and horse to move up progressively, they should be the same rider at the two-star CCI level that they were at the preliminary five years before.

Mike Huber competes on Quartermaster at the Rolex-Kentucky Horse Trials in 1988. USET
PHOTO BY MARY PHELPS

Mike Huber put three-day eventing on the map in the Southwest. He and Sir Oddity were the leading rider and horse in the U.S. Combined Training Association's Southwest region from 1975 to 1977. Next came Gold Chip, a $2,000 purchase. She took him to thirteen straight victories and the 1978 World Championships, where eighteen-year-old Mike and six-year-old Gold Chip finished thirteenth.

After breaking a bone in her knee in the 1980 Alternate Olympics, Gold Chip made a comeback and was USCTA Mare of the Year in 1985, as she had been in 1978.

Huber, who worked out of his parents' Tipasa Ranch in Norman, Oklahoma, runs a training business, the Gold Chip Corporation, named after his retired superstar.

The winner of the 1987 Pan American Games team and individual gold medals aboard Quartermaster, Mike had a successful season in Europe in 1989 with that horse, Nietzsche, and the homebred Phoenix.

GETTING STARTED IN EVENTING

Mike Huber

As a Southwesterner, my background is quite different than that of most eventers, since the sport is strongest on the coasts. Because of my location, I had to work quite a bit harder to acquire the skills of an international event rider.

I began my competitive career in the show ring, because in my home state of Oklahoma, riding English meant hunters and jumpers at that time. Through my mother, I also was involved in the Pony Club, which gave me my first opportunity to go cross-country. I was soon hooked on it.

My next problem was getting the proper training to switch from jumpers to eventing when there were no trainers in our region who worked with event riders. In 1975, when I got involved in eventing, I relied on instruction in jumping and dressage from separate trainers, and participated in clinics.

But I soon found that wasn't enough to make the kind of progress I sought. This became even more evident when I wanted to go to my first three-day event, the 1976 national junior championship in Radnor, Pennsylvania.

There were no three-day events within eight hundred miles of Oklahoma, so if I wanted to move beyond the preliminary horse trials level, I was going to have to travel a great deal. I've done so ever since.

Going to Radnor in 1976 was a great experience because it was the first time I could watch our country's top riders, such as Mike Plumb, Jimmy Wofford, and Bruce Davidson.

I realized then that I didn't have the background necessary to ride a three-day event properly. Even though I managed to finish at Radnor on my own, I needed someone to train with. I sought out Mike Plumb, making arrangements to work with him the following summer.

I went to several three-day events in 1977 with Mike. My time with him was invaluable. Trying to soak everything in was an experience in itself.

In 1977, I went to the Wayne DuPage Hunt three-day event in Wayne, Illinois, where my young horse, Gold Chip, won the USET screening trials. I continued to ride with Mike Plumb and participated in a training session with Jack Le Goff in South Hamilton, Massachusetts, which again was marvelous. I was learning a lot and gaining mileage in East Coast events.

I went to Michael Plumb to train again in 1978. I graduated from high school early so that I could go to Maryland, where he was living, to prepare my three horses for the World Championships trials. I didn't really know what was involved, just thought I would give it a try to see if I could make the team. I'd had a lot of experience handling big fences with my show jumpers, so the size of the obstacles didn't scare me. It was a matter of doing them properly, going at the right speed and getting the horses seasoned over the various types of fences.

Nietzsche, Mike Huber up, at Radnor, 1987. PHOTO BY FRED NEWMAN

I made the World Championships with Gold Chip and finished thirteenth—even though I didn't really know what I was doing. I had relied on my raw talent and the horse.

Following the World Championships, I had a brilliant opportunity: Jack Le Goff invited me to become a resident rider at the USET training center for the 1978–79 season, leading up to the 1980 Olympic Games. I was in college at the time, trying to figure out my future. I didn't have a major, but I loved horses very much and decided that was really what I wanted to do, so I left college. Having Jack Le Goff as a trainer on a daily basis was one of the best experiences of my life, and it put me in the sport full-time.

People often ask me what makes an international event rider, wondering if they have the talent to pursue the sport and go to the Olympics. I'm a firm believer that one must have short-range goals in order to progress in this sport. When I started, I never thought that I would go to the Olympics. Each year I set goals for myself, deciding what I wanted to accomplish and making the steps to get there as logical and reasonable as possible. I tried to achieve one thing before going on to the next.

Various elements go into forming a top rider. First, it's obvious one needs to feel comfortable with the horses and ride well. Training is also very important. I've been involved in teaching a lot of people to ride and know that training makes a huge difference. It certainly did in my case. Three-day eventing is quite complicated; it can't be done just out of the backyard. I had to go halfway across the country to get my training. Fortunately, now there are good trainers throughout the United States, so at least beginning riders can get the proper foundation. When I was starting, there were no top level eventers from my region, and I had the misconception that people in the East had a huge advantage. Though they did have an edge, it was one that could be challenged.

I've tried to teach my students that they can be just as competitive as riders on the East Coast. As a trainer, I have found it very rewarding when they succeed.

In 1986, John Staples from Kansas, who was a student of mine, won the American Continental Young Riders Championships. In 1987, Alexandria Tatham won the National Young Riders Championships at Radnor, and I also trained Cindy Collier, who was a resident rider with the USET and is now riding in Europe. This only proves that you don't have to be from a certain place or a certain standard of living to succeed. One has to make oneself available to the right instruction, the right competition, in order to progress. This brings up the next part of the makeup of an event rider: determination.

A rider must be determined to learn, determined to compete, and determined to deal with both success and failure. Our sport is very humbling. One weekend you're on top of the world and the next weekend you're literally lying in the dirt. You must overcome that and not give up. It's very important to have a positive attitude at all times.

Next, riders must be willing to work very hard and give up a lot of things, including social life, in order to train properly and sufficiently to make their horses ready for competition and better their riding skills.

It goes without saying that a rider must have horses available that can do the job. Good horses make good riders and good riders make good horses. They go together. It's always an advantage to have several horses, because not only do you have more opportunity to ride, but you also are dealing with varying traits and learn to deal with different horse problems. The other factor in maintaining riding at the upper levels is that a horse's career is not as long as a rider's. Therefore, one must continually come up with new horses in order to stay at the top of the sport. So you can't just ride and enjoy your advanced horses. You must always be bringing on new horses to take their place when those mounts are retired. Nor can you expect to go to the Olympics on your first horse. There are horses to learn on, intermediate horses, and advanced horses. The best horses are not suitable for beginners, so one must be willing to exchange mounts through the years to suit advancing riding skill.

The same philosophy, I believe, is true for the instructors you choose. No one is taught in college by their kindergarten teacher. Likewise, in riding you must move on as riding skills improve, from the person you started to ride with to an intermediate instructor, and later an advanced instructor.

In any kind of teaching, there are specialties. An international trainer might not be the best to start a beginner. Likewise, a beginning riding instructor cannot deal with the international training that is required to go to worldwide competitions. So a rider has to be willing to move on as skills improve. It's important that trainers do not try holding riders back to maintain their egos or their businesses. I always feel that when riders graduate, it's a compliment to the trainers, showing that they have produced someone who can go on.

Like riders, horses come to the sport from many different backgrounds. Riders may have raced, ridden pony club, shown horses, participated in dressage or perhaps, Western riding. Likewise, one of my first very successful mounts, Gold Chip, was an ex-racehorse Thoroughbred mare that I bought from Lois and Tex Raymond here in Oklahoma, at a farm only about three miles away. We have riders looking all over the world for mounts, but sometimes your best horses are right in your backyard.

Gold Chip was the horse that really brought me into the international circuit. I bought her as a four-year-old and she and I learned a lot together. She not only took me to the 1978 World Championships in Kentucky, but also was named with me to the Olympic team of 1980.

Another very successful horse was South Coast, whom I purchased from Kavar Kerr here in Oklahoma. He was a show hunter that was a bit too keen for the ring. He turned out to be a wonderful event horse who was very good cross-country and was short-listed for the 1984 Olympic Games. Following that, I sold him to John Staples, who won the 1986 Young Riders Championships on him.

Quartermaster, whom I rode to two gold medals in the 1987 Pan American Games, had been a jumper. An appendix-registered Quarter Horse, he was purchased by Lisa Whitecotton from Jeri Lou Paul in Virginia. He proved to be a bit too much horse for Lisa and she asked me to take over. Most of the horses I get are green and unstarted, but this horse had jumper mileage, though no eventing. From the beginning, he was wonderful cross-country, had a quiet manner in the dressage ring, and was obviously a good show jumper. He went on to be short-listed for the 1988 Olympic Games, finished fourteenth at Badminton in 1989, and has since moved on to the Spanish Olympic team.

My mother, who does quite a bit of horse breeding, came up with a homebred by the name of Phoenix. He is a Thoroughbred that did not race, and was one that I started from scratch.

Another horse, Nietzsche, was an import. I bought him as a two-year-old in Germany and he also has come up in the eventing ranks to be short-listed for both the 1987 Pan American Games and the 1988 Olympic Games.

At the 1978 World Championships in Kentucky, Mike Huber jumps into the water on Gold Chip, the horse he found "next door." PHOTO COURTESY OF MIKE HUBER

Whether you buy the horse out of the field or along the event circuit, you're looking for some special qualities. I found that my most successful horses, the ones that I've just mentioned, all have certain traits in common. They're all very brave, good movers and solid individuals jumping, with the boldness to attack the cross-country courses. All of these horses in their own way are a bit difficult and are not to be ridden by a beginner. They're like John McEnroe of tennis: while they may be difficult, this strong character is what it takes to be an event horse.

*Number one at the 1977 Pan American Games, Mike Huber stands alone at
Indianapolis after a terrific ride on Quartermaster.* USET PHOTO BY KARL LECK

They must be very strong-willed, and so must the rider, to succeed at the top. They
must be talented, they must be athletic, and they have to have the desire to go cross-
country.

Quartermaster, the horse that has given me the most success in recent years, is an
animal with a lot of desire. He didn't go to his first event until 1986 and, because of his
jumping background, I moved him along quite quickly. I started him in July 1986 at the
preliminary level. He did three preliminary horse trials and then moved right on to
intermediate. By November of that year, he had won an intermediate three-day event in
Arizona. I brought him out in 1987 at the advanced level in preparation for the Kentucky
international event. Each time, he got more confident and more used to his new job,
really enjoying it. Having a horse with the right attitude will enable you to move along
at a quicker rate. He had a successful go at Kentucky and was put on the shortlist for
the Pan American Games. In August 1987, he won a gold medal in his first team
appearance—just slightly more than one year after I started riding him.

Phoenix, on the other hand, had a more traditional upbringing because he was a homebred. We broke him as a two-year-old. As a three-year-old, we started him working lightly on the flat and longe. As a four-year-old, he did the novice level; as a five-year-old, he went training level. At six, he was preliminary, completing the year at Radnor in his first three-day event. In 1988, as a seven-year-old, he began the year in intermediate. Seeing his potential, success, and ease at that level, I moved him up to advanced in the fall. He finished fifth in his first CCI at Chesterland. In 1989, as an eight-year-old, I took him to Europe with Quartermaster and Nietzsche and he continued to grow and gain experience. In April I decided to compete him at Badminton, which is by most standards the ultimate three-day event. After finishing tenth in his first try at Badminton, he was chosen for the USET team that competed at Stockholm, where the World Championships will be held in 1990. He finished this CCI in second place and I believe he is the horse for me in the near future.

Spending the 1989 season in Europe, participating in new events with three lovely horses, was very exciting. Competing there against the world's best riders was an education, a fun experience, and a new challenge. For me, this was the logical next step of my development as a rider, having competed largely in the United States through my career up to that point. Riders, and their horses, always must be challenged. If riders are going to progress and become the best they can be, they must continue to educate themselves, never thinking they know everything.

I'll always remember what Jack Le Goff once told me: "The better you ride, the better your horses will go."

In his role as USET three-day event coach, Jack Le Goff offers a pat to Golden Griffin. USET
PHOTO BY SUE MAYNARD

*Jack Le Goff compiled a remarkable record during his years as the USET's three-day event
coach. His teams brought home gold medals in the Pan American Games, the World Championships, and the Olympics—twice.*

*The son of a French cavalry officer, he followed his father into the famed Cadre Noir. His
record as a rider approached that of his record as a trainer. He was the French three-day
champion twice, and a two-time Olympian who led his team to a bronze in 1960.*

*Before coming to America, he coached the fourth-place French team at the 1968 Olympics,
where squad member J. J. Guyon took the individual gold on Pitou.*

*After retiring from his USET coaching job following the 1984 Olympics, where the squad
won the team gold and the individual silver, Jack took on the task of developing young riders
and horses for the Team from his base in South Hamilton, Massachusetts.*

CREATING A WINNING TEAM

Jack Le Goff

There are four elements necessary to make a winning team: Planning, riders/horses, training/coaching, and competition.

Planning establishes your goal. You have to make a master plan for the World Championships or Olympic Games by asking a number of questions and taking stock of the time you have to achieve your goal. What are the requirements to be met? Must the rider and horse combinations have competed in a CCI two-star within so many months of competition?

And how about the horses, their health conditions, quarantines. When do you have to make your entries and express your intention of participating?

All of these things are out of your control, but you have to meet the appropriate requirements, so they become part of your master plan.

Then you must figure out what your resources are. Are you free to plan anything, or are you restricted financially?

In making your plan, you must have checkpoints along the way to your final goal to track your progress so nothing is left undone and you can monitor the pace at which your efforts are proceeding. Most important, I believe that nothing replaces competition, so you have to plan a schedule of competition leading to your final goal. A big part of that is international experience. No matter how good you are at home, you will be shaking in your boots when the flag is on your saddle pad unless you have competed internationally.

When picking the horses and riders for a team, I put the riders first, because the riders are very important in being able to ride made horses or, ideally, make their own at some point (though some riders who have been successful internationally have never made a horse in their lives).

One of the factors that figures in here is whether you can afford to buy a made horse. Time also plays a part, because it dictates whether you can make a horse, or enables a green horse to gain sufficient experience.

When I first came to this country, I had extremely short notice to put together a team before the 1972 Olympics in Munich. I didn't have two years. There were two intermediate events in this country; I went to one. I knew what my goal was and I tried to round up some riders to look at with the help of some friends. The pressure was on, but with Kevin Freeman, Bruce Davidson, Michael Plumb, and Jimmy Wofford on the team, we came through to win the silver medal.

In later years, happily, I had more time to find and select riders. Every four years, we had screening trials to look at young potential riders. Then after training sessions, we would select three or four for full-time training for the next cycle. Out of that system emerged all the teams that went on to take gold medals at the 1976 and 1984 Olympics.

Explaining the fine points of eventing, Jack Le Goff talks to a group of students at South Hamilton, Massachusetts. USET PHOTO BY JUDITH McCLUNG

Jack Le Goff with a group of the young riders he so enjoyed working with at the USET center in South Hamilton, Massachusetts. Mounted are Diane Whitaker, Lisa Anderson, Cindy Collier, and Carol Peters. USET PHOTO

Once you have the riders, then you need the best possible horses you can put your hands on. In England, sponsorship would bring in these horses. In the United States, people used to donate or loan horses to the team. Today, however, riders have their own sponsors to buy them horses.

The next item on the agenda is to train the best riders and horses your resources can obtain. If they are not prepared properly, you have a problem. No one was born knowing how to ride; no horse was born knowing how to do flying changes every stride or negotiate the cross-country at the Olympic Games or go up against a grand prix jumping course. The sport of eventing is probably the most complex of all equestrian disciplines because it combines all of the different aspects of classical riding—dressage, show jumping, conditioning. It takes a good horse, good trainer, good facilities, and lots of patience. There is no instant training.

You must put effort every day into preparation and training, whether it is cold or hot, whether there are mosquitoes or not. There is no such thing as five days a week. It takes most of seven days, and really, there are never enough days in the week.

After all this work, you still have to select the team. The most important factor is being honest about it. No selection system ever has been established that satisfies everyone. The only satisfied riders are those who make it. Only four make the team in the Olympic

Jack Le Goff in a familiar role, giving a clinic in 1986 at South Hamilton, Massachusetts. USET
PHOTO

Games, though sixty try. Obviously, fifty-six are unsatisfied. You have to be prepared for
that in trying to put together a winning team.

When you make the selections, you have to feel confident in your own judgment. You
can't care whose friends make the team. You just want the best team you can put together,
regardless of personal preference.

To me, the selection process is also part of the preparation process, and people must
compete under the same conditions when they are being chosen.

Once you have your team, it is time for your final preparation. If you can take the
squad to Europe, that will be the best preparation you can give a team. In this country,
riders all have a business and demands on their time. But if you take them abroad, they
can't drag their students with them; you must have their complete concentration.

Coaching is the last chapter. Once you have prepared the horses and riders on a technical
basis, when you get to a competition, the trainer has to leave and the coach has to move
in. At that point, you have to exploit what the trainer has done. Coaching for the Olympics
or World Championships is similar to what must be done for any big football game.

I don't believe in making the final selection decision until right before the event. You
take five horses and riders to the Olympics, and only four can start, but something always
happens to one of those horses or riders and the selection takes care of itself. Of course,
if mother nature does not do it, the coach or chef d'equipe must make the choice alone.
No one can act on his behalf.

Once the team is set, it is time to arrange the order of go, and be organized during the competition in order to keep tabs on what other riders have done so you can adapt your plans, depending on what is going on. There is, however, no point in taking chances if you don't have to.

By the time your third horse is ready to start on the cross-country course, you know what to expect. If the team has no chance, then your remaining riders can go for individual medals. But the team must come first, and sometimes a rider must sacrifice his shot at an individual medal to make sure the team gets a medal.

It's nice to get both, but the team medal is more important, because it reflects the strength of a country in the sport. Many countries have a top individual, but few have four people who can bring home a team medal. When the chips are down and it's a big competition, we're all on the same side. It's no time to get excited or hit the panic button; it's time to flow.

If the four horses and riders are well prepared, they're confident. Your plan has brought them to the point where they are able to do their very best.

Karen Stives splashes through the water on her 1984 Olympic mount, Ben Arthur.
USET PHOTO BY MARY PHELPS

Former USET eventing coach Jack Le Goff spotted Karen Stives in 1979 during her tryout for the Pan American Games dressage team. Hedging her bets, she had also ridden in the intermediate-level horse trials the same weekend that was an observation for eventing candidates.

Eventing turned out to be her forte, and she went on to take the individual silver medal at the 1984 Olympics, the highest achievement at the Games for a woman in the sport.

Several times U.S. Combined Training Association Lady Rider of the Year and the group's Rider of the Year as well, Stives has taken a break from competition but keeps an active interest in the sport.

ASK NO QUARTER, GIVE NO QUARTER

Karen Stives

"Karen is going to be all right, but she shouldn't ride again until September." It was May 1982, and the doctor was talking to someone in my hospital room.

I had fallen from Silent Partner at the first fence at Lexington. It was a freak situation, because the horse was such a wonderful jumper. We speculated about what had happened, and watched it on tape a million times. It was a vertical, near the steeplechase course. He brought his front end off the ground, then slapped it down again and hit the fence at chest level and flipped over. It was quite dramatic.

I sustained a severe concussion and didn't really recall anything much about my five days in the hospital.

September was the World Championships in Luhmühlen, West Germany. Despite what my doctor said, how could I wait until then to start riding?

I took it easy for most of June and started again in July. We left in August to train in Europe. I can't believe they even put me on the list. I think they just figured, "Well, she'll never go, so we'll be good guys and put her on."

When we were training in France, Jack Le Goff set up a cross-country school at a wonderful old castle, and I walked the course and felt good. But when I got on, I was scared to death. And then after riding it, I felt fine. I wasn't afraid of the jumps—I was afraid I wouldn't remember what to do, that my instincts wouldn't be there. But once it started happening for me, I felt relieved.

Then we went off to the World Championships. I was not on the team. I was an individual, rightfully so, and I was second on course, which made me a little nervous. I went on the slow side and had a great ride and that was that.

I finished somewhere in the middle, and was clear cross-country with time faults. My mother, Lillian Maloney, who is not what I would call a horsewoman in the strictest sense but has great instincts about whatever she does, decided I needed another horse. She got wind of the fact that Ben Arthur was for sale, and she asked me to contact New Zealand's Mary Hamilton, who had been riding the horse. Mary was working with Mike Tucker in England, and the horse was in his stable.

Mother asked me to get first refusal on the horse, which I did, though I was a little reluctant. I watched the gray gelding work. He seemed huge. He probably wasn't more than 16.2 hands and ½ inch, but he was so loose and up in front. His head and neck were up into the sky. Each step was forward and sideways and at an angle at the same time. Everything went in a different direction. He was like a big gangly baby, except that he was not a baby. I thought, "Oh God, my mother's crazy, but I'll do it to keep her quiet."

When I watched him go cross-country on the video, however, I was very impressed. He reminded me of The Gray Goose, with great instincts. When it was wrong, he either left it out or somehow backed up. I was very excited, until I watched the show jumping. He didn't just have four rails down—he had four fences down, the standards and everything. When Mary would go to steady him, all she would get would be his head and neck. The stride didn't shorten at all, he would just invert.

That made me very nervous. I had been so excited after cross-country that we had verbally agreed to buy him, pending a ride on him Monday morning and a vetting, of course.

I rode him on Monday and he was pretty rideable, but he had just finished the World Championships. The strange thing about this is that Mary did a wonderful job on the flat on him, and to this day, I can't figure out how she did that, because he was very difficult for me.

We went ahead and bought him, and when we got him home a local transport company went down to pick him up from quarantine in a two-horse trailer. To our surprise, we couldn't get him out of the trailer. He ran forward and pinned Mike Plumb, whom I trained with, against the wall. Finally, we dismantled the inside of the trailer and got him turned around. I was an absolute wreck. He had lots of backing-up lessons after that.

A lot of English horses (he was actually Irish, but he'd lived in England) are very uncomfortable in our closed-in barn, because they are used to living in open barns. It took Ben Arthur a long time to come around.

He was nervous about everything. He was eleven, but he didn't know any rules about cross-ties or wash stalls or even fly spray. When I took off his boots one day and tossed them aside, I thought he was going to have a coronary.

I couldn't take my jacket off while I was on him. I was afraid to hack him out in the woods. Heaven forbid a leaf should fall or a squirrel should rustle by. I decided they didn't have squirrels in England. He would take me sideways off into woods that only deer could get through. I don't know how we survived unscathed.

Proud individual silver medalist Karen Stives gets her award at the Los Angeles Olympics.
USET PHOTO

I wore my crash helmet in the indoor ring, even when I rode him on the flat. I never knew what was going to happen and was too afraid to tell my mother we had made a big mistake.

We bought him in the fall and went to Southern Pines that winter. I went training level for my first event and trotted around the course. The next event was preliminary level, and I cantered around. Mike was the next one out after me. He almost passed me, and then told my mother there was no way I could go to Ship's Quarters advanced because I wasn't riding very competitively.

I never knew what was going to happen in the dressage ring. I put a full bridle on him just to keep his head down, but he didn't really come through his back and move into the bridle the way he should. But he was such a good mover and so flashy it worked out anyway, though I held my breath through the whole test.

That initial year was the first time we had the bridge and water at Lexington and he was brilliant to finish third. He just had a way of galloping cross-country and he could be clever with no preparation on my part. It didn't matter what I did, because he didn't listen to me anyway.

I still was not happy riding the horse in the woods or across a road. I was always afraid he was going to wheel and slip. I went to Burghley in the fall of '83 on a USET grant and

*Karen Stives and Ben Arthur in a characteristic pose at the Brigstock Horse Trials in
England in 1985.* USET PHOTO BY FINDLAY DAVIDSON

I managed to get through the dressage. It was tense because a tractor came by with a
wagon full of trash cans on top, rattling during my warm-up.

I was having a brilliant, fast cross-country ride when I came to the third-to-last obstacle,
a difficult combination, an oxer-to-oxer bounce. I had never done anything like that and
I was afraid of it. I should have known that he could work those things out if I went
straight through. But I did the other route and didn't get him back enough and he ran
out at the corner, which was strictly rider error. That was disappointing and I finished
way down, but it was a very good lesson.

While I realized from Day One that I had a problem, during the next spring in Southern
Pines I knew that I wanted to go to the Olympics and that I had a horse who could do
it. Still, he reduced me to tears practically on a daily basis trying to do my flat work. It
was really frustrating, because I couldn't contain him. If I held on to the front end, the
back end was in the next county. If I had him going forward and picked him up from
behind, I couldn't capture the front end. He would be unruly, so he trained me not to

bother him, and he did a very good job of it. I couldn't do any of the exercises, like a turn around the haunches in the trot, that Mike had taught me to supple and develop my horses. I couldn't even ride in a straight line. He was unlike any other horse I'd ever ridden.

Ben Arthur resisted any approach, and the more definite you were, the more he resisted. Although I knew he needed the discipline that Mike was trying to instill, it didn't make him easier for me to ride.

I kept abandoning all the tried-and-true methods because they weren't working, so I put up my own rules—and they changed all the time. Whenever I thought I had made a little bit of progress, he wound up beating me every time.

I'd take him in pre-green hunter shows to school him because that was the only height where I could control him, unless we were going cross-country. I couldn't do a flying change because he wasn't hooked up from front to back.

But I did well at the Olympic trials, so that helped. He was always clear cross-country, and I could fake the dressage by putting a full bridle on. We were first at Ship's Quarters and second at Green Spring.

When I was at Burghley, I saw pictures of British eventers Lucinda Green and Richard Meade using Kimberwicke bits. Though I'd never thought that much of the bit, Ben Arthur loved it, and if I could have ridden my dressage tests in it, I know I would have done well. Mike was horrified when I started to ride him cross-country in the Kimberwicke, but it certainly made my life easier.

After I was selected for the Olympic team, things started getting better. I had some good days on the flat, and in our preparation at Unionville, Pennsylvania, Mike helped me a lot with the gallops, because it was hard to get the horse galloping in a frame.

Though I was nervous about how Ben Arthur would react to Santa Anita racetrack, where the dressage and show jumping would be held, there were so many walls that it was sort of like being in an indoor ring.

We had laid out five bridles for the dressage, but I wound up competing in a snaffle, and it was the best test I ever had. He had warmed up so well that I got off and stood around before it was time to go in the ring.

Afterward, I took off my competitor's badge and it went back with the grooming tools. Security intercepted me and I spent two hours trying to get back to the stables, asking them, "Do you think I would be dressed up like this if I weren't competing?"

Cross-country was held north of San Diego, where Ben Arthur handled the twists and turns on the course like a slalom skier. He was great and made up for all those tears.

In show jumping, I was thrilled with him. We had only one rail down, and maybe I was a little ahead of him there. Though I was disappointed at not winning the gold, I had done a good job, he had done a good job, the team had done a good job, and the team medal had been gold. That was the most important thing. My mother certainly had been right about this horse. One of the things that had kept me going on him was the fact that I was afraid to say anything to my mother. I had to make it work out, and I do my best that way, when I really have to reach inside myself and come through.

A few weeks after the Olympics, I was in Vermont competing at Green Mountain at training level. Someone said to me, "It must be a real letdown doing this after the Olympic Games." But I told them it was just as exciting to do well with this horse at his stage of training. That's what eventing is all about. You can't spend your whole life at the Olympics.

DRESSAGE

Hilda Gurney on Keen at the 1976 Montreal Olympic Games. USET PHOTO

After winning a team bronze medal at the 1976 Montreal Olympics, and two golds at the 1979 Pan American Games, Keen was sidelined by an unexplained paralysis, and turned out to pasture with little hope of recovery.

But fighter that he was, he came back at the age of eighteen to represent the United States honorably again at the 1984 Olympics in Los Angeles, where his rider, Californian Hilda Gurney, was the hometown favorite.

Keen died in 1989, but Gurney continues competing, teaching, and breeding dressage prospects at her farm, Keenridge, named after her old superstar.

KEEPING KEEN SHARP

Hilda Gurney

Keen and I were partners for fifteen years, from the spring of 1970 through the fall of 1985. In '85 he was promoted from the role of competition horse to dressage mentor.

A successful competition horse must have a sound constitution so that he can travel from show to show, while changing feeds and surroundings almost weekly. He must adjust to crowds and withstand the rigors of travel and, at times, extreme climatic changes. Keen was well suited to these challenges.

A California resident, Keen traveled almost annually to the East Coast, six times by trailer and twice by air.

When traveling cross-country by trailer, I have found that Keen arrived at his destination much fresher if I myself trailered and stabled him each night, exercising him lightly either an hour or so after arriving or in the morning before departing. Because he was very large (17.2 hands), Keen dehydrated easily, and I always kept water in his manger on trips that were longer than several hours. On the road, he was always fed the same grain as at home, but because of space limitations he got half California hay and half local hay to start out. I always tried to feed one-half ration California hay for at least three feedings before switching to a different hay. This colic preventive care, of course, is impossible on foreign flights, because hay is not allowed through quarantine. Happily, Keen never suffered from colic.

The younger Keen took more time adjusting to new surroundings. I would lead him around the show grounds in order to help him settle. Throughout his career, he performed best if he had the edge worked off in the morning. I would ride him until he worked consistently, even though the piaffe and passage were still slightly explosive. At show time later in the day, he would still be revved up, but not uncontrollable. At the age of nineteen, the morning after winning his last national dressage championship, I did not bother with his morning workout, thinking that by the fourth day of showing, he would not need it. With Keen exploding constantly throughout the warm-up, my final Intermediate II class had to be scratched for lack of time to defuse the Keen "bomb." Two weeks later, he won the gold team medal and the silver individual medal at the North American Championship at Old Salem Farm in North Salem, New York.

The older Keen settled in at new stables more quickly, but tired sooner from travel and work. My morning edge-smoothing schooling sessions were always necessary, but I never stuck to any specific amount of time. When Keen was quiet, I only schooled ten to twenty minutes. When he was hyped I either schooled until the edge was off or gave him a second early school after he had rested an hour or so. Keen was usually bathed and braided between the morning work and the competition. I avoided more than a twenty- or thirty-minute warm-up before his class so that he was not too tired to be brilliant. I found it much more difficult to have brilliant tests in international competition because my short final warm-ups made the coaches very nervous and they would insist on working Keen harder.

The bronze-medal winning USET dressage squad at the 1976 Olympics: Hilda Gurney on Keen, Edith Master on Dahlwitz, and Dorothy Morkis on Monaco. USET PHOTO

Hilda Gurney receives the USET's National Dressage Championship trophy from Colonel D. W. Thackeray as USET Chairman William Steinkraus offers his congratulations. USET PHOTO

Keen loved dressage. Even at the age of twenty-three, he eagerly waited at his paddock gate for his rider, moping if not worked. He seemed depressed when the competition horses left without him.

I was always Keen's rider, never his master, because his Thoroughbred temperament would refuse domination. Fortunately, he loved to dance and show off and easily won during his entire fifteen-year career. His only soundness injury resulted from my allowing another expert rider to attempt to master him.

Dressage was very natural for Keen. After I bought him for $1,000 plus tax from Alperson's Thoroughbred Farm, it took me three months to coerce the explosive three-year-old gelding to do a working trot instead of an extended trot or passage. When he was four and five years old, I evented Keen and showed him in hunter and jumper classes. He won two hunter championships as well as the training division at the Ram Tap horse trials. I soon found that the only way to have my "bomb" behave away from home was to make traveling part of his routine. Every week, I trailered my young horse somewhere. Once, I used him to lead an overnight Pony Club trail ride across the Santa Monica Mountains from the San Fernando Valley to the shore of the Pacific Ocean. Even leading the ride, he was extremely excited, passaging for most of the forty-mile trip. Passage is fun, but I don't recommend it for two days of mountain riding.

Passage was natural, but teaching piaffe to my explosive youngster was a challenging task. Colonel Bengt Ljungquist (the late U.S. Equestrian Team coach) tried touching Keen's hind legs with a whip just once. That resulted in Keen's launching through the arena

Hilda Gurney demonstrates Keen's skills at Gladstone in 1985. USET PHOTO BY
ALIX COLEMAN

mirror, followed by a lay-up for a cut head. I also tried unsuccessfully to work Keen in
hand, a method which is successful with most horses. Keen was always difficult to lead
and several times he swung me off the ground at the end of the lead rope. Just imagine
trying to tap this huge young horse's hind legs with a whip more than once. I didn't!
Using the whip on Keen's haunches from the saddle was no more effective than the
previous method. How could I ever teach him piaffe?

Creative training methods worked again! Fortunately, I lived in an area with wonderful
trails. Keen always passaged home from our almost daily trail rides. If another horse,

usually my mother's horse, Didit, went in front, Keen would canter in place. I tried having my mom ride slightly ahead of Keen, who of course passaged. Checking slightly behind while she halted her horse in front of me, I would get a few steps of piaffe. Later on, we practiced the same strategy while riding home on a paved and almost unused street. Keen, always aware of rhythm, would hear his footfalls and instinctively try to maintain the same beat throughout the piaffe that he had in the passage. The result was fabulous piaffe-passage transitions. Yankee ingenuity at its best.

Keen made every one of my childhood dreams come true. After his career ended, he remained at the farm I named after him, Keenridge, teaching a few select students how to ride grand prix. My two attempts to retire him to pasture proved disastrous. The first terminated with his running through a fence when lightning struck a nearby tree. A broken jaw for Keen was the result of the second attempt at pasture retirement. People often asked me, "Don't you wish that he were a stallion?" My answer was most emphatically, "No!" A 17.2-hand bomb doesn't need hormones, too.

I tried to share Keen's love of dressage with my students. I know that Keen has played a role in popularizing dressage in the United States. Watching Keen dance made so many of us aware of the beauty of grand prix dressage and inspired many riders to strive for the supreme expression of individual talent and character that grand prix dressage training gives a horse.

*Carole Grant competes with Percy III at the World Dressage Championships in 1982 at Lausanne,
Switzerland.* USET PHOTO BY FINDLAY DAVIDSON

*Carole Grant Oldford and Percy III, a 16.1 hand Hanoverian gelding, won the team and
individual gold medals at the 1983 Pan American Games in Caracas.*

*The next year, they were the USET's National Intermediate II Champions, and in 1985,
Percy took the U.S. Dressage Federation's Horse of the Year titles in grand prix freestyle and
Intermediate II.*

*Percy, who competed as a jumper in Germany, was trained to grand prix level by Grant
with help from Melle van Bruggen and George Theodorescu.*

*He also carried Carole's older daughter, Mary Ann, to the medals at the 1981 Continental
Young Riders Championship.*

MAKING THE TEAM: A POSSIBLE DREAM

Carole Grant Oldford

Can a normal, hardworking person make the U.S. Equestrian Team? My history speaks for itself.

Since 1964, there have been open selection trials by the USET. Candidates who have been observed by USET selection committee members at local shows, clinics, and screening sessions are put on the USET long lists. These people are invited to work with top European trainers at Gladstone. All expenses for horses and riders are paid by the USET. Some of these candidates also have received USET financial grants to travel to Europe for further training and competition.

The most successful of the long-listed riders are put on a shortlist and invited to Gladstone for the final open selection trials to choose the country's representation for international events.

A significant change since 1964 is that we in the United States no longer go to Europe to buy fully trained horses. Now we buy young horses and train in this country with help from American and European experts. Through experience, Americans have developed a good eye for horses with potential.

Another dramatic innovation is the large amount of news available. Magazines give dates of upcoming shows and clinics, as well as results and educational articles, few of which were available before 1964. Monthly bulletins from the AHSA and U.S. Dressage Federation also help the dressage competitor.

Carole Grant and Percy III in 1983. USET PHOTO

More Americans are becoming interested in dressage. They have greatly increased their activity in buying and importing horses into the United States from Europe. Increasingly, more quality trainers are developing here and are imparting their knowledge to the next generation.

At this time, we are acknowledged as having the best horses in the world and riders with enough experience to win medals. As a result of our great improvement in stock and training in America, a new market has developed, with our top-quality horses being sought for buyers in Europe. With luck, there will be enough sponsors here so that we can keep these good horses in America.

The American dressage riders have paid their dues to study the sport and have learned to develop good horses. It is a very difficult sport because it involves two individuals, each with opinions and good and bad days.

The secret to success is staying power, and the Americans have that. As I write this, the American team has just won the 1989 North American Dressage Championships. Our riders in Europe this summer won top ribbons at the major shows. I have been told by key European trainers that we are candidates to win a medal at the 1990 World Championships in Stockholm. In order to accomplish this task, we must have total dedication from our rider candidates and strong support from our sponsors.

My personal introduction to dressage began in 1961. Prior to that, I had ridden hunters and competed in equitation as a junior.

My first trainer was Chuck Grant, and at first, I found the work very difficult. Being a typical novice, I tended to blame the saddle instead of my poor seat. I was sure that the horses, even the trained ones, were not good because they would not perform to my liking. I became frustrated when I couldn't comprehend the difference between a turn on the forehand and a turn on the haunches.

Finally, I realized desire and performance are two different things. I then started the long process of learning to ride dressage. Continuous learning, and trying to communicate with horses in training, has been my life for the last twenty-seven years.

Gold medalist Carole Grant makes a victory pass at the 1983 Pan American Games in Caracas, Venezuela. USET PHOTO

Carole Grant and Percy III. USET PHOTO BY GALBRAITH

In 1973, I began studying with Cristilot Boylen, a Canadian Olympic competitor. By this time, I fancied myself a good rider. I soon found out, however, that I wasn't nearly so good as I thought.

I was able to lease a grand prix mare trained by Willie Schultheiss. After riding Bon Année at my farm in Michigan for six months, I returned to Christilot in Toronto. She was quick to analyze my progress.

"Carol, I know what you have done and what you haven't done," she said. We then worked on what I hadn't done. In 1975, I took Bon Annee to the open trials at Gladstone and finished sixth.

In 1976, I rode another grand prix horse in the selection trials for the Montreal Olympics. I worked with Bengt Ljungquist, the U.S. coach at that time, for one year on the basics with Bit O'Shine. He was very encouraging and said, "All you need now is a good horse to make the Olympic team." I found out later it was going to take more than that.

With my father's help and encouragement, I went to Europe in 1977 and purchased a grand prix horse from the world-famous Olympic rider, Joseph Neckerman of Germany. I truly felt I was on my way to the Olympic team with this horse. But to my consternation, I found I could not ride him. We never even made the show ring—it was a disaster.

I traded him for a fourth-level Trakehner stallion, Plast, whom several German trainers had worked with unsuccessfully. I found I was certainly no better than they were. At the 1978 selection trials, I finished dead last with Plast. This was one of the lowest points of my career, but it provided a good lesson about selecting a suitable horse. I gelded Plast and gave him to my daughter, Tonya, for a children's hunter.

In 1979, I acquired several horses from Europe, one of whom was an eight-year-old chestnut gelding named Percy III. He had been a jumper, and was considered the least likely of the group to succeed in dressage.

I enjoyed riding and training him, however. He learned so easily and quickly that I felt he must have known it from another life. By this time, I had given up my dream of being on the equestrian team, and concentrated instead on the daily work of being a good rider and trainer.

Percy improved rapidly from third level to grand prix by 1982, and we were selected for the World Championships team that would compete in Switzerland and major European shows that summer. Suddenly, my dream had come true.

But there were more good things on the horizon. In 1983, Percy and I were selected for the Pan American Games team. We won two gold medals in Caracas, and I felt very proud when I saw them raise the American flag after our victories.

After studying in Europe in 1984 with the help of a USET grant, I was looking forward to the Los Angeles Olympic Games. But Percy suffered a chronic bout of laminitis and was unable to train sufficiently for the trials. With much treatment, this brave horse went on to compete successfully for two more years. Though fate prevented us from competing in the Olympics, I was able to reach my goal of being a member of the USET and having the joy of a special relationship with a horse I trained myself.

In her eventing days, Sandy Pflueger rode Free Scot at Badminton in 1981. USET PHOTO BY
FINDLAY DAVIDSON

*An "A" Pony Club graduate who calls Hawaii home, the resourceful and determined Sandy
Pflueger has spent many years abroad pursuing equestrian excellence—first in eventing, then
in dressage.*

*She started riding for America in dressage in a big way at the 1982 World Championships,
where she was the highest-placed U.S. competitor, aboard the handsome Holsteiner gelding
Marco Polo. They were sixteenth on the sixth-place U.S. team at the 1984 Olympics, and
had the best American score again in the 1986 World Championships.*

EVENTING AND DRESSAGE

Sandy Pflueger

As the Duke of Edinburgh, former president of the FEI, has said: "Dressage may not strike the uninitiated as a very dramatic sport, but like so many of the really good things in life, it can easily become an acquired taste." Like other acquired tastes, such as wine and music, dressage takes years to figure out. You have to go through the pain barrier with patience, training, and years of experience before fully appreciating the magic of dressage, the very special symbiosis that has to build up between horse and human to achieve competitive advantage at the top international level. And patience is not something I have in abundance.

With eventing, you can do a bit of everything, and I was always like that. Dressage was a bore and although I had to do it for eventing, I couldn't wait for the cross-country to overcome the frustration. Not that eventing is devoid of technical skill, not at all; it's simply that the mindset is different. It is changing now, of course, in the United States and Canada, but in my upbringing, we never learned the appropriate mind-discipline and concentration essential for dressage. So in the beginning, there was just jumping.

Eventing was the only thing on my mind from age four on, through the pony clubs around the United States to boarding school on the East Coast and college in Denver, to the time I decided to go to the United Kingdom because I was told it was the best place to event. Dressage could not have been further from my thoughts. Little did I know what the future would hold.

Marco Polo performs the piaffe for Sandy Pflueger at the 1982 World Dressage Championships in Lausanne, Switzerland. USET PHOTO BY FINDLAY DAVIDSON

Tactically, I decided on three months in the United Kingdom, because with the Badminton and Burghley three-day events held there, it was the mecca of the sport. Since then, the three months have stretched to years with a formative detour to Germany.

If it hadn't been for sheer chance on a couple of occasions, I'd no doubt still be enjoying eventing but not savoring this acquired taste, dressage, which at the highest levels is the supreme test of riding.

Call it fate or serendipity, but at the end of 1974, I purchased a young horse for eventing that turned out to be excellent for dressage. While at the Waterstock Training Centre in Oxford, my attitude toward work on the flat was that it was something to be suffered in order to progress to the jumping—little realizing that dressage is a vital precondition to doing cross-country or jumping. The horse I brought with me, Patriot, did nothing to enhance my regard for dressage.

I found a young Thoroughbred, whom I named Hanalei Bay, after a place in my home state of Hawaii. After a lot of work to improve my strike rate at dressage, David Hunt, my trainer at the time, and I decided that Hanalei Bay was too nice a mover to risk his legs in the cross-country. We retired him from eventing to become a dressage horse. A horse for the sake of dressage! It was quite a turnaround for the books, but in retrospect, a prophetic decision. I remember the trainer saying that the horse was so talented, it couldn't do anything less than dressage. At the time, I can't honestly say I knew what he meant. But he taught me that the key is to put and keep the horse in a balance.

"In a balance" was the theme for all my work in those days. It took years to do what David did immediately with a horse, shifting the point of balance to the hindquarters so he moved more freely and harmoniously, looking smoother and more relaxed. This encounter left a little scratch on my mind that it is a question of controlled relaxation, as in skiing and tennis, although here you're dealing with another animal to achieve that very special chemistry required.

Although the mid-1970s were fruitful in terms of my progress in eventing, they actually were frustrating years for dressage. I could never get it right or match what my trainer could achieve on Hanalei. I began to travel to the major European dressage shows, however, where watching the world's top riders taught me that it wasn't enough just to sit over the center of balance. You had to get your horse "on the aids." It was the incredible balance and obedience required to ride for maximum collection and extension, to ride a horse "through." Finally, I understood what I was supposed to do, but it was only over a long and difficult period that I gradually was able to do it.

Then came the second turning point on the long road to understanding dressage. In the spring of 1978, I entered Hanalei Bay at the Royal Windsor Show and various other international shows in Vienna and Fontainebleau during the year and into 1979. Lady Inchcape, the former organizer of the Goodwood International Dressage Show and a great dressage stalwart, got to know Hanalei Bay. Coincidentally, I got to know her impressive gray horse recently purchased from Germany, which has always had a terrific reputation for producing winners. I had never seen anything like this 17-hand horse and wanted it very much, especially as it had been trained to grand prix level at the age of nine and was unknown in the United Kingdom. So we swapped. His name was Marco Polo and the rest is history. Though Hanalei was a wonderful horse with good movement, he was a Thoroughbred and the European judges seemed to prefer the way German horses went.

Suddenly, my horizons widened. I'd come to the United Kingdom to be a top event rider and now I was also thinking about competing at the highest levels of dressage. Though the horse and I went through rigorous training, I wasn't totally hooked on dressage. Eventing still meant a lot to me, and my event horse, Free Scot, was fast developing into a talented jumper. We were fourteenth at Badminton in 1980, and, wonderfully, second a year later. Because he'd performed so well, we were even invited by the USET to compete in the American eventing trials. Meanwhile, Marco Polo and I were beginning to get our dressage act together and I was loath to leave him idle while back in the States, so it was agreed I should try to qualify him for the dressage screening trials at Gladstone.

The only problem was that I had four months to compete in three eventing and three dressage competitions, all without my trainer. When I thought about it, I realized that what I'd learned was not a set of random actions, but a system—a whole methodology, with a set of equations and solutions.

I was beginning to realize that at each stage when you think you have reached the ultimate, you find there is more and perfection eludes you. That's the frustration, but also the challenge. Eventing fires the adrenaline. It's exciting, but it's not the same attainment. Like mountain climbing (to use another sporting metaphor), you feel you can't go any farther, and then you find another toehold.

Marco Polo and Sandy Pflueger demonstrate a relaxed walk across the diagonal at the 1986 World Dressage Championships in Canada. USET PHOTO BY FINDLAY DAVIDSON

So I resolved to make an all-out effort for both teams. Somehow (and it could be argued this was another turning point), I never managed to get it together with Free Scot in this period, while Marco Polo was improving dramatically. He won the Grand Prix Special, thus securing his place on the USET for the World Championships in Lausanne, Switzerland. So I'd come to the States to do eventing and ended up on the dressage team in August 1982. Marco Polo was the highest-placed U.S. entry, finishing eighteenth out of forty-four.

Partly by design, partly by accident, I decided to go for it with Marco Polo. The difference in learning to control the incredible power of the horse in a gymnastic way, thus creating a true athlete rather than just going as fast as possible, was becoming clearer to me. Another milestone was the German influence. Unlike the situation in the United States and the United Kingdom, the emphasis in Germany is on the proper control of the horse, rather than the fun bits. Put it down to history and culture, possibly. Eventing and dressage mix together, but at the highest levels, it is impossible in terms of logistics, training, and time to do both successfully. I had reached the proverbial crossroads. In eventing, speed is of the essence, the horse needs a galloping frame, whereas in dressage, collection is vital for the movements. I was finding that the degree of collection I was working on in dressage hindered my free forward flow across country. Equally, when I had been galloping the event horses too much to correct this, I lost perspective of the amount of collection I needed for the dressage horses. The viewpoints are different, a bit like top tennis players being unable to play squash.

My year of dressage was 1983. At the end of it, the USET told me that George Theodorescu from Germany had been hired as the coach for the Olympic year, so I had to train for a while in Germany, where he was based. It was a seminal experience. In 1984, Marco Polo made the Olympic team.

Through all that intense training in Germany, I realized finally that dressage is the basis of everything. Very simple things were always taken for granted, but dressage teaches that it is very difficult to do it properly, that it must be mastered, that there are no shortcuts.

Imperceptibly, I became hooked on the training of the horse and what the rider brings to enhance the horse's natural ability. It all takes time and training, hard work and a sense of humor. It's easy to write this, tougher to achieve it in practice. What was it Colonel D. W. Thackeray, one of the U.S. judges, said to me just before we shipped back to Europe after the U.S. trials? "Remember Sandy, lots of impulsion."

Impulsion, compression, more gas in the engine, brilliance, a supreme union of human and animal, are all phrases used to describe the essence of dressage. It's a sustained learning process for horse and rider, with each stage fitting into an overall strategy. It's that simple—or is it? All I know is that in the rest of my career I will continue to search for those elusive little toeholds that bring one closer to the understanding of this art, with the help of the right horses, of course! It's all really an acquired taste.

Robert Dover in 1988.
USET PHOTO
BY FRED NEWMAN

Beating the Europeans at their own game in the 1987–88 season, Robert Dover led their league in qualifying for the FEI Nashua Dressage World Cup finals with Federleicht. His fourth-place finish in the 1988 Cup was the best ever for an American.

While he has become known for his lyrical freestyle performances, Dover also excels in the bread and butter of dressage, the Grand Prix and Grand Prix Special. He rode in the 1984 and 1988 Olympics, as well as the 1986 World Championships, and has anchored several gold medal squads in the North American Dressage Championships.

Though his family moved around the country when he was growing up, Dover always managed to find a dressage instructor. His pivotal training came with the late Colonel Bengt Ljungquist, and Dover was long-listed by the USET in 1977. Jonathan Livingston Seagull, his prospective mount for the 1978 World Championships, died of an aneurysm, but Dover rebounded a few years later with Romantico.

He rode that horse in the 1984 Olympics, as well as taking national freestyle championships with him in 1983, '84, and '85.

The Northeast regional freestyle title went to Dover and Federleicht the next year, and in 1987, they took Europe by storm. After the World Cup, Dover went on to the Seoul Olympics, where he and Feder were thirteenth individually.

In 1989, he continued his winning ways on yet another horse, claiming the Miller's/USET National Grand Prix Championship with Walzertakt.

RIDING A WINNING FREESTYLE

Robert Dover

The freestyle is not just a test put to music. It is an interpretation of a story the rider would like to tell the audience, using the medium of a horse. Dressage is more than a sport. It is also an art, and in the freestyle, the competitor is able to use riding skill to portray emotions.

One begins to put together the Kür, or freestyle, by selecting the music that fits the character of the horse and rider. Then it must be choreographed so the horse can produce movements that coincide with the rhythm. But technical expertise can never be sacrificed in the process.

The Kür must be difficult enough to make the judges sit up and take notice. This means possibly doing changes on circles or serpentines, half-passes in passage, or just difficult transitions that will set your Kür in a different light from all the others.

When I first came to Europe in 1987, I already had ridden quite a few freestyles in the United States with some degree of success. The music that I selected always was pretty light and had a sense of humor. I enjoyed doing the freestyle both by myself and in quadrilles, as we did at the Washington International Horse Show, or the pas de deux that we performed at Madison Square Garden.

Arriving in Europe, I did my Kür at my first World Cup and placed toward the bottom of the class. I found it was not enough to have nice music that fit with the horse and a lot of interesting or difficult movements. One also had to be technically very correct.

Robert Dover at the canter on Federleicht during his test at the 1986 World Dressage Championships in Canada. USET PHOTO BY ALIX COLEMAN

Having performed a Kür that was insufficient technically, I went home and proceeded to work harder on requirements of the Grand Prix. A couple of months later, I went to Lipica, Yugoslavia, and rode the exact same freestyle on Federleicht, although now I had a higher degree of proficiency in the technical aspects of it.

What was interesting was that one of the officials who judged me there also had been at the World Cup a few months earlier. He came up to me after my ride, which was second place, and told me how much finer my new freestyle was than the one I had ridden at the World Cup, that the music was nicer and the new choreography was much better.

Well, of course, I laughed to myself, because it was the exact same freestyle I had ridden previously. But because it flowed with fewer technical problems, he thought it was completely different.

At any rate, my freestyle caught on pretty quickly with the judges. After having marked me quite low in the beginning of my tour, all of a sudden, the judges started waiting for my freestyle. They decided they liked the humor involved and the intricate movements, such as one-tempi flying changes on a circle in the center of the arena with pirouettes at each end of the center line, followed immediately by more one-tempi flying changes. So we moved through the season from Lipica to Venice to Lausanne and then on to Aachen. Until then, I had been second and third in freestyles. Coming into Aachen, I knew it would be very difficult, because my competitors were some of the most distinguished riders in the dressage world, such as Reiner Klimke, Jean Bemelmans, and some of the other German team riders.

Going into my Kür, I thought, "Well, I'll just do the best that I possibly can and see what happens." After I was finished, I received my score, and I remember sitting with Gabriella Grillo watching Reiner Klimke's ride, which he did fairly effortlessly, and then waiting for the score to come back. When Gabby Grillo came back with sort of a frown on her face, I said, "That's all right. Being second to Reiner Klimke is always an honor, anyway." And then her frown turned into a smile and she hugged me and told me that I had won. This was my first major victory in Europe.

After winning at Aachen, I realized that in order to do a good job riding a Kür, one must not only ride the technically difficult parts of the Grand Prix test with accuracy,

Robert Dover performs the half-pass on Romantico, his mount for the 1984 Olympics Games. USET PHOTO

Robert Dover on Federleicht, whom he rode to a fourth-place finish in the 1988 World Cup and later that year in the Olympics at Seoul. USET PHOTO BY HUGO CZERNY

but must also be able to do it so easily that the feelings a rider is trying to convey are projected to the audience with ease and harmony. So confidence plays a major role in riding a winning freestyle. This confidence comes from doing it again and again and feeling at home with the Kür, as well as feeling comfortable with the Grand Prix and riding your horse.

One should remember that the Kür should flow like a ballet or a dance set to music. The audience should be taken for a six-minute fairy-tale ride along with a beautiful dancing horse and rider.

We went on to Rotterdam, where we had the favorite show of my European tour. Not only was my horse the winner of the Kür, but he also had a super competition in the Grand Prix and Grand Prix Special, where he placed higher than some of the German team members' horses.

In Paris, I rode Juvel and placed well in both the Grand Prix and the Kür on him. But I chose not to ride Federleicht in Paris on the advice of Reiner Klimke. The interesting thing about dressage is that, whether it is the Kür or the Grand Prix, there is an element of politics involved, and one cannot really think that one can ride without having politics play some role in the results.

Dr. Klimke recommended that I wait for the results from Rotterdam to be written up in all of the magazines, so that by the next show politics could work for me, instead of against me. This seemed to work very well, because in my next show, which was Stuttgart, and then in Hannover, the horse won again and I was also the leading rider in both shows. By the end of the season, Federleicht had won enough Kürs to be the leader of the European league going into the World Cup finals in 's Hertogenbosch, Holland, where I received a silver whip to commemorate the achievement.

Going against many of the top riders of the world, Federleicht and I ended up fourth overall, having been third in the Kür and fourth in the Grand Prix. I was very happy to finish my tour this way and to go back to the United States to prepare for the 1988 Olympic Games.

Talking it over are Colonel D. W. Thackeray, Elkins Wetherill, and longtime team dressage rider John Winnett. USET PHOTO BY FREUDY

The only judge to be certified internationally to officiate in driving, dressage, jumping, and three-day eventing, Colonel D. W. Thackeray also can take credit for spending a decade or so writing the international rules for combined driving.

A West Point graduate and cavalry officer, he was stationed in Vienna as a military attaché. At that time, he noted, "People thought dressage was Lippizaners and the Spanish Riding School." He rode at the riding school "and when I came back, people thought I knew about dressage," he said, noting that opportunities to judge soon came his way. He since has officiated at many Olympics, World Championships, the Pan American Games, the World Cup, and numerous other competitions around the globe.

A former FEI vice president, Thack is the USET's vice president for driving and a member of the Team's executive committee.

THE TROUBLE WITH JUDGING

Colonel D. W. Thackeray

I won't say that we dressage judges don't often ask ourselves, "What are we doing here? Who in his or her right mind could possibly want to play a no-win game in which the best you can hope for is not to be hanged in effigy before the show is over?" And then, of course, we come right back and do the same thing next week.

The fact remains that dressage judging always has been the focus of a lot of controversy, and hard as we try administratively—making the rule book thicker, more specific, more complex; running mandatory and very comprehensive judging clinics—the controversy remains. The real trouble with dressage judging is that you can't run a competition without it, and this means in turn that the sport has got to keep coming up with otherwise normal citizens who are willing to stick their necks in a noose labeled Judge every weekend.

This is not to say that we haven't made a lot of progress. Back in the Dark Ages of our sport in the early equestrian Olympics, it was de rigueur for judges from certain countries that shall remain nameless to start really judging only after they'd put their own people on top and their nearest rivals at the bottom.

Most of us who watch gymnastics and ice skating have seen the same thing there much more recently, though there is also evidence that efforts to regularize judging in these sports are starting to bear fruit. But frankly, I think our task is even tougher, for the performance we judge is clearly much more complex. And thus even at our most important competitions with our very best and most experienced judges, you will see quite wide

*Colonel D. W. Thackeray accepts the new Equestrian Bowl for the USET National
Dressage Championship in 1979 from Charles Wickard, executive vice president of
the Franklin Mint.* USET PHOTO BY FREUDY

variances both in total scores and in ordinal placings. How can this occur? Is it right or
wrong? Do we have insoluble problems in arriving at truly fair, objective results?

One must recognize that judges' marks are based on a standard existing in each judge's
mind. This standard is derived from the judge's experience—whether from actual learner
judging, riding and training dressage, studying the FEI rule book, reading books by great
artists in dressage, and taking part in judges' clinics. You have all observed that judges
are among the first to check scores at the scoreboard. Actually, they are checking each
other's scores, as no judge wants to be far out of line.

So, what it comes down to is that judges are individuals and as such have their own
personal tastes. Even with all their background and preparation, judges' individual standards

and tastes are reflected in their scores. Judging is not an exact science and it should not be. Other sports also have judging troubles. Why do baseball managers rush out to the mound and jaw with the umpire? Why do we have the instant replay in football? It is typical to see figure-skating scores come up 9.8, 9.7, 9.9. The judges are dealing with an individual competitor and not included is a four-legged animal, the horse, a major factor in dressage.

The position where the judge is sitting can affect his scoring. Straightness and bending of the horse can be seen from the end but not from the sides. On the other hand, actual movements, paces, transitions, etc., are better observed from a side position. It can be said that scores from the side judges may run ten or twelve points lower than the end judges in higher level competition. It is also quite usual in the Grand Prix Special that judges' scores become more even after already having seen the horses once in the Grand Prix.

Then there is the halo effect. Well-known and capable riders and horses are sometimes given, on an off day, higher marks than they deserve. The FEI recognized this tendency and recently reduced the coefficients in the general marks for paces and rider from two to one in the Intermediate I and Grand Prix tests. The halo effect also is dimming somewhat because many of the people riding today are not as well known as were the Reiner Klimkes and Harry Boldts.

Another factor is nationalism—judges giving competitors from their home country noticeably higher scores.

It also must be mentioned that in Europe, because there are many international competitions, the judges get to know the horses and riders. Their placings evolve into the judges' scores being partially based on observations that the horse is doing either better or worse than, for example, last winter at Aachen. Therefore, when European judges come to America, they have no comparison basis and tend to mark lower (on the safe side). It is also quite strenuous for American judges to make the European scene for the first time.

All in all, however, dressage judging does not have any major troubles. Through training programs, clinics, courses, seminars, examinations, and lots of practice, subjective judging has been reduced and scores brought into line. However, as long as dressage scores are not derived through an exact mathematical process, but by human observation, there will continue to be differences, hopefully small ones. The computer has not yet taken over dressage judging.

Certainly, there is pressure on judges, and I think that helps your blood run a little better. I want to be sure I see everything. You can't go to sleep out there.

The 1964 Olympics dressage team: Patricia Galvin de la Tour, Karen McIntosh, and Jessica Newberry. USET PHOTO

Riding and equestrian committee work both get equal commitments from Jessica Newberry Ransehousen, who first rode internationally at the age of fifteen.

After winning the silver medal in the 1959 Pan American Games, she went on to be a member of the teams for the 1960 Olympics in Rome and the 1964 Games in Tokyo, where the squad placed fourth.

Then, after an absence from the Games of nearly a quarter-century, she came back to ride in Seoul and made the cut to compete in the Grand Prix Special on Orpheus.

The foreign representative to the FEI World Cup Committee, she is also the USET's vice president for dressage, an AHSA director and head of that group's young riders' committee. She is an FEI and AHSA judge who is admired worldwide for her diligence and great sense of humor.

FROM ROME TO SEOUL

Jessica Newberry Ransehousen

What is a woman supposed to do? I'm not complaining, mind you, only asking what a woman is supposed to do.

If she has reached high goals—the Olympics in Rome and again in Tokyo—and tradition calls for marriage and children, where does she stand after eight years of dedicated, hard, and intensive training? Lost? Boy, I'll say!

The realism of daily life had just begun to hit me. Previously, the cushioned routine of hard training and competitive preparation had been all that I thought about. But after doing two Olympics, it was time for me to get on with my life. I didn't even know what that meant!

A job? All the interviews were depressing. I would be starting at the bottom anywhere I applied and slowly working my way up. And the pay? That was the real rub. A week's pay about equaled what I could make in a day's clinic teaching dressage.

It began to occur to me that my credentials were impressive in the riding field and perhaps that was where I should remain. New vistas opened up: judging around the country in places I had always wanted to visit and had never had the time for, clinics, and pupils. All of these things were available now that I had more time.

But did I have more time? Suddenly there was a man on the horizon! Though he was not involved with horses, Jim Ransehousen was gradually taking up more of my time and thoughts.

Now, other interests began to grow; marriage and children didn't seem so foreign anymore. I could even combine them, and a little judging and clinics! It all looked very promising and I would be fulfilling the traditionally acceptable role for a twenty-six-year-old woman.

We were married in 1964, and for the next three carefree years, Jim and I traveled when we pleased. I stopped competing to concentrate on an old farm we bought in Vermont, where we kept busy renovating the house.

This was a breeze, and then came Clayton! What a cute baby, but I had no experience with infants and such a small bundle scared me to death. No more carefree trips with Jim. Every four hours I was on call to feed Clayton. As a matter of fact, I felt on call twenty-four hours a day! But slowly, Clayton grew and showed me that he was really an easy child, eating everything in sight and staying healthy. So, Jim and I felt brave and planned another child. Missy was everything Clayton was not. He was easy-tempered, brown-eyed and brown-haired at birth; Missy was ash blond, blue-eyed, small—and a devil. She could cry four hours without stop for little reason that I could see. For the first year of her life my hands were full, so clinics, judging, and pupils took a back seat.

By the time Missy was eighteen months old, however, I felt brave enough to map out an exciting trip to Africa with George Morris. We were going to conduct a combined dressage and jumping clinic. As I had never been to Africa, it was a fascinating plan.

Missy had her own plan. She had a wonderful way of preparing me for separation, beginning twelve to twenty-four hours in advance! That would include upset stomach, flu-like symptoms, and colds! This trip, perhaps because it was with three weeks' worth of luggage, was high on her list. I was up the whole night caring for her before leaving. Naturally, guilty feelings swamped me and I decided to curtail most of my trips until she was about four years old.

While the children were young, judging and committee work for the AHSA, USET, and U.S. Pony Club became important. A lot of paperwork could be done at home. I judged when my family's schedule would allow.

As the years went by, I began to ride competitively again on Fair Lad, son of my Olympic stallion, Forstrat. I wanted to train seriously in Europe and expose my children to life there. In 1978, we moved to Germany. We found a new townhouse to rent outside Münster, and moved Fair Lad into Reiner Klimke's stable.

The mornings were filled with riding. In the afternoon, I helped my children with their German homework. Here, English was taught only as a second language, and we learned together.

Missy rode Polly, the lovely gray pony Reiner had given her, for the duration of our stay. With all these activities we felt we blended into our surroundings quite well.

Dressage competitions for me were a little different. I remembered Germany in the late 1950s. Showing was almost a family affair. Everyone would gather after the show in one hotel room or another, either a dressage rider's—perhaps Liselott Linsenhoff-Reinberger's—or a jumping rider's—Hans Günter Winkler's—to joke, laugh, and enjoy each other while discussing the funnier details of our rides. The room and surrounding hallways would be filled with friends.

Now the shows seemed far more serious and businesslike. Riders were more involved in themselves, less in others. Polite talk, little humor, and no "hotel room" parties. There were far too many riders.

Jessica Newberry on Forstrat at the 1960 Rome Olympics. She finished twelfth individually. USET PHOTO

The classes I won this time were not as much fun, either, in this new, more impersonal atmosphere. Only working under Reiner's watchful eye and the hours of watching him work Ahlerich and others was the same as before, and the parties "à la Klimke" certainly had not lessened in fun, laughter, and interest over the years.

The sport had not changed drastically during my absence, but there were some differences. The need to ride precisely was the same, but now the inner bend was even more pronounced. The more natural frame of the high-level horse of the fifties had to be more elevated through the neck and shoulders. Extensions were more brilliant and the tests were putting greater weight on the piaffe and passage, and especially the transitions, and less on the perfection of the basic training.

It was fun watching the impressive, often unpredictable Granat with Christine Stückelberger piaffe and passage through the grand prix with ease and fluidity. She could really piaffe beautifully in place.

Returning to the States in 1980 was a difficult transition. Clayton was sad to leave his many friends and soccer games. His team had won the local championships and they gave Clayton their small trophy to remember them by. Missy bade Polly a tearful good-bye as their happy relationship ended. Horses were definitely going to be an important part of her life.

We had decided to move to a Pennsylvania farm with a one-hundred-and-fifty-year-old house. Missy and I enjoyed having the horses stabled fifty feet from the house, and Clayton and Jim fished in our small pond.

Missy became more and more involved in three-day eventing. Bruce Davidson helped find us Nina, our fifteen-hand insurance policy who carried Missy through baby novice, junior training, and up into preliminary eventing.

Meanwhile, I really enjoyed helping select some of the Pan American and Olympic dressage riders during the 1970s, and riders for the 1984 Olympic dressage team.

Then came Orpheus, a lovely bay stallion with a pretty, delicate face. With a name from Greek legend, Orpheus should have been something special, but much of his behavior in the first year made me wonder if I should send him back to his syndication owners, name, legend, and all! Most of his barn manners were reasonable, but when Jo, Orphy's firm and patient caretaker, wanted to walk him around the show grounds, he was so unpredictable that Jo never knew what to expect. He could rear, run backwards, and kick out with both hind legs almost simultaneously. He could even look elegant while doing it. Under saddle, he could be either steady or a bundle of nerves without warning. At one show, he put on a bucking act in the dressage arena that amused and delighted the judges. Who said dressage was as interesting as watching grass grow?

For the first year, I never knew what my warm-up before the class would be like or what the actual performance would include. I had never had an electric performer before and I had to think of many ways to keep several steps ahead of Orphy every time we went to a show. First, I always rode him at daybreak, even if my class was at 7:30 or 8 A.M. That gave him a chance to look around. We visited the competition rings and often I would be trotting around in the early morning fog as the show people were arriving to rake and prepare the competition rings. In this lovely, quiet part of the day, I enjoyed my rides on Orphy the very best.

Jo took Orphy for numerous walks during the day to help keep him calm. All of this proved to be helpful in the end, but there were many trying times in between. On one walk, Orphy suddenly began rearing and leaping around Jo, causing a horse on the other side of the bleachers to leap adroitly over the white fence into the arena beside the judge at C. It could have been all quietly excused except for the fact that it happened at the Eastern National Dressage Championships.

Orpheus became a definite member of the family, and even Clayton, who was not interested in horses at all, traveled with us to several shows to videotape my rides. Jim was a great supporter too, giving up his interest in golf for dressage shows along the East Coast.

The first two years showing Orphy were such fun because we did only the shows we thought were needed to further his education. But he started to place so well that the USET began to notice him. They suggested we apply for a grant to train and compete in Europe. At first, I felt threatened. I was all too aware of the responsibility and pressure placed on a rider representing the United States. Did I really want to become involved again? It seemed so nice "doing my own thing."

Somehow, with the wonderful support of my family and knowing that Orpheus was really well cared for by Jo, no matter where he went, I decided to try out for the USET again. We went to Germany on a USET training grant on October 19, 1987.

We competed in four shows and stayed seven and a half weeks. Our training took place near Gabriella Grillo's home in Mühlheim, where Robert Dover had several of his horses stabled. Robert was completing a very successful year's tour in Europe and agreed to help me, offering to put us up in the house he rented from Gabby and to compete in the same shows. The training program was appropriate for Orphy's stage of development, and although the first two shows were shaky because the new work made Orphy nervous, by the last two shows, he had settled down and the results were gratifying. In Zuidlaren, Holland, I placed third in the Intermediate II; in the Grand Prix, Robert placed first and I was third.

With my USET grant, I had to declare that Orpheus would be available for further Team selections and not sold, because if he were sold, I would have to pay back the grant. This was a real turning point because the new year was 1988 and the countdown to the trials for the Olympic Games was beginning. I needed to compete at two selection sites and I picked the Dressage Derby at White Fences in West Palm Beach, Florida, in March and the Spring Dressage Show in Lexington, Virginia, in May. Orpheus seemed agreeable and at White Fences, he won all three of his classes, the Intermediate II, the Grand Prix, and the Grand Prix Special. In Lexington, he again won both the Grand Prix and the Special.

We appeared to be on a wonderful high with everything going in our direction, but that was not to last. At our final competition, a month before the trials in June, Orphy was frightened by a horse kicking out at him. He flew, leaping across the warm-up arena. When we came to a stop Jo checked him out, but everything seemed in order. I rode into the ring directly after and found my test to be not very happy. When I gave Orphy the aids for the flying change, he kicked at the touch of my leg on every stride. During his bath back at the barn Jo found a very sinister-looking quarter crack on his right front hoof. This was just the beginning of a three-week worry session that kept Dr. Midge Leitch continually stopping at our barn. Not only did we need to have a special fiberglass patch with ten screws put on, but Orphy had strained his ankle and the tendon sheath. All of these things did not come to light immediately. As the trials approached, it looked as if we would be unable to start. But fortunately, the patch started to feel more natural and the new shoes he wore to equalize the pressure on both front feet became more comfortable. The ankle started to settle down. Orphy was eager to work again, and the week before the trials, we rode through our first Grand Prix in over a month. Each morning, Orphy came out bright and pleased. We left for the trials at the

USET headquarters at Gladstone, New Jersey, which were to stretch over two consecutive weekends.

At the first trial, we not only had to worry about what we were doing—we also wanted to spend time with Missy, who was competing in the Essex Young Riders Three-Day Event there. She rode cross-country on Saturday afternoon about two hours before my first Grand Prix ride on the first trial weekend. The cross-country course was challenging, and the weather hot and humid. My orders were to be at the end of steeplechase to bathe her horse, Der Kaper, and give Missy something to drink, as well as check that all shoes were still attached. Then I scurried back to the vet box to join Jo and Jim, who nervously waited for her to appear. My nerves were on edge, but thank heaven her cross-country was fast and clean. Her two-day total put her in first place—and now it was my turn. Orphy warmed up well and the first test of the trial was over in no time! Relief. Orphy placed second directly behind Robert Dover on Juvel. We were very happy. The next day, our Grand Prix Special brought the same result. And Missy had one rail down in the stadium jumping, which put her in second place also! We loaded Kaper and Orphy on the van and headed home to rest.

The week between the trials seemed very short, but Orphy rested well and in no time we were on our way back to Gladstone. Most of the other riders had stayed on at the Team during that week. It was nice to have a break but great to be back under Robert Dover's watchful eye and joking with Belinda Baudin and Kathy Connelly. The environment seemed quieter without the added excitement of the Essex Three-Day Event going on.

Jessica Ransehousen wins the Prix St. Georges on Fair Lad at the Dressage at Devon Show in 1977. USET PHOTO BY KARL LECK

Orphy's Grand Prix test was not so accurate and smooth on Saturday and I knew I had schooled too much in the transitions from piaffe to passage. My fears were confirmed when I placed third behind Robert on Juvel and Belinda on Christopher. Gabby Grillo agreed with me about the warm-up, so we laid better plans for the next day. Gabby came to watch my warm-up and supported my preparations. We moved back up to second in the Special.

The USET selection committee met to pick the riders to compete in the 1988 Olympics in Seoul: Robert Dover on Federleicht and Juvel, me on Orpheus, Belinda Baudin with Christopher, and Lendon Gray aboard Later On.

With a deep feeling of accomplishment, Jim and I took a week's vacation in the Bahamas, only to return to find Orphy sadly in the throes of a virus. What a shock! Was someone reminding us that life is full of setbacks? For ten days he was stall-bound while his temperature soared to 105 degrees. Midge was back again daily and Jim groaned at the thought that our vet bill was soaring to giddy heights!

The dressage team was expected to move into the USET stable at Gladstone on August 10 for a mandatory month of quarantine before leaving for Seoul, Korea.

Missy again had her plans well mapped out. She was going to the Continental Young Riders Championship in Illinois while we were busy in New Jersey during quarantine. She assured me she would call to keep me posted. She knew it was imperative for me to keep building Orphy's condition back up from the virus by riding him religiously twice a day. I couldn't be there to coach her or be with her if . . . ! The first call was loving and tearful. Kaper was not up to his usual standard, the footing in the dressage rings was terribly deep, and the weather was over one hundred degrees! What could I tell her from so far away that could sustain her through such anxiety?

We first worked out a riding schedule she could follow, making sure she stayed out of the deep sand until the last minute, and went over the dressage test.

She seemed happier, especially when we both agreed that she would prefer competing there, with all the disadvantages, to staying home. The next time she called her tone was cheerful. She survived the dressage test and Kaper was tenth. That was super! Tenth place would mean she could ride the cross-country with less pressure.

In the third phone call she was quite herself. Her cross-country was clean and fun! She had moved up to fourth and could face the stadium jumping with little pressure.

The fourth call: "Mom?"

"Hi, Pumpkin. How are you?"

"I'm fine. How is Orphy doing?"

"He is doing really well. How did you make out?"

"I won!"

"You did what?"

"I won the gold medal and the good sportsmanship trophy!"

What marvelous excitement and feelings of accomplishment she expressed. It was a turning point for her to do something so important by herself.

Now it was my turn and Seoul was not so far off. One of the best parts of being on the Seoul Olympic team was the caring attitude of the USET. The dressage horses were the first to leave the United States for Korea, and a vet flew with them. The USET provided excellent vet and blacksmith care in Korea, and it was clear that both horse and

Jessica Ransehousen on Orpheus, her mount for the 1988 Seoul Games, during the Olympic trials at the USET Training Center in Gladstone. USET PHOTO BY KARL LECK

rider mattered to them. In return, it was easy to prepare mentally and physically to do our best when we knew all was well in the stables.

Seoul was a marvelous experience in every way. September 23, 1988, will be engraved on my memory as the best Grand Prix test Orpheus and I performed. Against sixty-five of the world's best dressage riders, what was to be our very last Grand Prix test together placed us in the finals for the individual medals.

So, there it was, a culmination of nearly thirty-five years of hard work in so many directions. I won my first international dressage class at age fifteen, and as the mother of two, I was competing in the Olympics just before my fiftieth birthday. I had enjoyed marriage, raising a family, three Olympic teams, judging, clinics, and all the USET and AHSA committee work. I also learned a lot of lessons along the way.

It was a plus for me to take a break from intense competition when I had the kids and while they were young. I meet so many women who try to have it all—to raise their children and ride hard at the same time. Something has to give if you do that, and most often, it is the children who wind up on the short end of the stick. It is important that they not feel cheated.

I was there for my youngsters when they needed me, and I found that when I wanted to go to the 1988 Olympics, they were there for me. I could concentrate on what I had to do in the Games because Missy volunteered to stay home and run our farm while Jim and I were in Korea. The moral and physical support that they all gave me was invaluable. My appearance in Seoul with Orphy was very much a family achievement, and that made it one of the most rewarding experiences of my life.

On the cross-country course at the 1956 Olympics in Sweden, Major Jonathan Burton jumps into the water with Huntingfield. PHOTO COURTESY OF JONATHAN BURTON

A retired army major general who rode in Olympic three-day event competition for both the U.S. Army Equestrian Team and the USET, Jonathan Burton was the U.S. three-day eventing champion in 1947. Demonstrating his versatility, he was the top military show-jumping rider the same year at the National Horse Show.

Since retiring from competition, Jack has remained busy as a judge, technical delegate, chef d'équipe, and course designer. He also gives his time to a number of equestrian organizations, having served as president of the U.S. Combined Training Association, as a vice president and director of the USET, and as a director of the AHSA.

THE OUTLOOK FOR AMERICAN DRESSAGE

Jonathan R. Burton

Since the Europeans are the dominant dressage competitors, understanding where they are and how they arrived there may help us predict the future for American dressage.

Dressage has been a vital sport in Europe for centuries. As early as the eighteenth century, European countries established training facilities such as the Spanish Riding School in Vienna, Cadre Noir in France, Parke Alter Real in Portugal, German Cavalry School in Hannover, Tor di Quinto in Italy, Stromsholm in Sweden, and Weedon in England. Experienced instructors at these schools set up the basic philosophy and curriculum that serves as the text for developing riders and instructors to this day.

Systems were developed in Europe to provide standard dressage instruction by utilizing base schools—such as Warendorf in Germany— as the foundation of dressage training.

In Germany, for instance, all trainers have to attend courses at Warendorf on all phases of equestrian art, including stable management, veterinary subjects, and feeding, in addition to riding.

Candidates at Warendorf spend up to seven years as apprentices under master instructors and are subject to all-encompassing exams before they receive a license to train and instruct. As a result, almost every village in Germany has a riding hall and a licensed instructor who teaches "out of the book."

The German system is controlled and administered by the German Equestrian Federation and produces outstanding results, as proven by the records of the Olympics, European Championships, and World Championships.

Still riding for the Army in 1947, Burton participated in the Garmisch, West Germany, show with Nipper. PHOTO COURTESY OF JONATHAN BURTON

Contrast the European system with what we have. Before World War II, the only dressage riders were in the U.S. Army, which had the mission of producing Olympic equestrian teams. A few officers specialized in dressage. In some cases, the officers had been sent to European schools of equitation to learn. Others used the writings of the European masters and common sense to develop their horses. Since there were no dressage shows or classes at home, the riders received their competitive experience through exhibitions. In some cases, the specialist dressage riders had several horses and would mount regular cavalry officers on their spares to have enough people for a team. In 1948, the last Olympic Games where it furnished the equestrian teams, the Army used dressage horses captured from the Germans in World War II. In sum, the Europeans have a long tradition of dressage riding and training, and the U.S. base is far less experienced.

In addition, European dressage competitions at all levels are highly organized. Progression is controlled by the national federations, and all events are licensed. The European competitions are numerous and well attended, operating at a high standard.

Competitions in our own country have evolved since World War II and expanded rapidly. U.S. Dressage Federation statistics report that in 1974, there were thirty-four recognized competitions. By 1988, there were 483. In 1974, the USDF had 3,358 members while in 1988, the number had climbed to 17,845. So there has been a virtual explosion of dressage competitions in the United States, to the extent that although hunters and jumpers account for 65 percent of the people competing in AHSA events, dressage is second with 55 percent and eventing is third with 40 percent.

Yet results of Olympic Games, thus far, have found the Europeans dominant. The U.S. Army team was third in 1936 in Los Angeles, and second in London in 1948 on captured horses. In 1976, the United States was third at Montreal. But at Seoul in 1988, we finished sixth of twelve participating nations. A widely held opinion of U.S. dressage is reflected in something Wolfgang Niggli, chairman of the FEI Dressage Committee, said to me: "Much of the problem here is that the basic work is not clear enough and therefore the aids are not clear. It is so important to give the same aids for the same thing, or the horse is confused. Your horses are at least as good as the ones we have in Europe, but they come too quickly to too high a level and the basic problems always come through. My feeling is that because the horses are so good many basic things are neglected."

A riding candidate in the United States usually learns to post, canter, and jump across rails in a brief time, then enters a beginners' class, wins a ribbon, or changes instructors. In Europe, meanwhile, the neophyte rider spends months on a longe at the trot with no stirrups to develop a seat. To put it another way, they learn to ride before venturing on to more advanced work. The European neophyte also has the benefit of adequate licensed instructors who are teaching out of the same syllabus.

In the United States, instructors are not licensed and, in most cases, have not had the opportunity to attend courses and apprentice programs as in Europe. Fortunately, we have

Captain Jack Burton trains at Fort Riley, Kansas, on Air Mail. He was an alternate for the 1948 three-day event competitions. PHOTO COURTESY OF JONATHAN BURTON

Jack Burton watches the action at one of the many equestrian events he attends in a variety of capacities each year. USET PHOTO BY IRENE CROMER

some European instructors residing here, but they are few when you take into consideration the size of our country. A solution afforded a few U.S. riders is to train in Europe with one of the masters. European master instructors also give short clinics in this country at greater and greater frequency, much to our benefit.

Harry Boldt, German dressage team chef d'équipe, agrees that the United States now has the horses, but still needs the riders. The trend in dressage is to use European breeds. At the higher levels, fewer and fewer American Thoroughbreds are in evidence. There are several approaches to obtaining higher-level horses. One is to buy made European mounts and hope that the U.S. rider can handle them. The other is to buy less advanced horses, either in Europe or in the United States, and develop them here.

With either solution, it comes down to having an experienced instructor and a rider with enough talent to progress. The statistics show the trend. In 1986, we had one hundred riders competing at Grand Prix level. In 1988, we were up to 117. Prix St. George offers a few more—369 in 1986, 457 in 1988. Thus, we are expanding in the number of participants at all levels.

So what does the future hold for dressage in the USA? My first prediction is that the number of participants, shows, and horses will continue to expand at the current rate of about 3 percent a year. The number of instructors, both domestic and European, should continue to expand at about the same rate.

It is, therefore, easy to predict that dressage will provide more and more people with an increasing opportunity to compete and develop.

Anticipating where our international teams will be placing, however, is more difficult. But with the numbers expanding at the higher levels, with more adequate instruction becoming available, and with a good system of breeding or buying dressage-type horses, it looks as if our chances of success in international competition are improving. In the 1986 World Championships in Toronto, we placed ninth out of nine. At the Seoul Olympics in 1988, we finished sixth out of twelve. In 1990, in Stockholm at the complete World Championships, our mathematical projection should see us in the medal category, with a good measure of luck. No matter what happens, though, it is certain that dressage will provide an expanding opportunity for pleasant competitive sport for a growing number of riders.

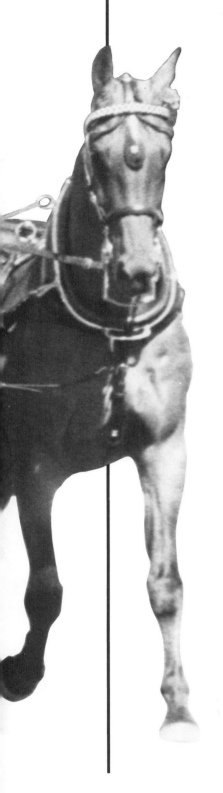

DRIVING

Holly Pulsifer teaches a clinic on hazard design and scoring. PHOTO BY NORMAN
HAPGOOD

Combined driving takes up a great deal of time in the life of Holly Pulsifer, who practically
qualifies as a professional chef d'équipe. She organized the team at Apeldoorn, Holland, in
1980, when the USET first participated in a four-in-hand World Championships. Similar
duties have been hers several times in Hungary and elsewhere, and she always handles the
demands with brisk organization and good humor.

    She is a recognized judge and technical delegate, who also competes with a pair of ponies.
A member of the FEI's Driving Committee, she is a director of the American Driving Society
and a member of its Combined Driving Committee and that of the AHSA. The native of
Virginia is a past director of the Carriage Association of America and serves on the USET's
Driving Planning Committee. She and her family live in Ipswich, Massachusetts.

COMBINED DRIVING IN AMERICA: A HISTORY

Holly Pulsifer

Combined driving turned twenty years old in 1989, a surprising fact that belies statements extolling this "new" sport, and warrants a summary of the accomplishments of the past two decades.

The organization and growth of international driving competitions is largely due to the interest of HRH Prince Philip, who not only instigated formulation of the rules during his tenure as president of the FEI, but was an active participant in the sport. As he relates in his book *Competition Carriage Driving:*

> At one of the annual general assemblies [of the FEI] I found myself talking to Eric Brabec, one of the Polish delegates, and he suggested that the FEI ought to produce some international rules for driving competitions. . . . I paid a visit to the Aachen Horse Show, where I saw twenty-four four-in-hand teams, mainly German and Hungarian, driving round the ring and it became very obvious that the idea was worth pursuing.

Prince Philip asked Sir Michael Ansell, a senior member of the Bureau of the FEI, to chair an international committee to produce some rules for driving competitions. The rules were formally adopted by the FEI in October 1969, and were first put to the test in Lucerne, Switzerland, in June 1970.

The rules were based on the ridden three-day event, and even today, the wording remains remarkably similar in the two disciplines. The similarity was fortuitous, because it enabled the new sport to be readily understood by a large base of capable horsemen.

Philip Hofmann, a respected horseman and driver of four-in-hands who was then CEO of Johnson & Johnson, organized the first show to be conducted in the United States under the newly adopted FEI Rules for Driving Competitions. The competition, held at Johnson Park, in New Brunswick, New Jersey, in June 1970, consisted of a dressage test, a fifteen-mile marathon, and obstacle driving "on an established course between plastic wastebaskets, with a 1 ft. clearance on each side of the vehicle," to quote the program!

Bernard N. Mills was the judge for the Johnson Park competition. Mills, the son of Bertram W. Mills, the owner and founder of the famous Bertram Mills Circus, became chairman of the first British Driving Trials Committee. He was a tireless and successful proponent of driving trials as an international horse sport, and a competent "whip" himself. As the sport developed in America, organizers here relied heavily on the experience gained in England, and Mills was among the first of many British enthusiasts who generously shared their knowledge with "the colonists."

Among the exhibitors at the Johnson Park International Driving Show were Mr. and Mrs. Harden L. Crawford III, then of Hamilton Farm, Gladstone, New Jersey. The Crawfords showed pairs and tandems of Welsh ponies, beautifully turned out with the professional assistance of Victor and Evelyn Shone.

Victor Shone had become involved with combined driving in a circuitous way. He began his career at a Welsh pony stud farm in his native Wales, went on to help Frank and Cynthia Haydon with their hackneys, then emigrated to the United States to join Commander Chauncey Stillman's Wethersfield Farm in Amenia, New York. He put together the Broadwell Morgan team for Cecil Ferguson, and the Crawfords' team of Welsh-Arabs. In 1972, he founded Shone's Driving Establishment, in Millbrook, New York, where his wish for perfection produced turnouts that set a high standard in early pleasure driving competitions. In 1974, the Shones organized a combined driving event judged by the Crawfords. The introduction to the program states:

> We . . . have organized this form of Driving Competition to introduce to you the type of competition which has become so popular in the British Isles and across Europe. We feel that this form of competition will help develop a more skillful driver, and a better understanding of your animal's paces and gaits under natural driving conditions.

Competitors in the Shones' events, held between 1974 and 1977, included many who have gone on to shape the sport as judges, organizers, and teachers: among them, Will Davisson, Jack and Barbara Weir, Ann Collins, Deirdre Pirie, the Kelloggs, Frank Kinsella, Judy Hall, Hopeton Kimball, Macy Hill, Jamie O'Rourke, and me. Many of those who competed at the Shones' became ardent supporters of combined driving, and continued the attention to detail and high standards of performance that the Shones espoused.

After the Shones' competitions, three events were started, which continue despite changes in locale, form, and scale. In 1975 in Massachusetts, Deirdre Pirie and I founded the Myopia Event. In 1977 in New Jersey, the Weirs, Halls, and Whaleys planned the first Gladstone Event; and in 1979, Judy Hall and Richard Nicoll (who directed the driving activities at the Halls') began the Millbrook Hunt Event.

Myopia resulted from a chance remark—someone suggested that there should be a driving competition concurrent with the Ledyard International Horse Trials, which Neil Ayer organized in Hamilton in 1975. Deirdre Pirie, who was tired of traditional coaching classes and enthusiastic about the competition at the Shones', accepted the challenge. When she approached me with the idea I had more sense; I said, "You're crazy, we can't. It's too complicated. We don't even know where to begin." I then went away for a weekend, only to discover on my return that Deirdre had ignored my advice and committed us both to a full-scale driving competition, to be held two months later.

To find out what to do, Deirdre and I went to England, to the Windsor Driving Grand Prix. We found our way into the Home Park to look at the hazards before the competition, and were bent over measuring the distances between some hay bales and fence railings (Yes, hazards were much simpler then!), when an official-looking Range Rover drove up. We were startled by a piercing whistle, and a shout, "What are you two birds up to?" Thinking we were about to be reprimanded for spying, we confessed our plans to run an event in the States, and were relieved to learn that we had been accosted not by officials, but by two popular competitors, George Bowman and Jack Collinson. George and Jack squeezed us into the already crowded car, showed us the whole course, and went on to introduce us to the people, papers, and procedures that make an event run. In years to follow, George's help saved the United States years of trial-and-error learning.

By 1977, there was enough interest in FEI driving to prompt the American Driving Society to approve the formation of a separate committee to oversee the competitions. A report of the first meeting records: "A number of combined driving enthusiasts . . . proposed some temporary modifications of the FEI rules to put into effect until American whips become familiar with the international level."

Instead, the "temporary" modifications became national rules for different levels of competitors, and served as a model for other countries tailoring the sport to beginners on up to candidates for international teams.

Although the first competitions in the United States were primarily for singles and pairs, four-in-hand drivers competed occasionally. Among them were Richard Nicoll, Jack Seabrook, Frolic Weymouth, Lutz Wallem, Deirdre Pirie, John Jenkel, Clay Camp, and Walter Sirrenberg. An interest in competitive driving—instead of exhibition coaching—was fostered by Liz Whitney Tippett, who in 1977 purchased the team that Emil Jung had driven to a silver medal in the World Championships at Apeldoorn, Holland, in 1976.

Jung came to the United States to show the horses at Myopia in October in what Charles Kellogg, editor of *The Whip*, called "the first-ever FEI combined meeting strictly for four-in-hands to be held in the United States." Even before the event started, calamities narrowed the field from sixteen to twelve. A rain-soaked course and a sick horse caused the withdrawal of two other would-be starters, and broken vehicles claimed four more. Mr. Kellogg's report concluded:

The outcome pointed out succinctly that with the notable exception of Deirdre Pirie, who was fresh from competing with a pair in England, American whips have a long way to go before they become equal to the experienced and talented Europeans who have been at this for at least a decade. Mr. Jung and his team were unforgettable, Mrs. Pirie was deft and smooth, and the steady competence of Walter Sirrenberg was equally

With the characteristic cigar clenched between his teeth, the late Phil Hofmann, the first American to compete internationally in combined driving, takes his team around an obstacle course. PHOTO BY PAM SHEEDY

notable. The other two finishers, Messrs Jenkel and Kellogg, can take considerable pride and find confidence in the knowledge that they went all the way.

By 1979, the events had become more demanding (the first Shones marathon was only eight kilometers long). Team drivers began to think of competing in the 1980 World Championships, held every even year, beginning with the first in Lucerne in 1970. Their ambition was fueled by the example of the British, who had won the championship at Frauenfeld in 1974. But before U.S. drivers could compete abroad, the national federation, the AHSA, had to approve. Since the United States had, from the start, followed the FEI rules closely, acceptance as a viable international sport was not a problem. More difficult was persuading the USET directors to take on driving as the fourth discipline for which they organized training, selection, and funding.

The directors had to be convinced that a large number of driving enthusiasts supported the idea of sending a team to the World Championships. At that time, Carriage Association membership was under two thousand and the fledgling American Driving Society had about eight hundred members. The percent that was informed about combined driving was tiny—most of the members thought of driving as a nostalgic recreation to be done with lovely antique carriages, and had little tolerance for "those cowboys who ram around trees in horse-drawn tanks." However, Phil Hofmann, the founding president of the ADS; Homer Easterwood, then presiding over the Carriage Association of America; and Colonel D. W. Thackeray, chairman of the AHSA Driving Committee and international judge, supported the idea, and made several persuasive telephone calls. Colonel Thackeray, in particular, is owed a debt for his efforts in supporting the infant sport of combined driving. Nonetheless, when I, as chairman of the ADS Combined Driving Committee, made the presentation asking the USET directors to take on driving, it was with considerable trepidation and the expectation of being turned down. I remember being absolutely dumbfounded when Josh Barney looked up and said the USET should adopt the sport. I hardly heard him say that the driving community would have to provide most of the financial support!

Between January 1979 and the debut of the USET drivers at Windsor in August 1980, a flurry of fund-raisers attempted to underwrite the cost of training and transporting a team. In faraway Colorado, Wes Spurry hosted a driving clinic for the benefit of the USET, and in other locales, carriage shows held USET benefit classes. The incentive of training for the World Championships encouraged organizers to institute several eve ts in 1979. In California, riding on the coattails of increased interest in the sport, W and Cathy Ashford initiated the Saddleback Horsemen's CDE, and in the East, Glenmore Farm, Radnor, Chesterland, and the Millbrook Hunt events were scheduled.

Although a sizable sum of money was raised, it was primarily through the generosity of the participants that the first U.S. driving team competed at Windsor. Jimmy Fairclough drove Liz Tippett's team, John Fairclough and Jamie O'Rourke handled Tish Hewitt's two teams of Hungarian horses, and Clay Camp and Deirdre Pirie drove their own teams. The United States did not distinguish itself at Windsor, finishing last of the countries entered. Of the five Americans participating, Deirdre Pirie was the only one to complete the meet, the other four being eliminated for one reason or another. But one quarter of the contestants were eliminated that year, and besides the United States, Germany and Holland each failed to finish as a team; in retrospect, we were in very good company!

In the fall of 1980, the USET, hoping to develop future candidates, offered the William Dreyer Memorial Challenge trophy for pair drivers. Fourteen drivers competed at the Hamilton Farm headquarters. The top five—Emil Jung, James Fairclough, Charles Cheston, Deirdre Pirie, and William Lower—drove in Madison Square Garden later that year, and introduced many spectators to the sport. The competition evolved into the USET National Pairs Driving Championship, and started the USET on its way toward developing strong contenders for international pairs competitions.

In 1981, Myopia hosted the first USET Championship, won by William Lower with horses belonging to the Team. Bill Long was second, and John Jenkel third. Tjeerd Velstra judged, and following the competition conducted a USET-sponsored instructional clinic highlighted by his delight in taking the reins of the various teams and rocketing through the hazards at speeds unthought of by their usual drivers.

In the early 1980s, competitions flourished. Competitors benefited from the increasing experience of officials and organizers, and from the stimulation provided by our participation in the World Championships. CDEs at Woodstock, Grazing Fields, Mannington Meadows, Connecticut Valley, Radnor, Gladstone, Chesterland, Millbrook, Genesee Valley, and Myopia filled the calendar for Eastern drivers. In the rest of the country, combined driving made a tentative start at events of the Saddleback (California), Pacific Northwest, and Rocky Mountain clubs.

Some events offered the newly defined training level for novice drivers; others were observation trials for the USET, thus marking a clear progression for ambitious drivers.

The long list for the 1982 Championships named eleven drivers, including the members of the 1980 squad, 1981 USET Champion Bill Lower and runner-up Bill Long. Emil B. Jung, who emigrated from Germany in 1978, was appointed trainer. This was a controversial move for the USET, but also an acknowledgment that no American had the competitive experience to bring our drivers up to international standards. Jung and Pirie went to Europe in May and competed in several events there in preparation for the World Championships in Apeldoorn, Holland. At Aachen, they won the first driving medal ever for the United States, placing third among nine countries. At the awards ceremony, the crowd cheered enthusiastically as Pirie was presented with a huge bouquet, not only for her driving, but also for her birthday!

At the World Championships in Apeldoorn that August, the United States finished seventh. Jimmy Fairclough drove Clay Camp's Gelderlanders to twelfth place individually, Pirie finished nineteenth, but Jung was eliminated on the marathon when he bent a pole in the third hazard too badly to continue safely.

The enthusiasm generated by the USET's entrance into world-class driving continued into 1983, when eleven teams entered Myopia for the USET's team championship, won by Jung. Almaden Vineyards was a USET corporate sponsor, and hazards replicating vineyards, wine cellars, and stacks of wine barrels adorned USET-sponsored events. Charles Cheston leased horses abroad to compete in the inaugural European pair driving championship in Italy, then returned to the United States and applied his experience to win the USET Pairs Championship at Gladstone with his own Appaloosas.

The rapid expansion of the sport did not continue into 1984. Events began at the University of Massachusetts and Middletown, but Charles Kellogg wrote, in an editorial in *The Whip*:

> CDE had a very good year in 1983, but the ranks have thinned materially so far as venues in 1984. For various reasons, some in common and some unique to themselves, previous CDE fixtures have defected from the calendar. Radnor, Millbrook, Chesterland, and Genesee are among the more prominent of past years to come up missing, and some of 1983's first-time starters also are not on the '84 agenda. It has to be recognized that, regardless of the reason why individual CDEs are not active, at least this year, every one of them, living or dead, requires an outpouring of volunteer workers 'on the ground' which far surpasses that required by any other equine sport, and some of the duties demanded call for expertise few localities can provide.

Even so, the American team continued to improve. After selection trials at East Oaks, Maryland, and Equifest, Massachusetts, the team went to Europe to train. Paced by Bill Long driving Mr. and Mrs. Finn Caspersen's bays to a seventh place, the team finished fourth in the 1984 World Driving Championships at Szilvasvarad, Hungary. The marathon put a premium on the stamina of the horses, and our knowledge of conditioning stood the team in good stead. Deirdre Pirie was sixteenth, Jung was eliminated on the marathon again, and Sem Groenewoud, driving as an individual for Dr. Alan Weintraub, placed twenty-second.

Pair driving flourished. Eighteen pairs competed at Myopia in June, with Bill Lower finishing first and Charles Cheston reserve. Later in the year at Gladstone, Cheston again won the pairs championship. That feat effectively laid to rest the rising controversy over using large European horses instead of American-bred animals for international competition, since the champion drove a pair of Appaloosas under 15 hands. Much of the interest and increasing skill shown could be attributed to instruction at clinics at the USET for both pairs and teams. A USET report noted that the Team "has committed to developing and training pair drivers as well as team drivers for international competition. . . . Certainly the results of the pair class at Myopia are encouraging evidence that the program is already showing results."

In 1985 Larry Poulin, with Margaret Gardner's Kennebec Morgans, won the USET Pairs Championship over sixteen pairs at Myopia, then went on to finish eighth at the World Championships in Sandringham, England. Sharon Chesson, driving with a hand broken on the flight over, after tangling with an unruly horse, finished thirty-fifth, and Charles Cheston was twenty-first, putting the team in sixth place among fourteen countries. Canada joined the roster for the first time as Rick Hardman competed.

To stir up renewed interest on the home front, Finn Caspersen formed the Gladstone Equestrian Association and launched an intensive campaign to tell the public about combined driving in general, and the September Gladstone Event in particular. Videos, champagne, driving demonstrations, and a roster of experts combined to interest press representatives from national magazines, equestrian publications, and newspapers. Harry Buurman and Joep Brink of the Netherlands were commissioned to design the hazards, and the premier team drivers in the world—Laszlo Juhasz of Hungary, the 1984 world champion; Tjeerd Velstra, the 1982 world champion, and Jan Erik Pahlsson from Sweden—were flown over to compete, and thereby expose thousands of spectators to the driving skill familiar to European enthusiasts. The resulting television exposure on ESPN, and the videotapes made from the television shows, informed the public about the sport far better than previous local efforts had been able to do, and developed much-needed visibility for driving and Chrysler Corporation, the USET corporate sponsor.

Across the United States, many clubs began small competitions, and although these did not make up for the demise of the larger events, they made combined driving accessible to more drivers. Events in California included Fresno, Oakdale, Borrego Springs, Woodside, and Coto de Caza. Among other events were Foggy Bottom and Arroyo Seco in Texas, not to mention fixtures in Washington, Kansas, Colorado, Arizona, Paumanok on Long Island, Sangamon Valley in Illinois, and The Laurels in Pennsylvania. The proliferation of these smaller events holds hope for expanding interest in combined driving, and for developing a pool of potential international competitors.

The 1986 USET Team Driving Championship at Fair Hill was won by Jung once more, closely followed (0.1 point!) by Bill Long. The class included Jung, Long, Groenewoud, Pirie, Camp, and Fairclough—with a disappointing lack of new talent. On the other hand, the pairs were won by Tucker Johnson in his first season as an advanced driver, but within two points of his marathon score were Philip Hanneman (Texas), Doug Kemmerer (New Jersey), and Canada's Rick Hardman. At the USET Pairs Championship at Gladstone in the fall, Larry Poulin retained his title, defeating Eckert Meinecke of Germany and Heiner Merk of Switzerland, both medal winners at the 1985 World Championships. Poulin's success over the Europeans, and the close contest among all the pairs was an encouraging sign of the progress in the standard of pairs driving in America, as was the rating of Poulin as the second-best pairs driver in world competition by *L'Année Hippique* editor Max Ammann.

At the World Four-in-Hand Championships in Ascot, England, the Americans placed fourth, despite a freak accident in which Sem Groenewoud broke his elbow while walking the course before dressage. Bill Long was ninth individually, and Deirdre Pirie sixteenth. Once again, the cones course was the downfall of the team, as the Americans added four balls down to let the German team's clear rounds carry them to the bronze medal. Jung, competing as an individual, was consistent once more—he was eliminated on the marathon.

In 1987, the American pairs drivers posted unspectacular results on the testing Championships course at Riesenbeck, Germany. Poulin placed twenty-third, Cheston thirty-second, Johnson thirty-seventh, and Bill Lower was forced to withdraw after one horse became lame from shoeing problems before the event, and his spare developed a muscle spasm during the marathon. Numerous shoeing and veterinary problems plagued the team, which finished a disappointing eighth among fourteen nations. However, the Canadians, who had trained at the American selection trials, finished fourth, with Udo Hochgeschurz posting the third-best score of the marathon, so we could not blame the preparation given our drivers.

The quality of competition in the United States reached a new level at the 1987 Gladstone event. Catherine Tyler in *Driving Digest* reported:

> For the first time in America, horse teams from seven countries competed in an FEI CAI event, stepping up a notch from the Gladstone Driving Event's '85/'86 CAA status. The chance to reaffirm his status at Gladstone drew twice World Champion Tjeerd Velstra out of recent retirement from four-in-hand competition for an exciting match which ended first, Velstra (Holland); second, Ysbrand Chardon (Holland); third, Laszlo Juhasz (Hungary)—the same top three order as the '86 World Driving Championships at Ascot. Fourth was Bill Long (USA), who as the highest placed American, claimed the Chrysler-USET National Four-in-Hand Championship.

Another promising development in national activities was the formation of a "circuit" of three competitions in the Southwest with the goal of improving events by sharing equipment, leadership, and competitors. Stuart Morris pioneered the concept, which culminated in the Rocky Mountain Carriage Club's first sanctioned CDE at the Tomora Training Center in Greeley, Colorado, in May of 1988. Phil Hanneman and Charles Smith respectively topped the pairs, and Randy McFarland and Anne Wolfe the singles. The achievement earned the pairs drivers invitations to USET training sessions, and brought McFarland a chance to be on the Gladstone Equestrian Association's Master's Cup Team at Windsor in early 1989.

At the '88 World Championships, held at Apeldoorn for the third time, the American team of Long, Pirie, and Groenewoud finished seventh. Individually, Long was thirteenth, below the form he had shown in previous competitions in Europe, Groenewoud seventeenth after a weak dressage test, but an excellent marathon, and Pirie a disappointing forty-second after unusual problems on the cones course. Camp, competing as an individual, finished thirty-fourth, and Jung, an American citizen now, but living in Germany, was eliminated after a marathon fraught with confusion.

Larry Poulin again won the USET Pairs Championship, besting Udo Hochgeschurz (Canada), and world champion Laszlo Kecskemeti (Hungary) in the CAI at Gladstone.

Noteworthy additions to the Gladstone competitors were the "outlanders"—Charles Smith of Dallas, Texas, who received the Trammel Crow grant, and Veronica Wood, who traveled from Missouri.

The 1989 season was ushered in by the April selection trial for pairs at Gladstone at Tampa, part of the Volvo World Cup festival. The Gladstone organization distinguished itself by moving en masse—or en trailer to be exact—to Florida, where they and The Florida Whips proved that local volunteers and imported administrators can put on a first-class event. In response, an unexpectedly large entry resulted as drivers convened from California, Illinois, Vermont, Texas, and points between to enjoy the sunshine and their favorite sport.

In May at Windsor, Bill Long (New Jersey), Lana Wright (Maryland), and Randy McFarland (California) made up the American team for the Masters Cup, a new type of competition for which the team consists of a four-in-hand, a pair, and a single. The Americans each placed second in their class, and won the Masters Cup from seven other nations. The American driving community greeted this success enthusiastically, for it recognized not only the four-in-hands and pairs, but the singles, which are accessible to all—and in particular, not a single from the East, but McFarland, a Western driver of an Appaloosa/Thoroughbred cross.

Following Tampa, the pairs traveled to Canada, New Jersey, and Myopia before Poulin, Chesson, and Wright, with Kelly Valdes as alternate, were selected to go to the World Championships in Balatonfenyves, Hungary. There they astounded many by leading after dressage, Sharon Chesson placing first, Lana Wright fifth, and Larry Poulin eighth. The

Holly Pulsifer and her son, Nathaniel, compete with Aquila Pan and Aquila Snowflake. PHOTO COURTESY OF HOLLY PULSIFER

team was not competitive in the marathon, however. Although they made the section times handily, none of the three were able to push their horses through the hazards as fast as was needed to win. Larry Poulin finished tenth overall. There was some solace in the fact that Udo Hochgeschurz of Canada won the individual gold medal. Udo prepared for the championships at all the American events.

On the twentieth birthday of international combined driving and the tenth anniversary of USET involvement, it can be said that the sport has produced drivers of great ability, both as reinsmen and trainers, whose horses accomplish maneuvers on the marathon and exhibit suppleness in the dressage ring that were not even imagined twenty years ago. Through increasingly sophisticated competitions and USET training programs, as well as local efforts that encouraged new talent, American drivers have kept up. Indeed, our pairs drivers have become leaders in dressage, but we have not yet achieved the all-around excellence that wins a medal. Nor has America solved the problem of nurturing a sport in a country where vast distances make it difficult for experienced organizers, judges, and competitors to help each other. Without assistance and stimulation from other nearby events, local enthusiasts burn out. Without spectators and sponsors, large sources of financing, which have up to now been available only from the USET and the Gladstone Equestrian Association, are required to produce events. The future will tell whether the many small local competitions can spread the interest, and provide the underlying support for the international aspirations of the United States.

Finn Caspersen on the back of the vehicle as his team makes a tight turn in the marathon at Flyinge, Sweden, in 1985. PHOTO BY KRISTER LINDH

Beneficial Corporation CEO Finn Caspersen has become the driving force behind American driving, tirelessly promoting and benefiting the sport he loves.

As chairman of the Gladstone Equestrian Association, he helped make the Gladstone Driving Event one of the world's finest, and a place for Americans to test their skills against European drivers.

On a larger scale, he was behind Beneficial's deeding of the Gladstone training center to the USET in 1988, assuring the Team a permanent home forever.

Finn himself participates in driving as a groom-navigator, having three World Championships to his credit and aspiring to many more. In 1990, he added another title to his portfolio and became the USET's president.

A GROOM'S-EYE VIEW OF DRIVING

Finn M. W. Caspersen

Little did I know what lay ahead in 1976, when my wife, Barbara, suggested we take up driving because she had been advised not to ride during her pregnancy. Driving seemed an innocuous sport that easily could be pursued with a minimal investment of time, effort, and resource, but with a great deal of consequent pleasure.

Several pleasure driving shows quickly disabused us of that notion. While we did well, first with a pony, then a horse pair, there was always a turnout that was just a bit better, at least in the eyes of the judges who beheld it. The subjectivity involved was most frustrating, causing us to yearn for a more objective standard. Human nature and our competitiveness took their inevitable course as we continually strove to improve.

Bill Long joined us about this time as our farm manager and suggested that we try our luck at combined driving, a discipline of which we knew nothing, where measurable performance in the marathon and cones was absolute and even dressage allowed only limited subjectivity. We all agreed to make this change and Bill became the prime driver, though Barbara still drove occasionally with either Bill or me as groom. The die was cast, however, and I became the permanent owner-groom and brass polisher, either to Barbara or Bill.

As with all such enterprises, success—and even failures—bred ever-higher aspirations. At first, we drove Norwegian Fjords, marvelous animals and still my favorites, but not competitive in dressage or the walk section of the marathon. After several years with them,

Keeping a watchful eye going through the water at the 1988 World Championships in Holland is Finn Caspersen, whose titles include Beneficial Corporation CEO and groom. PHOTO BY ALIX COLEMAN

including one year when we tried to compete in vain with a unicorn hitch (two horses behind and one in front) in the national team championship, we switched to an Arabian/ Fjord-cross pair. We were quite successful, except that we could never be sure whether on any given day they would be classified as horses or ponies. Rather than continue to fight that battle, we switched for a short, notably unsuccessful period, to a team of Canadian crossbreds. Then we became involved with Holsteiners and Dutch warmbloods, which we continue to utilize to this day.

We purchased the Holsteiners through Emil Jung, the most knowledgeable and successful American combined driver of that era. Though Phil Hofmann was unquestionably the pioneer and father of combined driving in this country, Emil brought from Germany the most modern and successful training methods. (On a side note, I always regret that Phil Hofmann's participation and mine in the sport did not overlap more, as he personified the competitiveness and élan the sport needs.)

Emil was kind enough to take Bill and me under his wing as he taught Bill the skills necessary to succeed in the national and international arena.

Emil even attempted to teach me how to time a marathon, but this was one area where the German and American methods could not mesh. Despite my failures in Teutonic timing, I continued as Bill's owner-groom, competing up and down the Eastern Seaboard.

What I do in the marathon comes easily for me. It's a natural inclination to use your weight against where the carriage wants to go. Even on small planes these days, I find myself leaning over the other way when we bank to land.

When things go well in the marathon, it's art in motion. When they don't, it's frustrating to be groom-navigator, because you don't have control of the horses and you're there to get the vehicle out of trouble.

During this period my wife, Barbara, recognized the scarcity of shows (still a problem today) as a severely limiting factor on our competition. In 1982, she took it on herself to revive the Gladstone Driving Event, which had been defunct for several years. The format of Gladstone was different from other shows in the United States in that it encompassed a number of social and sponsor activities that provided funding for the show and other driving-related activities.

Barbara attempted to follow Phil Hofmann's axiom that driving was only worthwhile if it was fun, something we all should remember. The Gladstone Event continues to honor his contributions to the sport through a marvelous perpetual trophy, an antique silver tea service for the winning team driver, which his family donated in 1989.

As the show progressed, its funding activities became so successful that European pairs and teams could be brought to Gladstone to raise the level of U.S. competition. Foreign judges, technical delegates, and course designers also were imported, and clinics given so that U.S. and European standards would be equivalent. American drivers were sent abroad so they could benefit from the high level of European competition. Competitors at Gladstone routinely are offered grants if they otherwise cannot afford to participate. Widespread interest in the sport was encouraged through the electronic and print media.

Those Gladstone-sponsored activities did not bloom overnight, but were the product of eight years of hard work by a dedicated committee and board who have immeasurably improved the sport.

After the first Gladstone, Bill and I became interested in testing our skills against the Europeans. We conferred with Emil, who gave us crucial encouragement, and we succeeded in making the 1984 U.S. team that would compete in the World Championships in Hungary. After weeks of arduous training on a farm there, we were pleased to finish in the top ten in the world, despite a disappointing dressage test. That single experience addicted us to European competition. The Europeans were the best, and a combination of individual and national pride compelled us to attempt to compete successfully against them on their home ground.

In the beginning, the Europeans regarded American drivers with amusement, and even occasional contempt. One judge in Hungary (not a Hungarian) was so sure Americans could not drive a dressage test that he never even bothered to look at our test, much preferring to chat up his attractive scribe.

The year following the Hungarian experience, we competed at Windsor and began our love affair with the Royal Windsor Horse Show. Thanks to great driving by Bill, as well as a little luck, we won the show. But just as important, we came to know many of the best European drivers and appreciate their true love of the sport. Further, Windsor provided a partial model for Gladstone and what it could become. While Gladstone could never replicate the backdrop of Windsor Castle, it could provide an atmosphere of fun and competition on a high level. Windsor's good-humored emphasis on the pony steeplechase

Queen Elizabeth greets Finn Caspersen after his team won at Windsor in 1985.
PHOTO COURTESY OF FINN CASPERSEN

and pony club games gave us an added dimension for Gladstone and taught us the value of crowd-pleasing activities.

Finally, Windsor and Gladstone became in many respects "sister shows," with squads from Gladstone (team, pair, and single) competing at Windsor for the Master's Trophy, which was in residence at the USET Training Center in Gladstone after America won it in 1989.

The Queen even personally donated a trophy for advanced single horse competition at Gladstone. Indeed it was at Windsor that the odd amalgam of groom-owner, a concept difficult for many Europeans to understand, was formally recognized by the Queen.

When I was presented (in full groom's livery) to her after our victory, she noted the uniqueness of my position and then inquired about my function on the marathon. I replied that I lowered the center of gravity and she, noting my middle-aged spread, graciously though accurately stated that I was admirably suited for the job.

During the following years, we continued to compete abroad and at home, sometimes successfully, sometimes not. We have won the U.S. Championship three times, more than any other team in history, and have placed well in many European shows. Unfortunately, an individual or team medal in a World Championships continues to elude us. Part of the problem is the necessity of going to Europe to compete in top shows with the concomitant significant financial hardships. Additionally, Americans have great difficulty in acquiring top driving horses, since the Europeans invariably have first pick and the American breeds just do not appear to be consistently competitive. Finally, despite massive efforts at publicity, there is significant difficulty in recruiting young, dedicated drivers, with lack of sponsorship contributing to the problem.

Despite all these obstacles and our persistent individual and national failure to gain World Championship medals, we continue to love the sport. It is truly an amateur sport in the best sense of the word. Our total winnings over a decade have been less than $1,000. We have become fast friends with our strongest competitors, both in victory and defeat. Royalty and commoners compete on equal ground, learning from and respecting one another.

Driving is a family sport. Linda, Bill's wife, contributes immeasurably by handling the incredibly complex logistics of European trips, and has been U.S. chef d'équipe for several international events. All Bill's children and mine have assisted in preparation and grooming. Milton, Bill's youngest son, may well follow in his father's footsteps.

Contrary to popular belief, combined driving is not necessarily a sport of the rich. One of the best drivers in the world is Hanspeter Rueschlin, an artisan from a Swiss village who, through superb training, has turned horses from a nondescript background into arguably the best dressage team in the world.

And as for being a groom, where else can a middle-aged man participate in a world championship arena, have the best seat (or standing room) possible, and the continued opportunity to travel to new venues and meet truly wonderful people?

On a more personal level, grooming affords me the opportunity to abandon the mantle of a CEO and become a participant and even second fiddle in a real-life sport, with all the inherent tribulations and joy.

Driving is a great sport and I love participating in it. Combined driving will continue to evolve and advance rapidly, as it has over the past decade, and there must be every effort to make the United States more competitive. But we must never forget that it is the sport that counts first, last, and always—though a medal now and then certainly would be welcome!

At Windsor in 1985, Bill Long's effort with Finn Caspersen's team won him the event. USET
PHOTO BY FINDLAY DAVIDSON

In the 1984, 1986, and 1988 World Four-in-Hand Championships, Bill Long was the top-scoring driver for the USET.

The three-time national champion, who trains his own horses, scored the first American international four-in-hand combined driving victory with his win at Windsor, England, in 1985.

Bill lives in Andover, New Jersey, where he manages Finn Caspersen's Westby Farm. His wife, Linda, and sons William and Milton are actively involved in the success of the Caspersen team as well.

WINNING AT WINDSOR

Bill Long

During the months leading up to the Windsor driving event in England in 1985, I experienced many ups and downs in my training program.

First, my horses arrived from Germany only ten months before the selection process began for the 1984 World Four-in-Hand Championships in Szilvasvarad, Hungary. None of these Holsteiners owned by Finn Caspersen had any previous experience, but after only two months, I had them all driving, working both in pairs and four-in-hand.

The selection trials were beginning and I knew I had to do exceptionally well to earn a spot on the team with my youngsters. The first trial was held in Gladstone, New Jersey, at the USET Training Center. Dressage went fairly well, but I knew I could do better and felt sure that with the summer to work, we would be much improved.

The next morning, the first marathon hazard drove fine, but then came the water hazard. It was the first time the horses had been in any water off the farm. I knew as soon as I approached the first gate that I was in trouble. One of my leaders, my mare, took off with the reins and bolted up, out and over the railroad ties, bringing the other leader with her, leaving my two wheelers, crew, and carriage behind in the water. This was the worst feeling I had experienced in competition. After all of the work, training, and effort, there we sat. I saluted the hazard judge and proceeded to unhook. While walking the horses back to the barn, I thought that if I had entered a little more slowly or taken another option, things might have gone better. But even after that bad showing,

Full speed ahead is Bill Long's usual way of handling a marathon. USET PHOTO BY FINDLAY
DAVIDSON

I had a warm feeling in the back of my mind, because after four sections and one hazard
I had proven to myself that I had a good team. With some luck and more intensive
training, I could and would drive for the United States in a World Championship.

After the accident, I took my mare out of the lead. She was never to return to that
spot, but became one of the most brilliant wheel horses that I have ever driven and
competed with.

We did quite well in the remaining selection trials and were chosen to represent the
United States in Hungary, where we were more than pleased to finish third in the cross-
country and seventh overall.

I felt our team was everything I had hoped and knew they could be. As a result of that
fine showing, we were the USET's four-in-hand national champions.

In December 1984, while I was training in our outdoor dressage ring, Mr. Caspersen
came down the driveway, stopped his car, and hopped on the carriage with me.

"Bill," he said, "how would you like to compete at the Royal Windsor Horse Show this
coming May?" I was thrilled and didn't hesitate to answer yes.

"It would be wonderful," I told him. We then took about a ten-mile drive discussing
exactly what it would entail to make such a trip so early in the season. We knew we
would have to train very hard over the winter in order to have the team in shape for the
marathon.

Back to reality and the barn, I was having problems. My leaders, after the grueling marathon in Hungary, were a little upset in their hazard training. They thought they had to rush, making it difficult to keep them flat on the ground concentrating on the job they had to do. So I started all over again, doing single driving and pair driving to see if I could regain their confidence in me. It took until February to achieve what I wanted, but by then, the horses were back in form and going quite well.

Time was getting short before we were to leave for England. My wife, Linda, coordinated the entire trip—a task that entailed a tremendous amount of paperwork, arranging the arrivals and departures of animals, and determining what shots and health certificates the British required. The lists seem endless, and without someone like Linda to do this work, it would be next to impossible to leave the farm.

Finally, five horses, two carriages, and all the tack trunks were loaded into vans and we were on our way to JFK Airport. The morning before we left, Mr. Caspersen paid us a visit to check that all was in order. After he was assured everyone and everything was ready, he said to me, "Just remember, Bill, we are going to Windsor to give it our best shot."

During the trip, I thought long and hard about what Mr. Caspersen had said. At one point, I went down to the plane's cargo section to check the horses. Just being alone with them caused many things to race through my mind. I looked at the animals as they stood there so quietly, then said to each of them, "You know we can do this if we just work together." I have always realized that if you treat horses with the respect they deserve— asking them to give what you know they can, but not more than is possible—they in turn give you their very best. You hope that will make a winning team.

We landed at Heathrow Airport, where we were met by our transport agent. He immediately made Linda and me feel very welcome and has since become a dear friend. He told us we were stabling our horses in the Royal Mews, which to me clearly was the sign of a great beginning.

We were greeted at the mews by Roger Oliver, who was in charge of the Queen's horses and carriages and all other facets of the Royal Stables for over twenty-five years. He couldn't have been nicer. Our horses were stabled directly opposite Prince Philip's and next to his carriage collection.

After feeding the horses and bedding them down, I asked Roger where we could train. He advised us to get some much-needed sleep and he would show me the facilities the following morning.

The next day, I was back in the stables mucking the stalls with my son, Bill, Jr., when there was a shout from the courtyard, "Bill, are you in the stables?"

Continuing to muck and feed I answered yes. "Well," the voice called back, "if you want to see where you can train, be ready and hooked in an hour."

"Fine," I said, thinking that it was Roger Oliver with whom I was speaking. I walked into the courtyard to thank him, but much to my embarrassed surprise, I found Prince Philip standing there instead. Not knowing exactly what to say or do, I bowed slightly and said, "Thank you, sir."

He shook my hand, asking how our horses had traveled and if everything was in order.

To reach Prince Philip's training facilities, we had to go down the "Long Walk" located in the Great Park. It was absolutely beautiful. The red deer and birds of every variety throughout the park were magnificent to observe from atop our carriage.

But now we had to get down to the task of preparing for the show. After training for a couple of hours, Linda and I were on our way back to the stables when we spotted Prince Philip's team trotting down the opposite side of the Long Walk, also going toward the stables. I asked Linda to put the stopwatch on him and see how fast his Cleveland Bays were trotting. When she told me they were going briskly between nineteen and twenty-two kilometers per hour, I was quite surprised. We continued back to the mews and began bathing the horses. Spotting Prince Philip's groom walking by the stable yard, I approached him and said, "Boy, those horses can really trot!" He replied that they get up speed when they are on their way back to the stable. That, he explained, is the reason this particular stretch of track always is used for the speed section in the Windsor marathon, where they will ask the horses to do twenty kilometers per hour.

I grinned to myself, having discovered the competitive spirit leaves no one untouched in this sport. Immediately thereafter, my grin was replaced with a frown of concern when I realized my horses never had been asked to give that much speed before and I would really have to push them to their maximum.

I spent the days before the show working on both dressage and speed/endurance, which is very difficult. You ask them to get round and supple and on the bit for the dressage, and then turn around and give them their heads and ask them for twenty kilometers per hour. Even so, the training was going well. Mr. Caspersen had arrived in Windsor along with his wife, Barbara, to get ready for one of the biggest shows to date in our combined driving career.

On the first day, our dressage went well, but the team was distracted by the nearby train, which is a Windsor trademark and very difficult to prepare for unless you happen to live next to a railway station. The horses decided they would make a very close inspection of the X marked with sawdust in the middle of the dressage field.

All in all, we did fine, but at the end of the first day, Prince Philip took home the crystal trophy and we had to settle for fourth place in dressage.

We knew now that we would have to put in a good marathon to better our standing. The next morning we were anxious to be on our way over the twenty-five-kilometer course. It started at the home of the famous Windsor Polo Club in the Great Park.

Section A bent around fields and streams and paved roads through the park. Section B, the walk section, was not easy going, up and down mostly on riding trails and over wood chips, used often in the park for footing. We were only in time by six seconds.

Section C, the fast trot, was very difficult, doing twenty kilometers per hour in slick footing. We had gotten caught in a shower on Section B and knew then that it would be hard to maintain the speed required in Section C. About halfway through, the track started to wind around some trees and tight corners and down steep embankments. We figured the time almost perfectly. At the third kilometer, Mr. Caspersen had me ahead by almost a minute and a half, which was time we desperately needed. At the finish of Section C we were nineteen seconds ahead of our allotted time. The only other teams finishing on time in that section were Prince Philip and George Bowman.

Section D was uneventful and we started Section E in a slight drizzle. The horses were a little tired, but that didn't seem to stop them from taking quite a hold on me as we approached the first of eight hazards. There were four gates to negotiate, all difficult because of the short distance between the letters, but this was the direct route. We had to attempt it in order to win. After the first hazard, I decided that if we could keep up the same pace in the next seven, it would take quite a good team to beat us. As I crossed the finish line I knew I had driven every hazard and all the sections to the best of my ability and my team had given me their greatest effort. My grooms had done a superb job, and now we just must wait for the results to be tallied.

At least an hour passed before we learned we would take home the crystal. Our score in the marathon not only earned us the win in that competition, but put us into first place overall. We had about a ten-point lead to maintain in the cones the next day, so we had a chance for an overall victory.

The cones started early on Sunday in the main ring, directly in front of the grandstands and box seats, with the Queen herself and the Royal Family in attendance. The top six competitors drive the cones course late in the afternoon, when the crowd gathers to view the end of the show.

So I had several hours to stew and keep reminding myself that I really was in first place at this prestigious show in Windsor, England. That only made me more nervous than I already was.

I was haunted by a saying that my wife used with our children in their competitive sports events to paraphrase Yogi Berra: "It's not over till it's over."

Prince Philip's team, which was in third place, had a clear round. The second-place team of Alwyn Holder also was clear. The very English announcer publicly played up the fact that, if I incurred any faults, I would be out of first place. I cannot explain just how nervous and apprehensive I was as I drove into the arena and saluted Her Majesty the Queen.

Then the bell sounded and I headed across the starting line. The first nine sets of cones

Polished to the nines, Bill Long drives the dressage test. USET PHOTO BY FINDLAY DAVIDSON

After his victory at Windsor in 1985, Bill Long shakes hands with Queen Elizabeth.
USET PHOTO BY FINDLAY DAVIDSON

drove very well. I was just about to take a deep breath when I drove into the U and my off-leader's trace broke away from the lead bar. It was swinging recklessly and this horse was very nervous. To have this happen to him spelled definite doom for me. Every time the trace would touch the horse, he became a little stronger and harder to hold—to say nothing of how difficult it was to drive him with one trace undone. But stopping meant losing everything and I was not willing to give up just yet.

My son, Bill, and Mr. Caspersen, who served as my grooms, were facing backwards on my presentation carriage and could not figure out why the crowd gasped at every move and turn. They could see that the balls were staying on the cones as we drove through them, and could not figure out the spectators' peculiar reaction.

Finally, I made it through the last set of twenty cones. Though my trace still was flying free, all of the balls remained in their rightful places on top of the cones. We headed for the finish line at a full gallop and I knew what it felt like to win at an international driving event.

Mr. and Mrs. Caspersen, my grooms, my wife, and the entire American contingent—but I most of all—could not have been any prouder or happier than we were that night. With beautiful Windsor Castle lit up in the background, the United States team took home the crystal.

At the 1984 World Four-in-Hand Driving Championships in Hungary, Deirdre Pirie negotiates the charcoal burners' obstacle. She finished in sixteenth place. USET PHOTO BY FINDLAY DAVIDSON

Known as a "homecomer" who always finishes an event, Deirdre Pirie is the only American-trained driver to have successfully completed five World Championships.

The Hamilton, Massachusetts, resident, who names all her horses after Indian tribes, was the first woman to drive at the Hamburg Driving Derby, where she was in the ribbons. At Aachen in the same year, 1982, she and teammate Emil Jung won the bronze medal.

Deirdre was the U.S. reserve national four-in-hand champion in 1984 and 1986. When she isn't on a carriage, she is active as an organizer. Deirdre is the co-founder of the Myopia Driving Event, America's oldest combined driving competition. A member of the AHSA's Driving Committee, she also has served on the American Driving Society's Combined Driving Committee.

FUN AND GAMES TRAVELING WITH HORSES

Deirdre Pirie

A million years ago—or so it seems—there were only one or two combined driving competitions annually in the United States, and none of the same caliber as those found in Europe. As I began to have notions of World Championship participation, it became obvious that to play the game in that league, I would have to take myself to Europe.

I had at my disposal a team of very ordinary Canadian crossbreds of mostly Clydesdale persuasion. They were neither fast nor good movers, and so they hardly seemed worth hauling to Europe. When an English friend invited me on a horse-shopping excursion in Hungary, off I went. I bought a group of unbroken horses (one sight unseen) and had them shipped to England.

The next spring, I moved myself bit by bit to England, figuring that it was a logical place to locate, as I knew the language and had friends to look after me.

It wasn't as easy as I thought, however, and I soon discovered that English as I knew it was not the language spoken there. While I could speak the language of social conversation, the vocabulary of ordinary things to do with horses and carriages was a different matter. Our vocabulary soon expanded to include terms such as ironmonger (for hardware store), spanner (wrench), and bonnet (car hood). My daughter even started an English-American dictionary.

Deirdre Pirie in the grand main arena at Aachen, West Germany, in 1982. USET PHOTO BY
ROLAND VON SIEBENTHAL

My plan was to conduct as self-sufficient and economical a campaign as possible. No
hotels, local trainers, or facilitators were used. I rented what sounded like a cute sixteenth-
century milk barn, converted to a cottage. In actuality, little had been done to it with
the exception of pouring a concrete floor and washing the walls. Plumbing was of the
Middle Ages variety. As there was a shortage of heating fuel worldwide at that time, I
found that we must make do with five gallons of oil for many months. No thought of
hot baths or heat. We found a public pool with hot showers down the road and went
out for our "Saturday" baths.

The horses fared better. Their living conditions were quite acceptable and certainly not
as primitive as those they had experienced in Hungary. Nevertheless, to take five rather
wild and barely handled horses and get them ready to compete as a team proved quite
an undertaking. I arrived on the first of March and that year we saw snow as late as June
in our part of England. (Another mistaken notion was that the Gulf Stream kept England
free of all that cold white stuff. That year the Gulf Stream must have moved to Spain or
somewhere.)

Our first competition was about five weeks after my arrival, and while I didn't expect
to do well, I did want at least to be presentable, a rather difficult task as I had only one
groom. We had arranged to borrow a "dressed" groom from a friend, and I had little
realization of the necessity of staff. As I sat on the carriage waiting to go to presentation,
my groom went to dress and suddenly my lead horse chose to remove his bridle. No one

was in sight or hearing as I plaintively called in sweet soothing tones for help. That was just one of a string of frightening moments that plagued me that year.

Water crossings with green horses are always a problem, and we determined to practice. A friend showed us a super stream to cross and the next morning we set off for it. It lay at the end of a tight path, and when we arrived we realized that the preceding night's rain had turned the nice little stream into a dangerous torrent. The leaders would have no part of it and climbed up on the side of the bank. We decided to unhitch them, but then couldn't find a spot to take them to. A nearby resident offered assistance and suggested that we lead them over a humpbacked stone mule bridge, which was about eight feet above the water. What I couldn't see from the carriage where I remained was that the bridge had no rail and was only a couple of feet wide. The helpful samaritan, having failed to inform us that he had never even touched a horse before, led one of the leaders onto the bridge. The horse turned his head to look down at the water and the man pulled him in the wrong direction, causing the horse to fall off the bridge and land on his back in about five feet of boulder-strewn water. Amazingly, he scampered up. The fact that we didn't have any serious injuries made the incident amusing in retrospect, though it was perturbing at the time.

Our next adventure with water was at an old quarry we found. Much of it was only two feet deep. We soon got in the lazy habit of galloping in there every day using that water to cool and refresh our horses at the end of their work. It took us nearly a month to realize the water was very limy and caused scratches and skin trouble.

Life in England was interesting. I had never lived in such a big "small" town. At home in the United States, no one seemed to care about my driving. In England, every villager took a keen interest. Each merchant commented on my state of ability, and the local butcher used to park his car and watch me practice. Later, he would give me hell and tell me I would never get anywhere. After a while, we learned to do without meat.

But the interest, support, and help of the British competitors was astounding. I was loaned anything and everything from grooms to trucks and horses. With their kind help and support, we managed to get around five courses that season with dressage scores starting in the triple digits and gradually improving.

The 1980 World Championships were at Windsor, England, and we returned to Europe in time to compete at several warm-up shows. We enjoyed extremely elegant lodgings provided by a friend and had smooth sailing through the season. It ended successfully as I placed highest of the Americans, despite competing as an individual.

World Championships are on alternate even years, and 1982 found me with a new idea of how to play the game. This time, having been selected as part of the team, I decided to try living in Germany because it was more central to competitions in general and to the upcoming World Championships in Holland in particular.

In Germany, we learned different techniques and customs for horse care. One, only muck stalls once a month (deep bedding carried to the extreme). Two, daily turnout—let alone turnout with grass—is never provided for competition horses. We encountered vets who tested for lameness with dowsing rods (the rod supposedly pulled toward the "hot" spot). We tried pointing out that the hot spots could usually be felt by palpitation, but that was considered not scientific. Blacksmiths, too, were a problem. Sharing the egos and patience of their American counterparts, they were resistant to any suggestions and insisted on shoes that were twice as heavy as what we were used to. Every night's prayer

The dressage phase at the World Four-in-Hand Championships at Ascot, England, in 1986, when Deirdre Pirie was tied for fifteenth. USET PHOTO BY FINDLAY DAVIDSON

pleaded with powers above to intercede and make it unnecessary ever to need a vet or blacksmith. Weather and footing being much kinder in central and northern Europe than in most parts of America, we seldom needed any emergency care.

That year, we and the horses learned what it is that driving horses must endure. Aachen is the most prestigious show in Europe in part because of the very large prize money offered. But we were surprised to find that our stalls were a wall in an empty hay barn, tied with other horses who could and did regularly get loose and molest ours.

German shows have a custom of requiring your presence in harness several times a day. Aachen, for instance, has a marathon that starts on the other side of a very busy city, more than an hour's hack from the stable. We had no transport, so were required to hack over, complete a very difficult twenty-five-kilometer marathon and hack back. Then several hours later, we had to return to the show ring with our same horses and marathon gear to put on a display of galloping among the grand prix stadium jumps in the pouring rain. Lining up in the ring with forty or fifty teams is always traumatic because many drivers have at least one horse that hates parades, music, flags, applause, or a combination of the above, and reacts accordingly.

Little regard is given to the fact that horses or grooms might be tired. Often, the horses are in harness for as much as six hours. At shows like Aachen, there is never time to eat. Sometimes, you do not leave the ring at night until ten o'clock. All this does train the horses to be bombproof, however, and, in spite of the exhaustion factor, it really is fun to participate in shows of that caliber where the public is so enthusiastic.

The 1982 championships were at Apeldoorn, Holland, a wonderful location with a beautiful castle at the center of the show grounds. Here we were treated to every civility, and by now we had all gotten used to the crowds, music, and flags. Or so we thought. Seventy thousand people is a great number even when spread throughout the marathon, and it was often difficult not to collide with pedestrians who were all over the paths.

In 1984, I went to Holland to get ready for the coming World Championships in Hungary, thinking that proximity to the previous gold medal winners might improve my technique.

Here we lived in a school dormitory, cooking all our meals on a single-burner hot plate. The training conditions were ideal, which made up for many inconveniences.

Getting to and from Hungary was an adventure. I traveled with the Dutch one thousand miles across Europe. Hungarian border officials would not allow horses to cross until midnight of the Monday before the competition. At midnight, trucks were lined up for miles. The Dutch contingent—forty-two horses in about fifteen vans and trucks and nearly sixty people—gave us a taste of the feeling that the early settlers must have had crossing the United States in wagon trains.

So many things we take for granted at home are not available in Europe. For instance, my American Ford pickup truck had an automatic transmission, and fluid for automatic transmissions is nearly impossible to find outside large German cities.

Also, my carriage trailer springs proved not to be up to the load, causing the bad one to press down and rub the tire. After one tire was bald and the other starting to go, we pulled over at midnight in Austria and improvised. Looking through our junk, I decided our best shot was to take screw eyes off the buckets, cut the straight ends off, and put them behind the wheel as spacers. The fact that the lug nuts would barely thread on seemed less important than just keeping moving, as we had a plane waiting for us in Frankfurt, ten hours' drive away. The rubbing stopped and we made it to the plane. However, I managed to forget that particular improvisation when I got home. The following spring, on the way home from the first show, the wheel spun off.

The Hungarian competition was exciting and difficult. The cross-country course took a huge toll, knocking out many previous medal winners. The rain made the going very dangerous and the last hazard in the main ring was a slippery wooden dance floor on which many horses could not even keep on their feet. The Americans came squeaky close to winning the bronze, ending up fourth.

The 1986 Championships in England at Ascot racecourse seemed like home ground. We came over at the last moment, which proved to be a mistake, as there is no substitute for competing with the international players. This time, we had to undergo very strict quarantine in the United States, which meant that my entire stable area had to be roped off and no strangers allowed to come or go for thirty days. Blue hospital gowns and rubber boots that had to be dipped into disinfectant on each entrance or departure from the building were worn by all. In theory, one could not leave the immediate grounds for exercise, which made it difficult to keep horses fit without breaking quarantine.

Once again, we just missed a team medal and it was a bitter disappointment, but we were pleased to have done as well as we did, despite one team member having been forced to withdraw from competition after sustaining an injury walking the course.

We had a second try at the Apeldoorn course in 1988. This time, we based ourselves in a small German town. Our accommodations were two bedrooms in a barn with two

*Sometimes the peripatetic Deirdre Pirie stays home. Here she competes at Gladstone
in 1986.* USET PHOTO BY FRED NEWMAN

horse stalls, so our dining room became the wash stall area and we shared every meal
with two staring horses. Rather akin to living arrangements with Mr. Ed of television fame.

Here we had a crazy landlady who did such things as lock our horses in the barn
without food and water when we left for a show. Our lack of knowledge of German always
made shopping and traveling amusing. A series of horse injuries made this try disappointing,
but the summer was full of adventure. In July, we took the horses to Stockholm, scene
of the 1990 World Equestrian Games. Here the cross-country course went right through

the city and pedestrians scattered like chickens in all directions. The Americans placed second as a team, which was the best we had done to date and a memorable moment.

We are seasoned travelers, but often long for little reminders of home. For a New Englander to go all summer without fresh corn on the cob is a serious deprivation, so we searched all the cow cornfields diligently to find the best-flavored variety and then kept very quiet as we cooked our bounty and tried to imagine the taste of the real thing. Buying food is always peculiar in foreign places and no place more so than Germany. Here, every supermarket has forty or more feet of a meat counter, of which 39.5 feet is devoted to pork products. Fresh chicken, beef, or lamb are out of the question. In our desperate search for variety, we resorted to cooking a pheasant killed by my car. It was the best meal of the summer.

There are still new things to discover and laugh at. In 1989, in Germany, I discovered that at smaller national-level shows, they give prizes to all who place in any division. In the evening following dressage, for instance, all the people who placed during the day are called to receive their awards. These prizes, down to at least sixth place, are donated by local merchants and tend to be hams, waffle irons, toasters, and the like. After one class is "pinned," the winners are expected to dance around the room to the accompaniment of live band music, holding their prizes aloft while onlookers clap in rhythm. If only I had a video camera to capture a fellow American skipping around the room with a waffle iron held high over his head, I could have made a fortune with the tape.

Now back in Germany once more, mounting the final campaign of my career (my family has heard that line so often they don't believe it), I wonder what has kept me at this madness.

Traveling in Europe on the do-it-yourself plan without sponsorship, as I have, has been a series of wonderful and exciting moments. Self-reliance, ingenuity, and a sense of humor have been essential, as has the ability to deal "in house" with all emergencies of a medical or blacksmith nature.

Why do I do it? Reasons include the advantage gained by having many competitions to enter, superb training areas with miles of perfect footing, and freedom from mosquitoes, summer heat, and hard ground. The fun derived from international living, as well as the disease that makes a competitor always feel that greater success is just around the corner, are certainly key elements. Clearly, it helps to have some gypsy blood, as I must have, in order to enjoy moving around the globe with six horses, two trucks, a trailer, an assortment of motorcycles, bicycles, and better than one hundred pieces of "luggage." Logic, common sense, and practicality must not be essential, for they seem to be missing from my repertoire, else I long since would have stayed at home.

Tucker Johnson in the World Pairs Championship at Riesenbeck, West Germany, in 1987, when heavy footing was a problem. USET PHOTO BY BOB LANGRISH

Coming late to driving after a youth spent hunting, showing, and playing polo, Tucker Johnson made up for lost time by getting deeply involved in the sport as soon as he decided it was for him.

He has scored several important victories in Europe and represented the USET in the 1987 World Championships, as well as always being an impressive competitor at events in this country.

When he is not involved with his horses, Tucker works in the field of real estate.

DO TWO PAIRS MAKE A TEAM?

S. Tucker S. Johnson

When I was nine, my maternal grandfather (who grew up in the Midwest riding a pony to grade school) glibly told me that any pony I was riding could be driven. Because he was my white-haired grandfather and an eminent psychologist, I believed him.

The carriage he provided me with was a dilapidated old breaking cart that had been sitting in his dairy barn since the Korean War. It had two flat tires, and there was a family of bantams nesting in the foot boot. After relocating the chickens and replacing the tires, I had my first carriage. Regrettably, my grandfather had not been so generous with tack and left me to improvise.

Lacking leather, I borrowed the webbing belts from my grandfather's grain sorter and pop-riveted together a one-piece harness for my pony, Susie, who despite this and other indignities, lived to a ripe old age. The beauty of this harness lay in the simplicity of its design rather than its material. Having one strap all the way around the pony held in place with two other straps, one at the withers and one at the rump, and with two tracelike straps similarly attached coming out behind the shoulder, I was able to slip it over her head without any buckles. By the time Susie and I had gone one eighth of a mile, I was hooked on driving. The thing that amazed me then, and to this day holds my fascination, is the unmatched excitement of flying through the woods behind an unsteady steed.

My Boston Brahmin paternal grandmother was not impressed with what my maternal grandfather called Yankee ingenuity and dismissed my homemade tack as dangerous and unsightly. She then provided me with a proper patent show harness and a governess cart with red leather seats—one faster than its predecessor.

By the time I was nineteen, my horse interest was still a major focus in my life. I had retired Susie, however, and I was concentrating on polo and foxhunting. It wasn't until the fall of 1983 that I discovered the organized sport of combined driving at the Gladstone Driving Event. As soon as I saw the pairs and four-in-hands going through their paces, I knew I was watching grown-ups enjoy the same thrills I had experienced with Susie. I had found an equestrian sport that looked like it had been custom made for me.

It took me two years to locate and finance my first pair. During those two years, my interest was directed and kindled by three of my neighbors who were participating in this sport. They were Sharon Chesson, who is known worldwide as "the queen of dressage" for her elegance and success in this phase; Doug Kemmerer, who found the hazard at every opportunity; and Finn Caspersen, who sponsors and navigates on the best four-in-hand in the country. With much lobbying from my three friends and early mentors, my mother was convinced that her Cedar Lane Farm should have a pair for combined driving. She sent me to Emil Jung with instructions to learn about driving and find a quiet pair of black or gray horses. One month later I returned with a pair of excited four-year-old bays and far too little knowledge. Like all good coachmen, I will still not know enough when I crack my whip through the gates of St. Peter.

Determined to start competing as soon as possible, I began a summer-long crash correspondence course in driving. My long-distance tutor was Emil Jung, German champion four-in-hand driver who was centered in Millwood, Virginia. During our weekly phone lessons, he never failed to remind me that it was a three-phase competition and that an hour of dressage practice a day would not slow the horses in the hazards. I, of course, would dutifully stay out of the woods and in the dressage field for at least an hour (some days), as I had set my sights on the Gladstone Driving Event in September.

The first thing I realized was that my pair seemed more prepared than I was. The amount of organization and teamwork it took was overwhelming compared to my previous experience managing a polo team and competing in horse shows.

Gladstone was a great competition all the way around. Kirsten Reimer, my groom, won the groom's award, and I won the preliminary pairs with a clean sweep in all three phases. This was all I needed to send me headlong into the big leagues.

A lot of training went forward through that next winter. Having made many trips to Emil's farm in Virginia, I felt that I was ready for a season of advanced competitions. That season provided me with placings at Ingleside, Virginia, and East Oaks and Fair Hills, Maryland. I ended the season at Gladstone, finishing fourth in the National Championships. I had learned that there were many subtle factors that make the difference between winning and placing, and to be competitive at the international level, I would have to make a total commitment to the sport.

In January 1987, I took my pair and my life to Germany to train with Emil. There were some difficult things I had to adjust to: cold weather, a language barrier, and isolation. These same difficulties, however, allowed me to concentrate totally and form a strong bond with my horses, which proved to give me an edge that season.

Traveling from country to country, combined with the stress of European competitions, gave me some up-and-down results at the first three shows. For example, at Windsor in

In the advanced pairs at the 1986 Gladstone Driving Event, Tucker Johnson goes well through the water. USET PHOTO BY FRED NEWMAN

mid-May, I was sixth in dressage, but first in the marathon, which moved me into second place. I thought I was ready to take first in the cones when I mistook cone nine for cone six, and I was eliminated.

I knew that I could not let that happen again if I were to make the team for the World Championships at Riesenbeck, Germany, that August. In two months, I crammed in three Dutch competitions, knowing that the best performance possible and success were mandatory. Suddenly everything began to click. My horses and I were in sync. We won at Exloo, and two weeks later won decisively at Lochem. Everything seemed to get better and better, and we won our third straight at Beek Bergen. With just three weeks before the World Championships and now training with the other three team members, Larry Poulin, Charlie Cheston, and Bill Lower at Opstalan Stable in Holland, I felt I was finally on my way to the big time.

At this point, humility and I shook hands again. During a team training session with Heiner Merk, my gelding Orpheus turned his ankle badly enough to make him very questionable for the World Championships only two weeks away. This left me with Carrington and Lesco, a horse that had been generously loaned to me to use as a spare. Unfortunately, Lesco, who was in training as a four-in-hand leader, was not up to the job required of a pair horse at Riesenbeck. As things ended up, I represented the USET as an individual and finished in the middle of the pack.

Through the water in the "Gladstone at Tampa" meet in 1989 is Tucker Johnson with his pair.
USET PHOTO BY KARL LECK

Fortunately, over the winter, Orpheus made a full recovery at Cedar Lane Farm. He and Carrington were joined by a Dutch warmblood, Pershing, that Santa Claus brought from Holland in December. The way these three horses were working together and progressing, I was in good condition for world competition in 1988. Once again, Finn Caspersen encouraged my mother and me, convincing us that I was ready for Windsor.

On the first of May, Carrington, Pershing, Orpheus, two carriages, and too much equipment to list; my groom, Kirsten; Bob Dryer, an old school friend, and I found ourselves at the Brighton Horse Driving Trials at Stanler Park, just outside Brighton, England. In every competitor's mind, there is always the question of whether to have a warm-up show or go cold into a major competition like Windsor. But because I had not competed with Pershing, I felt it was essential to do Brighton, even though the marathon there offered a serious challenge with its steep hills. Though Brighton was only a week before Windsor, it could not have been a better start. After dressage, Carrington and Pershing put us in first with a score in the low thirties. The hills in the marathon proved to be no problem for Orpheus and Carrington, and my score from this phase of the competition gave me a commanding lead going into the cones. I decided to risk using Pershing with Carrington for this phase. The gamble paid off, for Pershing gained valuable experience, we were clear in the cones, and we won the competition.

I went to Windsor with newfound confidence. Carrington and Pershing were working perfectly together, and Orpheus had never been more ready for a marathon. The excitement of the Royal Windsor Horse Show always provides an unknown factor. With Windsor Castle looming over the show grounds, and the marathon course traversing the home park, the serene and majestic beauty can be distracting to any competitor.

During the warm-up for dressage I was the only creature on the grounds more nervous than my horses. Miraculously, just minutes before my start time, Carrington and Pershing became soft and supple, working together as they never had before. When I entered the dressage arena, every movement of the test and every step the horses took was exactly how I had dreamed of the perfect pair dressage. As I turned down the center line and started my final extended trot, it seemed the horses knew they were the stars of the day, reaching farther and higher with every step. The judges awarded us a score of twenty-seven, the best score ever given for dressage at Windsor to that date.

The marathon course somehow seemed to have deceived me. During the course walk, it seemed relatively straightforward. But on the course, the space I had imagined in the hazards filled up so quickly that I found myself fighting, not only for each split second, but also to make my intended route. There was a Ben Hur quality to my trip. In the sixth hazard, as we were galloping out after completing the mandatory gates, the referee bounced off the carriage when the horses jumped and the vehicle sprang over a log. Fortunately, there were no penalties assessed and the referee was game to go on. In the seventh hazard, I hit a tree and had to back up and turn to continue, which cost me valuable seconds. This mistake on my part allowed Christine Dick, the many-times British National Pairs Champion and a fierce competitor, to beat me by one second on the marathon. However, we still held first overall going into the cones.

Having been eliminated the previous year in the cones at Windsor, I was particularly nervous entering the final phase. The competitor before me, who was Christine, had a clear round, which increased the pressure. I entered the ring, saluted the judges, and as the bell rang, I made a point of driving the horses aggressively. As I galloped across the finish line, clear of time penalties and faults, I knew I had won.

But it did not really hit me until I was in the awards ceremony with Mrs. James L. Johnson, my mother and sponsor, to my left, receiving the trophy and ribbons from Her Majesty Queen Elizabeth.

"Do two pairs make a four?" I must think back to the first four I ever saw. The year was 1979, it was autumn, and I was driving a 1945 Willys Jeep across Cedar Lane Farm, looking for the best spot from which to watch some of the horses and carriages in the Gladstone Driving Event as they went through. My own driving at this point was limited to my experiences with Susie in our governess cart. I was struck by the speed and size of the first carriage coming toward me in the woods. The driver was Phil Hofmann, the first American to compete internationally in combined driving with a team. At breakneck speed, Phil and his four pounded toward a steep downhill with a ninety-degree turn around trees at the bottom. Just as he was making the turn, something went wrong. Within a split second the carriage came to a dead stop, and the lead pair faced the driver. Through concentrated communication, using his voice and the whip, Mr. Hofmann was able to straighten his team and continue unscathed. This was terrifying and exciting, and ten years later, having competed internationally in pairs, I was challenged by the image of Phil Hofmann mastering his four-in-hand in those woods to make my two pairs into a team.

Two weeks before my first four-in-hand competition in 1989 I had to ask myself, "Do *my* two pairs make a team?" This question would be answered after the final phase of the Gladstone Event. I planned to use the pair with which I had won at Windsor—Carrington and Orpheus—as the wheel pair, and Pershing along with a new Dutch warmblood named MX as the lead pair. With two weeks to go, both pairs were doing all three phases well. The difficult part was getting them to do it together as a team.

With over one foot of rain falling in seventy-two hours just prior to Gladstone, hurricane Hugo clearly was not on the side of my competitors—not to mention me. In the dressage warm-up, my two pairs were making a good four. However, when I crossed the woods into the holding area for the dressage ring, my left wheeler, Orpheus, was spooked by the mud and crowd. He became wildly excited. His head went up and I feared he was going to bolt. In the first minutes of our dressage test, Orpheus was able to relax slightly. But that was not enough. I did not give the dressage test I was dreaming of. I felt lucky to place second, within one point of the leader.

After walking the marathon course and hazards, my regular navigator, Kirsten, and I were nervous. But Sharon Chesson, who was assisting me by riding with us for the marathon, felt confident. On the marathon, we had the fastest time for several hazards. With the combination of bad weather and occasionally lapsing into pair timing, I overshot several turns. Even in adversity, my horses remained calm and patient. Once again finishing second, I entered the cones with a chance at first.

The skies had cleared for the final day of the competition, which looked like a good omen. Having two pairs attached to each other seemed an overwhelming challenge. I felt I had something to prove. I needed to drive the cones smoothly, without any knockdowns. As I crossed the start line, I drew the breath that would have to last to the finish. Fortunately, I did not pass out from lack of oxygen, and no ball fell. With only two time faults, I was first in the cones for my division and second overall.

So back to the question: Do two pairs make a four? They can. They will. My horses performed admirably at Gladstone, and the only thing holding them back was my inexperience. Fours are the future for me—as soon as I cover some more ground with a pair.

Clay Camp on the obstacle course, his favorite segment of a driving event. USET PHOTO

A successful international bloodstock agent specializing in Thoroughbred pedigrees, L. Clay Camp has been successful with both pairs and four-in-hands.

The alternate to the World Pairs Championships in 1985, the year he was third in the USET's National Pairs Championship, Camp represented the United States in the 1980 and 1988 World Four-in-Hand Championships.

A native of South Carolina who lives in Kentucky, with his wife, Barbara, Camp showed saddlebreds, hunters, and jumpers before becoming involved with driving.

THE CHALLENGE OF DRIVING

L. Clay Camp

Long before driving became a challenge to me, it was merely a way of life. I was lucky enough to have been born in rural South Carolina in the 1930s. Tractors were something that would come later to that area, so all of the work was done with horses and mules. The mules worked the cotton and tobacco fields and the draft horses worked in the logging woods.

My father and his friends showed hackney ponies and fine harness horses in the Carolina area. The show and working stock were mostly driven single, except in the hayfields. Our part of South Carolina was very flat, so teams were not necessary. Occasionally, we showed the hackneys in tandem; but even that was a far cry from the present-day coaching or combined driving. (The current use of the two-hand system for the marathon phase makes me feel right at home!)

When I left South Carolina for the more sophisticated hunt fields and hunter shows of Virginia, I thought I had left driving in my wake. Only after entering a much more profitable area of the horse business, Thoroughbred sales, did I take up driving again. "Pleasure driving" with Amish horses and some Canadian crossbreds soon gave way to the challenge of competition in the show ring again. As my technique and knowledge improved, I began searching to upgrade my horses. A visit to England to watch the four-in-hands show in private driving and then watching a combined driving event really established my goals.

Going cross-country, Clay Camp and his team are reflected in the water during a 1980 outing.
USET PHOTO BY HAAUI MORREIM

The Dutch Gelderlander seemed to be a dual-purpose horse. (The Dutch warmblood had not yet been introduced to driving in 1977. The warmbloods would do in the show ring and also perform for combined driving. Indeed, our first team showed at Devon and the Royal Winter Fair before competing in the combined events. Then in 1980, they represented the United States in the World Championships in Windsor, England, and in the same year, were champions at the Toronto Royal Winter Fair.) I brought a team of Gelderlanders over from Holland in 1977, but they had not been broken to drive. I set about breaking them and found later, in driving the hazards, that I had done the wrong thing with my leaders by keeping them in draft. It took Emil Jung and myself the better part of a year to overcome this. The only good thing about my early training of the team was that I had made them fast, mostly because I had been told the fault with the Gelderlander was that they were too slow for competition.

My next challenge was being coached by Emil Jung, an episode that could make a book all by itself. Emil trying to teach a former draft horse driver the Achenbach style was quite a chore for both of us. His favorite expression when he would look down at the reins from behind me (he always stood behind me so he could beat on my shoulders for emphasis) was that I had a "bowl of spaghetti" in my lap.

The times with Emil were a great learning process, and in the following years Emil taught me—and everyone else in this country who was into combined driving—the basic techniques that we use today. He was the best driver in America.

At this point, my team needed an upgrade in type. A lighter and more fluid horse was indicated as the hazards became more demanding and the standard for dressage higher.

The new Dutch warmblood and the improved German Holsteiner seemed to be the ticket. Anyone watching or driving with world champion Tjeerd Velstra could come to no other conclusion.

Velstra brought the two-handed system to perfection in the hazards. Bill Long of the United States had learned "the touch" from him, and I tried to learn it from Bill. He used a soft, small loop and drove the team with voice commands and the whip as a guide. The change from large loops and resistance gave the leaders an easier time of it and kept them calm and more easily under control. Not to mention that it was so much faster. Faster has become the name of the game in the hazards. They have been shortened between the turns and we have learned to turn through places that would have seemed impossible when we started.

An amateur or part-time athlete in any sport who tries to meet the demands of competition on a level with the "amateur" full-time competitor is up against the odds. At least team driving lets you enlist the aid of another driver to get your horses fit. Without this help, there is no way to do it. Trying to hold a job and properly do a four-in-hand while getting yourself fit and your timing perfected takes great determination and lots of

Clay Camp steadies his pair in the water at Ledyard in 1985. USET PHOTO BY NORMAN HAPGOOD

Driving his four-in-hand through the water at Gladstone in 1986, Clay Camp is a picture of intense concentration. USET PHOTO BY FRED NEWMAN

encouragement from all sides. My hat is off to those competitors who have to train their bodies to such a high level and also work for their livelihood.

Just to "put-to" your horses takes about thirty-five minutes. Then there's two hours of training and another hour to unharness and cool them out. With a team, there is also a spare horse to be kept as fit and well trained as the other four. This three and a half hours does not include travel from your work place. When there is a competition, it is miles away from home base. Our combined driving squad suffers greatly from lack of experience in competition. Those without the wherewithal to spend the summer in Europe with their teams are out of luck.

The lack of events in this country really discourages any new driver from taking up the four-in-hand division. It is hard to start out against the more experienced drivers, and a preliminary division would certainly be of help.

The heat of July is not the best time to be practicing hazards, dressage, and, of course, speed over a distance. When there is only one event in the spring and one in the fall you are beholden to a less than ideal schedule. Overtraining is easy to do when you have no coach and no other team with which to compare yourself. Too much hazard practice (which is really the most fun) could get you a team of maniacs by the time of the event. Emil taught me to practice my timing slowly through the hazards and to work up to the speed with practice. Therein lies the problem. No time to practice. The quickness of timing in the hazard is born in drivers such as Bill Long and Jim Fairclough. Those not as gifted have to compensate with practice and training and responsive horses. You also have to choose your route in the hazard to take advantage of your training and ability level.

I said earlier that I was lucky to have had the start I had, but I am also fortunate to have had the best of help. Boo Coles came to me from one of the best hunter stables in America and Janie Gramley was a schoolteacher from Oregon. Amazingly, she and Bill Long's wife came from the same town. They have been the best grooms my horses have had in the last twelve years. Jane is doing an excellent job on her own now that Boo has retired.

My alternate driver is a former British team junior medal winner. Vance "Coco" Coulthard has helped with the driving and words of advice for the past eight years. He has been an invaluable asset, and also works full-time on the farm. The cheerful help of these people has made the difference in my ability to drive in competition on a world-class level.

Competition is the real challenge in life. We meet it every day. Nothing anywhere is more exciting or challenging to me than driving a four-in-hand in combined driving. The thought of driving in a meet has all the apprehension and thrill that football held for me in my college days and much more challenge than the show ring demanded. The feeling of power of the four horses going together as one unit in dressage and the feeling of accomplishment when you do your circles with the team well-bent is rewarding. It is hard to describe how you feel with that power in your hands as they settle into their extended trot across the diagonal.

The marathon course walk gets the adrenaline flowing and you only half-listen while Coco and Barbara discuss the possible problems on the first sections. In your mind you are already thinking about what is to come later. In your mind you are waiting for that granddaddy of all thrills, Section E, with those oh-so-tricky hazards. There are so many options, routes, and possibilities. Each is dependent upon your ability and that of your horses. Sometimes the turn you take is dictated by which wheeler is on that side. One is always better than the other.

Once you and all that horseflesh and that suddenly huge vehicle get inside the hazard, it's amazing how that seemingly easy turn now looks not so clever. When your wheelers clear the posts, your leaders are already through the next gate! You had better have a good eye and lots of control when you come at that two-and-a-half- or three-meter opening between two immovable trees at a fast trot with those four big horses. That is the time that your hair stands up on the back of your neck and you take a deep breath, because you know you must make a nearly ninety-degree turn into another three-meter opening right after the first one. What a feeling! What a thrill to rise to the challenge with just a touch on the reins and a word to your wheelers. They move in close to the pole and the leaders flirt around the tree with only a hint of pressure.

The challenge lies in the competition for me. The long hours of training and seeing myself and the horses improve are only a part of it. The horrible hassle of getting to the competition and the repeated checklists embedded in my brain are but another step toward the ultimate hour. It is intimidating to see so many other teams at the World Championships; it raises self-doubts. So does seeing the course for the marathon. But you take all of that in stride when you are well prepared and have the confidence that you are as good as possible.

To go to a competition and represent your country is a source of great pride. Your anthem has never meant so much. I have met the challenge and here I am at that goal, this driver from South Carolina who set out so long ago.

Sem Groenewoud drives Mr. and Mrs. John Kluge's all-gray team in the dressage segment at Stockholm in 1988. PHOTO BY M. M. MINEKUS

A native of Holland who was on the Dutch gold medal team at the 1982 World Four-in-Hand Driving Championships, Sem Groenewoud moved to the United States subsequently and now drives for America.

A veteran of seven World Championships (four for the Netherlands and three for his new homeland), Sem won the four-in-hand event at the 1988 Royal Windsor Show in England.

His all-gray team, owned by Mr. and Mrs. John Kluge, is always an eye-catcher. The two-time national champion and his family live in Virginia.

THE TRANSATLANTIC WORLD OF DRIVING

Sem Groenewoud

I started working with horses at my father's riding school in the Netherlands. During the week, the horses did their riding school work, and on the weekends, I went with them to the shows. My father and I were the first to drive Dutch warmbloods in competition, something that has since become a trend as other drivers abandoned their slower, heavier Friesians or Gelderlanders.

During this period, I had only one carriage to use—it had to do for the dressage, the marathon, and obstacle driving. It was a wooden antique vehicle, very nicely restored, but not really sturdy enough for rough terrain. So I always drove very carefully, because the pole or a wheel could break, or parts would come off—not to mention the fact that I was afraid to scratch it up.

These days, you have to compete with a new marathon carriage with disc brakes and standardized measurements. For the dressage and obstacle course, we utilize a sturdy replica of an antique carriage with disc brakes and measurements set by FEI rules.

In the twenty years since combined driving became an official FEI sport, it has grown so rapidly that it is hard to keep up with all its new rules and the equipment that has been developed.

Luckily, since I became involved in driving full-time, different people have sponsored me, giving me better horses (mostly Dutch warmbloods), better carriages, and better equipment.

At Szilvásvárad, Hungary, Sem Groenewoud drives one of his first teams before coming to America.
PHOTO BY FINDLAY DAVIDSON

All this is necessary because the competitions continue to get more difficult. I can remember when the marathon hazards were so wide-open, it was possible (though admittedly difficult) to drive through them with a big coach and a team of Shires. If I knew then what I know now about driving, I would already have been a world champion.

At the moment, dressage is judged on a demanding scale. You need a team of flashy, good-looking riding horse types, with the right conformation and movements. They must show suppleness, bending, balance, and accuracy at each gait. It goes without saying they must be working as a team, not as four individual horses.

The hazards today are very tight, and the times you must make in them are faster. They are built from the ground up, rather than made with natural material at the site. They are sturdy, to keep horses and drivers safe, with an eye toward making sure there are no sharp edges or points. In the future we will see fewer natural tree hazards, simply because the trees need to be preserved from being hit and scratched.

Obstacle courses are now more technical, with nice flowing lines but tighter circles, box obstacles, bridges, and water crossings. To make the time allowed, drivers must proceed at a faster trot or at a gallop.

The distance between cones varies now from 180 centimeters to 190 centimeters, with carriage width only 160 centimeters standard under FEI rules.

The new FEI rules include the presentation phase in the dressage test as part of the overall impression. Formerly, presentation was done at the halt. Judges would mark you down on minor things, a scratch on the carriage, perhaps, or the fact that the driver's socks were the wrong color. It got to the point where it was a matter of who had the most money to purchase the nicest gear in the world. In effect, you could buy your presentation. While that's fine for a *concours d'élégance*, which is based entirely on appearances, it was not right for the sport of combined driving.

Now the judge looks at things of a more practical nature. He has to see if the harness fits well, if the horses are braided and groomed well, and if the whole combination—carriage, driver, grooms, and horses—fits well together.

Working for Albemarle Driving Centre and Carriage Museum, I have the opportunity to compete with a four-in-hand of warmblood horses here and in Europe. When I first returned to Europe to compete, after driving only in America for a few years, I thought I would beat everyone. Of course, that wasn't true. Combined driving is still young in America, and the European drivers have progressed, too. They aren't fooling around over there.

Competing in America, where there are only six or eight teams, does not give you enough experience and real competition. And there are only three meets a year in America, which means you run into the same drivers over and over. After a while, you know each competitor's strengths and weaknesses extremely well.

In Europe, it's a completely different situation. Even in a tiny country like Holland, there are at least ten shows a year. Then you can travel to even more shows in England, Germany, Hungary, Switzerland, and elsewhere. You actually are able to choose among

Winning the USET Four-in-Hand National Championship, Sem Groenewoud navigates Dr. Alan Weintraub's team through the brandywinery hazard at Fair Hill in 1986. USET PHOTO BY IRENE CROMER

shows, and you meet different drivers at each. The advantage is learning different techniques and methods of driving from each of the other participants.

That is not to say that the shows in America are not good. Gladstone, Fair Hill, and Tampa are among the world's top-level competitions, and can be compared with such shows as Deurne, Aachen, and Windsor. The hazards in this country are built very professionally (by European course designers). Show grounds are big and open, so there is a lot of space to work with. Many of the European shows are not up to these standards.

And the drivers we have in America are high quality. The Europeans know that we are coming up and take us very seriously when we go abroad. And we Americans have good horses and equipment.

But I think the European warmblood horses are still the best for this sport. They have good temperament, nice conformation, and a long-strided walk and trot. Of course, you have to look for the right bloodlines in the warmbloods, because too much Thoroughbred is not good for driving. We still have to go abroad to look for these horses, but maybe in the near future we can find them over here, since so many Americans have started breeding warmbloods.

For me, driving started as a hobby, but now it is my profession. If you want to do well and are trying to be on top, you must be a professional and do it full-time.

It's also important to note that combined driving is a team sport in every way. Without the support of my wife and grooms, I couldn't be successful.

APPENDIX: THE AMERICAN RECORD

Compiled by
Max E. Ammann

OLYMPIC GAMES

1912 Olympic Games
Stockholm, Sweden

Jumping:	Lt. Benjamin Lear/Poppy	
	Capt. Guy Henry/Connie	
	Lt. John Montgomery/ Deceive	
	Team: 4th place	
Dressage:	Capt. Guy Henry/Chiswell	13th
	Lt. John Montgomery/ Deceive	20th
	No team competition	
3-Day:	Lt. Benjamin Lear/Poppy	7th
	Lt. John Montgomery/ Deceive	9th
	Capt. Guy Henry/Chiswell	11th
	Lt. Ephram Graham/Connie	12th
	Team: 3rd place (bronze medal)	

1920 Olympic Games
Antwerp, Belgium

Jumping:	Maj. Henry Allen, Jr./Don	7th
	Maj. John Downer/Dick	12th
	Maj. William West, Jr./Prince	18th
	Team: 5th place	
	(Capt. Harry Chamberlin/ Nigra; Capt. Karl Greenwald/Moses; Capt. Vincent Erwin/Joffre; Maj. Sloan Doak/Rabbit Red)	
Dressage:	Maj. Sloan Doak/Chiswell	14th
	Capt. Harry Chamberlin/ Harebell	14th
	Maj. John Barry/Singlen	14th
	No team competition	
3-Day:	Capt. Harry Chamberlin/ Nigra	6th

Maj. William West/Black
Boy — 7th
Maj. John Barry/Raven — 16th
Maj. Sloan Doak/Deceive — elim.
Team: 4th place

1924 Olympic Games
Paris, France

Jumping: Maj. John Barry/Nigra — 25th
Maj. Sloan Doak/Joffre — 29th
Capt. Vernon Padget/Little
Canada — elim.
Lt. Frederic Bontecou/Bally
McShane — elim.
Team: eliminated

Dressage: None

3-Day: Maj. Sloan Doak/Pathfinder — 3rd
Lt. Frank Carr/Proctor — 8th
Maj. John Barry/Miss
America — elim.
Capt. Vernon Padget/Brown
Boy — elim.
Team: eliminated

1928 Olympic Games
Amsterdam, Holland

Jumping: Maj. Harry Chamberlin/
Nigra — 17th
Capt. Frank Carr/Miss
America — 23rd
Capt. Adolphus Roffe/Fairfax — 33rd
Team: 9th place

Dressage: None

3-Day: Maj. Sloan Doak/Misty
Morn — 17th
Capt. Frank Carr/Verdun
Belle — 22nd
Maj. Charles George/Ozella — elim.
Team: eliminated

1932 Olympic Games
Los Angeles, United States

Jumping: Maj. Harry Chamberlin/
Show Girl — 2nd
Capt. William Bradford/Joe
Aleshire — 4th
Lt. John Wofford/Babe
Wartham — elim.
Team: eliminated

Dressage: Capt. Hiram Tuttle/Olympic — 3rd
Capt. Isaac Kitts/American
Lady — 6th
Capt. Alvin Moore/Water
Pat — 7th

Team: 3rd place (bronze
medal)

3-Day: Lt. Earl Thomson/Jenny
Camp — 2nd
Maj. Harry Chamberlin/
Pleasant Smiles — 4th
Capt. Edwin Argo/Honolulu
Tomboy — 8th
Team: 1st place (gold medal)

1936 Olympic Games
Berlin, Germany

Jumping: Capt. Carl Raguse/Dakota — 5th
Maj. William Bradford/Don — 25th
Capt. Cornelius Jadwin/Ugly — 34th
Team: 4th place

Dressage: Capt. C. Stanton Babcock/
Olympic — 23rd
Capt. Isaac Kitts/American
Lady — 25th
Maj. Hiram Tuttle/Si.
Murray — 27th
Team: 9th place

3-Day: Capt. Earl Thomson/Jenny
Camp — 2nd
Capt. Carl Raguse/Trailolka — 16th
Capt. John Willems/Slippery
Slim — elim.
Team: eliminated

1948 Olympic Games
London, England

Jumping: Col. Franklin Wing/
Democrat — 4th
Capt. John Russell/Air Mail — 21st
Col. Andrew Frierson/Rascal — elim.
Team: eliminated

Dressage: Lt. Robert Borg/Klingsor — 4th
Col. Earl Thomson/Pancraft — 8th
Lt. Col. Frank Henry/Reno
Overdo — 13th
Team: 2nd place (silver
medal)

3-Day: Lt. Col. Frank Henry/Swing
Low — 2nd
Lt. Col. Charles Anderson/
Reno Palisades — 4th
Col. Earl Thomson/Reno
Rhythm — 20th
Team: 1st place (gold medal)

1952 Olympic Games
Helsinki, Finland

Jumping:	William Steinkraus/ Hollandia	11th
	Arthur McCashin/Miss Budweiser	13th
	John Russell/Democrat	24th
	Team: 3rd place (bronze medal)	
Dressage:	Robert Borg/Bill Biddle	11th
	Marjorie Haines/Flying Dutchman	17th
	Hartmann Pauly/Reno Overdo	27th
	Team: 6th place	
3-Day:	Charles Hough/Cassavellanus	9th
	Walter Staley/Craigwood	18th
	John E. B. Wofford/Benny Grimes	31st
	Team: 3rd place (bronze medal)	

1956 Olympic Games
Stockholm, Sweden

Jumping:	Hugh Wiley/Trail Guide	11th
	William Steinkraus/Night Owl	15th
	Frank Chapot/Belair	27th
	Team: 5th place	
Dressage:	Robert Borg/Bill Biddle	17th
	Elaine Shirley Watt/ Connecticut Yankee	30th
	No team	
3-Day:	Jonathan Burton/ Huntingfield	elim.
	Frank Duffy/Drop Dead	elim.
	Walter Staley/Mud Dauber	elim.
	Team: eliminated	

1960 Olympic Games
Rome, Italy

Jumping:	George Morris/Sinjon	4th
	Hugh Wiley/Master William	7th
	William Steinkraus/Riviera Wonder	15th
	Team: 2nd place (silver medal)	
	(George Morris/Sinjon; Frank Chapot/Trail Guide; W. Steinkraus/Ksar d'Esprit)	

Dressage:	Patricia Galvin/Rath Patrick	6th
	Jessica Newberry/Forstrat	12th
	No team competition	
3-Day:	Michael Plumb/Markham	15th
	Michael Page/Grasshopper	17th
	David Lurie/Sea Tiger	elim.
	Walter Staley/Fleet Captain	elim.
	Team: eliminated	

1964 Olympic Games
Tokyo, Japan

Jumping:	Frank Chapot/San Lucas	7th
	Kathy Kusner/Untouchable	13th
	Mary Mairs/Tomboy	33rd
	Team: 6th place	
Dressage:	Patricia de la Tour/Rath Patrick	8th
	Jessica Newberry/Forstrat	14th
	Karen McIntosh/Malteser	17th
	Team: 4th place	
3-Day:	Michael Page/Grasshopper	4th
	Kevin Freeman/Gallopade	12th
	Michael Plumb/Bold Minstrel	15th
	Lana duPont/Mr. Wister	33rd
	Team: 2nd place (silver medal)	

1968 Olympic Games
Mexico City, Mexico

Jumping:	William Steinkraus/ Snowbound	1st
	Frank Chapot/San Lucas	4th
	Kathy Kusner/Untouchable	21st
	Team: 4th place	
	(Mary Chapot/White Lightning; Kathy Kusner/ Untouchable; Frank Chapot/San Lucas)	
Dressage:	Kyra Downton/Kadett	21st
	Edith Master/Helios	23rd
	Donnan Plumb/Attaché	24th
	Team: 8th place	
3-Day:	Michael Page/Foster	3rd
	James Wofford/Kilkenny	6th
	Michael Plumb/Plain Sailing	14th
	Kevin Freeman/Chalan	elim.
	Team: 2nd place (silver medal)	

1972 Olympic Games
Munich, West Germany

Jumping:	Neal Shapiro/Sloopy	3rd
	Kathy Kusner/Fleet Apple	10th
	William Steinkraus/	
	Snowbound	22nd
	Team: 2nd place (silver medal)	
	(Neal Shapiro/Sloopy; Kathy Kusner/Fleet Apple; Frank Chapot/White Lightning; William Steinkraus/Main Spring)	
Dressage:	Edith Master/Dahlwitz	18th
	John Winnett/Reinald	22nd
	Lois Stephens/Fasching	31st
	Team: 9th place	
3-Day:	Kevin Freeman/Good Mixture	5th
	Bruce Davidson/Plain Sailing	8th
	Michael Plumb/Free and Easy	20th
	James Wofford/Kilkenny	30th
	Team: 2nd place (silver medal)	

1976 Olympic Games
Montreal, Canada

Jumping:	Frank Chapot/Viscount	5th
	Dennis Murphy/Do Right	22nd
	Buddy Brown/A Little Bit	29th
	Team: 4th place	
	(Buddy Brown/Sandsablaze; Robert Ridland/South Side; Michael Matz/Grande; Frank Chapot/Viscount)	
Dressage:	Dorothy Morkis/Monaco	5th
	Hilda Gurney/Keen	10th
	Edith Master/Dahlwitz	14th
	Team: 3rd place (bronze medal)	
3-Day:	Tad Coffin/Bally Cor	1st
	J. Michael Plumb/Better and Better	2nd
	Bruce Davidson/Irish Cap	10th
	Mary Anne Tauskey/Marcus Aurelius	21st
	Team: 1st place (gold medal)	

1980 Alternate Olympics
Rotterdam, Holland

Jumping:	Melanie Smith/Calypso	3rd
	Terry Rudd/Semi Tough	10th
	Norman Dello Joio/Allegro	22nd
	Team: 5th place	
	(Katie Monahan/Silver Exchange; Norman Dello Joio/Allegro; Terry Rudd/Semi Tough; Melanie Smith/Calypso)	

Goodwood, England

Dressage:	*Gwen Stockebrand/Bao	17th
	*Lendon Gray/Beppo	25th
	Linda Zang/Fellow Traveller	26th
	John Winnett/Leopardi	28th
	Team: 7th place	

Fontainebleau, France

3-Day:	*James Wofford/Carawich	2nd
	*Torrance Watkins/Poltroon	3rd
	Karen Stives/The Saint	34th
	*Michael Huber/Gold Chip	ret.
	Washington Bishop/Taxi	ret.
	*J. Michael Plumb/Laurenson	elim.
	Team: eliminated	

1984 Olympic Games
Los Angeles, United States

Jumping:	Joe Fargis/Touch of Class	1st
	Conrad Homfeld/Abdullah	2nd
	Melanie Smith/Calypso	7th
	Team: 1st place (gold medal)	
	(Joe Fargis/Touch of Class; Leslie Burr/Albany; Conrad Homfeld/Abdullah; Melanie Smith/Calypso)	
Dressage:	Hilda Gurney/Keen	14th
	Sandy Pflueger-Clarke/Marco Polo	16th
	Robert Dover/Romantico	17th
	Team: 6th place	
3-Day:	Karen Stives/Ben Arthur	2nd
	Torrance Watkins Fleischmann/Finvarra	4th
	J. Michael Plumb/Blue Stone	10th
	Bruce Davidson/J. J. Babu	13th
	Team: 1st place (gold medal)	

(*denotes Team members)

1988 Olympic Games
Seoul, South Korea

Jumping:	Greg Best/Gem Twist	2nd
	Anne Kursinski/Starman	4th
	Joe Fargis/Mill Pearl	7th
	Lisa Jacquin/For the Moment	57th
	Team: 2nd place (silver medal)	
	(Greg Best/Gem Twist; Lisa Jacquin/For the Moment; Anne Kursinski/Starman; Joe Fargis/Mill Pearl)	

Dressage:	Robert Dover/Federleicht	13th
	Jessica Ransehousen/ Orpheus	17th
	Belinda Baudin/Christopher	33rd
	Lendon Gray/Later On	43rd
	Team: 6th place	

3-Day:	Phyllis Dawson/Albany	10th
	Bruce Davidson/Dr. Peaches	18th
	Ann Sutton/Tarzan	ret.
	Karen Lende/The Optimist	elim.
	Team: eliminated	

PAN AMERICAN GAMES

1955 Pan American Games
Mexico City, Mexico

Jumping:	Charles Dennehy/Pill Box	8th
	Arthur McCashin/Mohawk	9th
	John R. Wheeler/Little Mac	14th
	William Steinkraus/Volco's Duke	15th
	Team: 4th place	

Dressage:	Robert Borg/Bill Biddle	2nd
	No team	

3-Day:	Walter Staley/Mud Dauber	1st
	Frank Duffy/Passach	8th
	John E. B. Wofford/ Cassavellanus	elim.
	Team: eliminated	

1959 Pan American Games
Chicago, United States

Jumping:	Frank Chapot/Diamant	
	Hugh Wiley/Nautical	
	William Steinkraus/Riviera Wonder	

	George Morris/Night Owl	
	No individual competition; team: 1st place (gold medal)	

Dressage:	Patricia Galvin/Rath Patrick	1st
	Jessica Newberry/Forstrat	5th
	Karen McIntosh/Scipio	6th
	Team: 2nd place (silver medal)	

3-Day:	Michael Page/Grasshopper	1st
	Michael Plumb/Markham	2nd
	William Haggard/Bold Minstrel	9th
	Walter Staley/Sebastian	elim.
	Team: 2nd place (silver medal)	

1963 Pan American Games
São Paulo, Brazil

Jumping:	Mary Mairs/Tomboy	1st
	Frank Chapot/San Lucas	4th
	Kathy Kusner/Unusual	15th
	William Steinkraus/Sinjon	ret.
	Team: 1st place (gold medal)	

Dressage:	Patricia Galvin/Rath Patrick	1st
	No team	

3-Day:	Michael Page/Grasshopper	1st
	Kevin Freeman/Reno Pal	2nd
	William Haggard/Bold Minstrel	6th
	Michael Plumb/Markham	elim.
	Team: 1st place (gold medal)	

1967 Pan American Games
Winnipeg, Canada

Jumping:	Kathy Kusner/Untouchable	5th
	Mary Chapot/White Lightning	7th
	Frank Chapot/San Lucas	7th
	William Steinkraus/Bold Minstrel	9th
	Team: 2nd place (silver medal)	

Dressage:	Kyra Downton/Kadett	1st
	Diana Firmin-Didot/Avaune	4th
	Donnan Plumb/Attaché	10th
	Team: 2nd place (silver medal)	

3-Day:	Michael Plumb/Plain Sailing	1st
	Michael Page/Foster	3rd
	James Wofford/Kilkenny	4th
	Rick Eckhardt/The Stranger	5th
	Team: 1st place (gold medal)	

1971 Pan American Games
Cali, Colombia

USET did not participate because Venezuelan Equine Encephalitis was endemic there at that time

1975 Pan American Games
Mexico City, Mexico

Jumping:	Buddy Brown/A Little Bit	2nd
	Michael Matz/Grande	3rd
	Dennis Murphy/Do Right	7th
	Team: 1st place (gold medal)	
	(Michael Matz/Grande; Dennis Murphy/Do Right; Joseph Fargis/Caesar; Buddy Brown/ Sandsablaze)	

Dressage:	Hilda Gurney/Keen	2nd
	Dorothy Morkis/Monaco	3rd
	John Winnett/Leopardi	4th
	Team: 1st place (gold medal)	

3-Day:	Tad Coffin/Bally Cor	1st
	Bruce Davidson/Golden Griffin	2nd
	Beth Perkins/Furtive	5th
	Mary Anne Tauskey/Marcus Aurelius	7th
	Team: 1st place (gold medal)	

1979 Pan American Games
San Juan, Puerto Rico

Jumping:	Michael Matz/Jet Run	1st
	Melanie Smith/Val de Loire	5th
	Team: 1st place (gold medal)	
	(Michael Matz/Jet Run; Melanie Smith/Val de Loire; Norman Dello Joio/ Allegro; Buddy Brown/ Sandsablaze)	

Dressage:	Hilda Gurney/Keen	1st
	Gwen Stockebrand/Bao	2nd
	Team: 1st place (gold medal)	
	(Hilda Gurney/Keen; Gwen Stockebrand/Bao; Linda Zang/Fellow Traveller) (Unofficial because only two teams participated)	

No 3-Day

1983 Pan American Games
Caracas, Venezuela

Jumping:	Anne Kursinski/Livius	1st
	Michael Matz/Chef	3rd
	Team: 1st place (gold medal)	

(Michael Matz/Chef; Leslie Burr/Boing; Donald Cheska/South Side; Anne Kursinski/Livius)

Dressage:	Carole Grant/Percy	1st
	Hilda Gurney/Chrysos	2nd
	Team: 1st place (gold medal)	
	(Carole Grant/Percy; Hilda Gurney/Chrysos; Kay Meredith/Encore)	

No 3-Day

1987 Pan American Games
Indianapolis, United States

Jumping:	Rodney Jenkins/Czar	2nd
	Lisa Jacquin/For the Moment	19th
	Team: 2nd place (silver medal)	
	(Greg Best/Gem Twist; Rodney Jenkins/Czar; Lisa Jacquin/For the Moment; Katharine Burdsall/The Natural)	

Dressage:	Caroll Lavell/In the Black	4th
	Ann Guptill/Maple Magnum	5th
	Team: 2nd place (silver medal)	
	(Ellin Dixon/Windsor; Ann Guptill/Maple Magnum; Caroll Lavell/In the Black; Nancy Polozker/Klee)	

3-Day:	Mike Huber/Quartermaster	1st
	Emily MacGowan/Jet Set	2nd
	Packy McGaughan/Tanzer	3rd
	Nanci Lindroth/Landino	14th
	Team: 1st place (gold medal)	

WORLD AND EUROPEAN CHAMPIONSHIPS

Jumping

1953 Paris (France)
World Championships

| John Winnett/Sultan and Buffalo | unpl. |

1955 Aachen (West Germany)
World Championships

| John Russell/Bally Bay and Lonie | unpl. |

1956 Aachen (West Germany)
World Championships

William Steinkraus/First Boy and Night Owl	5th
Hugh Wiley/Master William	9th

1958 Aachen (West Germany)
European Championships

William Steinkraus/Ksar d'Esprit	5th
Hugh Wiley/Nautical	6th

1959 Paris (France)
European Championships

William Steinkraus/First Boy and Ksar d'Esprit	5th
Hugh Wiley/Nautical and Master William	6th

1960 Venice (Italy)
World Championships

William Steinkraus/Ksar d'Esprit	4th
George Morris/Sinjon	10th

1961 Aachen (West Germany)
European Championships

Warren Wofford/Hollandia and Huntsman	unpl.

1965 Hickstead (England) Ladies'
World Championships

Kathy Kusner/Untouchable and That's Right	2nd

1966 Lucerne (Switzerland)
European Championships

Frank Chapot/Good Twist and San Lucas	2nd
William Steinkraus/Snowbound and Sinjon	withdrew

1967 Fontainebleau (France) Ladies'
European Championships

Kathy Kusner/Untouchable and Aberali	1st

1970 La Baule (France)
World Championships

Frank Chapot/White Lightning	6th
William Steinkraus/Bold Minstrel	9th

1974 La Baule (France) Ladies'
World Championships

Michele McEvoy/Mr. Muskie and Sundancer	2nd

1974 Hickstead (England)
World Championships

Frank Chapot/Main Spring	3rd
Rodney Jenkins/Idle Dice	8th

1978 Aachen (West Germany)
World Championships

Michael Matz/Jet Run	3rd
Conrad Homfeld/Balbuco	12th
Dennis Murphy/Tuscaloosa	30th
Buddy Brown/Viscount	48th
Team: 3rd place (bronze medal)	

1982 Dublin (Ireland)
World Championships

Melanie Smith/Calypso	10th
Peter Leone/Ardennes	12th
Michael Matz/Jet Run	13th
Bernie Traurig/Eaden Vale	17th
Team: 4th place	

1986 Aachen (West Germany)
World Championships

Conrad Homfeld/Abdullah	2nd
Michael Matz/Chef	5th
Katharine Burdsall/The Natural	9th
Katie Monahan/Amadia	20th
Team: 1st place (gold medal)	

Dressage

1958 Wiesbaden (West Germany)
European Championships

Jessica Newberry/Archimedes	11th

1961 Aachen (West Germany)
European Championships

Karen McIntosh/Heraldik	19th

1966 Berne (Switzerland)
World Championships

Diana Firmin-Didot/Avaune	21st

1967 Aachen (West Germany)
European Championships

Diana Firmin-Didot/Avaune	17th
Martha Knocke/Englishman	32nd
Barbara McGuinness/Four Seasons	34th

1970 Aachen (West Germany)
World Championships

Edith Master/Helios	23rd
Lois Stephens/Fasching	25th

1974 Copenhagen (Denmark)
World Championships

Edith Master/Dahlwitz	15th
Elizabeth Lewis/Ludmilla	15th
John Winnett/Leopardi	19th
Sidley Payne/Felix	32nd

1978 Goodwood (England)
World Championships

Hilda Gurney/Keen	7th
Dorothy Morkis/Monaco	11th
Gwen Stockebrand/Bao	16th
Edith Master/Dahlwitz	17th
Team: 4th place	

1982 Lausanne (Switzerland)
World Championships

Sandy Pflueger-Clarke/Marco Polo	18th
Alexandra Howard/Bull Market	27th
Carole Grant/Percy	37th
Kim Beardsley/Woodimix	38th
Team: 10th place	

1986 Cedar Valley (Canada)
World Championships

Sandy Pflueger-Clarke/Marco Polo	22nd
Key Meredith/Encore	34th
Dianna Rankin/New Ladykiller	36th
Robert Dover/Federleicht	41st
Team: 9th place	

3-Day

1959 Harewood (England)
European Championships

John E. B. Wofford/Cassavellanus	33rd

1966 Burghley (England)
World Championships

Kevin Freeman/M'Lord Conolly	9th
Rick Eckhardt/Gallopade	elim.
Kevin Freeman/Royal Imp	elim.
J. A. B. Smith/Bean Platter	elim.
J. Michael Plumb/Foster	elim.
J. Michael Plumb/Chakola	elim.

1967 Punchestown (Ireland)
European Championships

Mason Phelps/Gladstone	15th

1970 Punchestown (Ireland)
World Championships

James Wofford/Kilkenny	3rd
Mason Phelps/Rowen	elim.

1974 Burghley (England)
World Championships

*Bruce Davidson/Irish Cap	1st
*J. Michael Plumb/Good Mixture	2nd
Beth Perkins/Furtive	6th
*Edward Emerson/Victor Dakin	14th
*Donald Sachey/Plain Sailing	21st
Caroline Treviranus/Cajun	ret.
Team: 1st place (gold medal)	

1978 Lexington (Kentucky)
World Championships

*Bruce Davidson/Might Tango	1st
Ralph Hill/Sergeant Gilbert	4th
*James Wofford/Carawich	10th
Mary Anne Tauskey/Marcus Aurelius	12th
Mike Huber/Gold Chip	13th
Torrance Watkins/Red's Door	15th
Mary Hazzard/Cavalistic	20th
*Tad Coffin/Bally Cor	22nd
Caroline Treviranus/Comic Relief	elim.
Desiree Smith/Foxie	ret.
Story Jenks/Toughkenamon	ret.
*J. Michael Plumb/Laurenson	elim.
Team: 3rd place (bronze medal)	

1982 Luhmühlen (West Germany)
World Championships

*Kim Walnes/The Gray Goose	
Peter Green/Branch Water	

(*denotes Team members*)

Bruce Davidson/J. J. Babu   13th
*Nancy Bliss/Cobblestone   17th
*Torrance Watkins/Southern Comfort   21st
Karen Stives/The Saint   25th
*J. Michael Plumb/Blue Stone   31st
Team: 3rd place (bronze medal)

1986 Gawler (South Australia)
World Championships

J. Michael Plumb/Blue Stone   8th
*Karen Lende/Lutin V   18th
*Karen Stives/Flying Colours   elim.
*Torrance Fleischmann/Finvarra   ret.
Kim Walnes/The Gray Goose   ret.
*Derek di Granzia/Sasquatch   ret.
Team: eliminated

Driving—Teams

1980 Windsor (England)
World Championships

Deirdre Pirie   27th
James Fairclough   33rd
John Fairclough   36th
L. Clay Camp   38th
Team: eliminated

1982 Apeldoorn (Holland)
World Championships

James Fairclough   12th
Deirdre Pirie   19th
Emil-Bernhard Jung   37th
Team: 7th place

1984 Szilvásvárad (Hungary)
World Championships

William Long   7th
Deirdre Pirie   16th
Sem Groenewoud   22nd
Emil-Bernhard Jung   38th
Team: 4th place

1986 Ascot (England)
World Championships

William Long   9th
Deirdre Pirie   16th
Emil-Bernhard Jung   37th
Sem Groenewoud   ret.
Team: 4th place
(*denotes Team members)

1988 Apeldoorn (Holland)
World Championships

William Long   13th
Sem Groenewoud   17th
L. Clay Camp   34th
Deirdre Pirie   42nd
Team: 7th place

Driving—Pairs

1983 Montemaggiore (Italy)
(open)
World Championships

Charles S. Cheston   11th

1985 Sandringham (England)
World Championships

Lawrence E. Poulin   8th
Charles S. Cheston   21st
Sharon Chesson   35th
Team: 5th place

1987 Riesenbeck (Holland)
World Championships

Lawrence E. Poulin   23rd
Charles S. Cheston   32nd
S. Tucker S. Johnson   37th
Team: 8th place

1989 Baloton (Hungary)
World Championships

Lawrence E. Poulin   10th
Kelly Valdes   46th
Lana Wright   56th
Sharon Chesson   57th
Team: eliminated

NORTH AMERICAN DRESSAGE CHAMPIONSHIPS

1985 North Salem, New York, United States

Hilda Gurney/Keen 2nd
Team: 1st place (gold medal)
(Debbie Bowman/Falstaff; Robert Dover/Romantico;
Hilda Gurney/Keen; Dianna Rankin/New Ladykiller)

1989 Ste-Justine de Newton, Quebec, Canada

Carol Lavell/Gifted 1st
Robert Dover/Walzertakt 2nd
Team A: 1st place (gold medal)
(Robert Dover/Walzertakt;
Heidi Ericksen/Prego; Carol Lavell/Gifted;
Marie Meyers/Dimitrius)
Team B: 3rd place (bronze medal)
(Belinda Baudin/Christopher;
Kathy Connelly/Enterprise; Nancy Smith/Felit)

NATIONS' CUPS

1976 Aachen, West Germany

5th   to ITA–FRA–HOL–GBR

Lucerne, Switzerland

1st   Dennis Murphy/Hummer; Michael Matz/
Grande; Robert Ridland/Almost Persuaded;
Buddy Brown/Viscount

Washington, D.C., United States

1st   Frank Chapot/Coach Stop; Michael Matz/
Grande; Dennis Murphy/Do Right; Buddy
Brown/Flying John

New York, United States

1st   Frank Chapot/Coach Stop; Michael Matz/
Grande; Dennis Murphy/Tuscaloosa; Buddy
Brown/Flying John

Toronto, Canada

1st   Frank Chapot/Coach Stop; Michael Matz/
Grande; Dennis Murphy/Tuscaloosa; Buddy
Brown/Flying John

1977 Calgary, Canada

5th   to FRG–GBR–CAN–MEX (USA disq.)

Washington, D.C., United States

1st   Conrad Homfeld/Balbuco; Joe Fargis/
Pueblo; Michael Matz/Jet Run; Buddy
Brown/Sandsablaze

New York, United States

1st   Conrad Homfeld/Balbuco; Michael Matz/
Jet Run; Buddy Brown/Sandsablaze;
Rodney Jenkins/Idle Dice

Toronto, Canada

2nd   to CAN

1978 Aachen, West Germany

8th   to FRG–GBR–IRL–FRA–BEL–SUI–HOL

Hickstead, England

2nd   to GBR

Rotterdam, Holland

1st   Conrad Homfeld/Balbuco; Dennis Murphy/
Tuscaloosa; Robert Ridland/Nazarius;
Michael Matz/Sandor

Calgary, Canada

3rd   to GBR–CAN

Washington, D.C., United States

2nd   to CAN

New York, United States

1st   Dennis Murphy/Tuscaloosa; Buddy Brown/
Flying John; Melanie Smith/Val de Loire;
Bernie Traurig/Gucci

Toronto, Canada

1st   Robert Ridland/Nazarius; Scott
Nederlander/Southside; Dennis Murphy/
Tuscaloosa; Michael Matz/Sandor

1979 Calgary, Canada

2nd   to GBR

Washington, D.C., United States

1st   Norman Dello Joio/Allegro; Peter Leone/
Semi Pro; Melanie Smith/Calypso; Michael
Matz/Jet Run

New York, United States

1st   Melanie Smith/Val de Loire; Terry Rudd/
Fat City; Norman Dello Joio/Allegro;
Michael Matz/Jet Run

Toronto, Canada

2nd   to CAN

1980 Paris, France

3rd   to FRA–SUI

Dublin, Ireland

1st   Armand Leone/Wallenstein; Katie Monahan/Silver Exchange; Norman Dello Joio/Allegro; Melanie Smith/Calypso

Rotterdam, Holland

5th   to CAN–GBR–AUT–FRG

Calgary, Canada

5th   to GBR–HOL–CAN–SUI

Washington, D.C., United States

1st   Peter Leone/Semi Pro; Leslie Burr/Chase the Clouds; Norman Dello Joio/Allegro; Melanie Smith/Calypso

New York, United States

1st   Armand Leone/Wallenstein; Leslie Burr/Chase the Clouds; Norman Dello Joio/Allegro; Melanie Smith/Calypso

Toronto, Canada

2nd   to FRA

1981 Calgary, Canada

4th   to HOL–FRA–GBR

Washington, D.C., United States

1st   Melanie Smith/Calypso; Rodney Jenkins/Coast Line; Michael Matz/Jet Run; Norman Dello Joio/Johnny's Pocket

New York, United States

1st   Melanie Smith/Calypso; Rodney Jenkins/Coast Line; Michael Matz/Jet Run; Norman Dello Joio/Johnny's Pocket

Toronto, Canada

1st   Norman Dello Joio/Johnny's Pocket; Donald Cheska/Southside; Anne Kursinski/Third Man; Melanie Smith/Calypso

1982 Lucerne, Switzerland

6th   to GBR–SUI–FRA–FRG–ITA

Aachen, West Germany

3rd   to FRG–GBR

Paris, France

5th   to FRG–FRA–GBR–SUI

Calgary, Canada

2nd   to GBR

Washington, D.C., United States

1st   Katie Monahan/Noren; Norman Dello Joio/I Love You; Donald Cheska/Southside; Melanie Smith/Calypso

New York, United States

1st   Katie Monahan/Noren; Donald Cheska/Southside; Rodney Jenkins/Coast Line; Melanie Smith/Calypso

Toronto, Canada

2nd   to SUI

1983 Rome, Italy

1st   Anne Kursinski/Livius; Joe Fargis/Touch of Class; Katie Monahan/Noren; Melanie Smith/Calypso

Calgary, Canada

1st   Joe Fargis/Touch of Class; Norman Dello Joio/I Love You; Katie Monahan/Noren; Melanie Smith/Calypso

Washington, D.C., United States

1st   Katie Monahan/Noren; Norman Dello Joio/I Love You; Joe Fargis/Touch of Class; Michael Matz/Jet Run

New York, United States

1st   Katie Monahan/Noren; Conrad Homfeld/Corsair; Joe Fargis/Touch of Class; Norman Dello Joio/I Love You

Toronto, Canada

1st   Anne Kursinski/Insolvent; Donald Cheska/Eaden Vale; Michael Matz/Chef; Norman Dello Joio/I Love You

1984 Calgary, Canada

4th   to FRG–SUI–CAN

Washington, D.C., United States

1st   Joe Fargis/Touch of Class; Leslie Burr/Albany; Conrad Homfeld/Abdullah; Melanie Smith/Calypso

New York, United States

3rd   to CAN–GBR

Toronto, Canada

1st   Katie Monahan/Amadia; Jeffrey Welles/
Ardennes; Michael Matz/Chef; Norman
Dello Joio/I Love You

1985 Aachen, West Germany

1st   Joe Fargis/Touch of Class; Louis Jacobs/
Janus de Ver; Christian Currey/Manuel;
Conrad Homfeld/Abdullah

Falsterbo, Denmark

1st   Lisa Tarnopol/Adam; Joan Scharffenberger/
Nataal; Michaela Murphy/Ramzes; George
Morris/Rio

Dublin, Ireland

3rd   to GBR–IRL

Calgary, Canada

5th   to GBR–SUI–CAN–FRA

Washington, D.C., United States

1st   Michael Matz/Bon Retour; Louis Jacobs/
Janus de Ver; Katie Monahan/The
Governor; Joe Fargis/Touch of Class

New York, United States

1st   Katie Monahan/The Governor; Lisa
Tarnopol/Adam; Michael Matz/Chef; Joe
Fargis/Touch of Class

Toronto, Canada

3rd   to FRG–CAN

1986 Dublin, Ireland

2nd   to GBR

Rotterdam, Holland

8th   to GBR–SUI–FRG–AUT–FRA–HOL–ESP

Chaudfontaine, France

5th   to GBR–HOL–BRA–FRG

Donaueschingen, West Germany

2nd   to FRG

Calgary, Canada

1st   Robert Ridland/Mon Bambi; Jennifer
Newell/Nero; Joan Scharffenberger/
Winnipeg; Hap Hansen/Juniperus

Washington, D.C., United States

1st   Anne Kursinski/Montreal; Katharine
Burdsall/The Natural; Lisa Tarnopol/Adam;
Katie Monahan/Bean Bag

New York, United States

2nd   to CAN

Toronto, Canada

2nd   to GBR

1987 Rome, Italy

4th   to SUI–FRA–FRG

Lucerne, Switzerland

4th   to FRA–BEL–SUI

Hickstead, England

1st   Anne Kursinski/Starman; Deborah Dolan/
Albany; Joan Scharffenberger/Victor; Katie
Monahan Prudent/Special Envoy

Aachen, West Germany

1st   Anne Kursinski/Starman; Lisa Tarnopol/
Revlon Adam; Joan Scharffenberger/Victor;
Joe Fargis/Mill Pearl

Calgary, Canada

1st   Anne Kursinski/Starman; Deborah Dolan/
VIP; Beezie Patton/Medrano; Joan
Scharffenberger/Victor

Washington, D.C., United States

2nd   to FRA

New York, United States

3rd   to CAN–FRA

Toronto, Canada

1st   Chris Kappler/Concorde; Deborah Dolan/
Albany; Debbie Shaffner/Don Carlos; Joan
Scharffenberger/Victor

1988 Rotterdam, Holland

5th   to SUI–HOL–GBR–ESP

Calgary, Canada

1st   Peter Leone/Oxo; Leslie Burr Lenehan/
Pressurized; Joan Scharffenberger/Victor;
Katie Monahan Prudent/Make My Day

Guadalajara, Mexico

1st   Norman Dello Joio/Aga Khan; Deborah Dolan/Albany; Beezie Patton/Northern Magic; Michael Matz/Bon Retour

Washington, D.C., United States

3rd   to FRG–FRA

New York, United States

1st   Katie Monahan Prudent/Make My Day; Anne Kursinski/Starman; Greg Best/Gem Twist; Joe Fargis/Mill Pearl

Toronto, Canada

2nd   to FRA

1989 Rome, Italy

1st   Joe Fargis/Chef; Deborah Dolan/VIP; Beezie Patton/Northern Magic; Katie Monahan Prudent/Special Envoy

Copenhagen, Denmark

1st   George Morris/Slinky; Gary Young/Claudius La Silla; Joan Scharffenberger/Victor; Beezie Patton/Northern Magic

Hickstead, England

2nd   to FRA

Aachen, West Germany

2nd   to GBR

Geesteren, Holland

2nd   to SUI

Oberanven, Luxembourg

3rd   to GBR–FRA

Stockholm, Sweden

2nd   to FRG

Dinard, France

9th   to HOL–FRA–SUI–GBR–AUT–BEL–FRG–ITA

Calgary, Canada

2nd   to GBR

Washington, D.C., United States

1st   Anne Kursinski/Starman; Beezie Patton/Northern Magic; Joan Scharffenberger/Victor; Jeffrey Welles/Webster

New York, United States

1st   Anne Kursinski/Starman; Joe Fargis/Mill Pearl; Beezie Patton/Northern Magic; Jeffrey Welles/Webster

Toronto, Canada

3rd   to GBR–CAN

WORLD CUP FINALS

Jumping

1979 Göteborg, Sweden

Katie Monahan/The Jones Boy	2nd
Norman Dello Joio/Allegro	3rd
Dennis Murphy/Tuscaloosa	7th
Conrad Homfeld/Balbuco	11th
Melanie Smith/Val de Loire	13th
Bernie Traurig/The Cardinal	13th
Scott Nederlander/Southside	16th

1980 Baltimore, United States

Conrad Homfeld/Balbuco	1st
Melanie Smith/Calypso	2nd
Michael Matz/Jet Run	5th
Rodney Jenkins/Third Man	6th
Leslie Burr/Chase the Clouds	9th
Terry Rudd/Fat City	10th
Dennis Murphy/Tuscaloosa and Lyrical Lou	20th
Bernie Traurig/Eadenvale	24th

1981 Birmingham, England

Michael Matz/Jet Run	1st
Donald Cheska/Southside	2nd
Leslie Burr/Chase the Clouds	5th
Melanie Smith/Calypso	6th
Norman Dello Joio/Allegro	9th
Jamie Mann/Signal Point	10th
Buddy Brown/Felton	12th
Bernie Traurig/Eadenvale	15th
Dennis Murphy/Lyrical Lou	27th
Robert Ridland/Island Discovery	29th

1982 Göteborg, Sweden

Melanie Smith/Calypso	1st
Peter Leone/Ardennes	5th

Mark Leone/Tim	9th
Donald Cheska/Southside	11th
Hap Hansen/Faon Rouge and Hai Karate	15th
Norman Dello Joio/Allegro	16th
Anne Kursinski/Livius	17th
Armand Leone/Loecky	24th
Harry de Leyer/Dutch Crown	27th
Bernie Traurig/Eaden Vale	29th
Cece Younger/Henley	32nd

1983   Vienna, Austria

Norman Dello Joio/I Love You	1st
Melanie Smith/Calypso	3rd
Conrad Homfeld/Touch of Class	4th
Barney Ward/Eclair de l'Ille	6th
Donald Cheska/Southside	8th
Katie Monahan/Noren	9th
Michael Matz/Jet Run	11th
Anne Kursinski/Livius	12th
Mark Leone/Tim and Loecky	21st
Debbie Shaffner/Abdullah	24th
Hap Hansen/Fil d'Argent	26th
Kevin Maloney/Turf Fire	28th
Rob Gage/Dutch Harry and Sage	31st

1984   Göteborg, Sweden

Norman Dello Joio/I Love You	2nd
Michael Matz/Chef	5th
Donald Cheska/Southside	8th
Leslie Burr/Corsair and Boing	10th
Rob Gage/Fürst	11th
Barney Ward/Pico	12th
Anne Kursinski/Insolvent	13th
Peter Leone/Jonker	17th
Lisa Jacquin/For the Moment	26th
Jeffrey Welles/Easter Jubilee	27th
Mark Leone/Arizona	30th
Kevin Maloney/Turf Fire	36th
Conrad Homfeld/Abdullah	38th

1985   Berlin, West Germany

Conrad Homfeld/Abdullah	1st
Hap Hansen/May Be	6th
Armand Leone/Jonker	11th
Lisa Tarnopol/Adam	12th
Michael Matz/Chef	13th
Peter Leone/Oxo	14th
Joe Fargis/Touch of Class	16th
Anne Kursinski/Medrano	20th
Christian Currey/Manuel	22nd
Mark Leone/Arizona	28th
Melanie Smith/Monroe	31st
Leslie Burr Lenehan/Boing	34th
Lisa Jacquin/For the Moment	36th
Norman Dello Joio/Ardennes	42nd

Louis Jacobs/Janus de Ver	44th
Katharine Burdsall/Pot Luck	45th

1986   Göteborg, Sweden

Leslie Burr Lenehan/McLain	1st
Conrad Homfeld/May Be	3rd
Lisa Tarnopol/Adam	8th
Lynne Little/Ommen	10th
Jay Land/Leapy Lad	12th
Peter Leone/Joe and Oxo	14th
George Lindemann/Sans Pardon	17th
Christian Currey/Manuel	18th
Lynn Witte/Hawkeye	20th
Katie Monahan/Bean Bag	26th
Diana Shaw/Logo	30th
Jeffrey Welles/The Girl Friend	31st
Deborah Dolan/San Marco	38th
Hap Hansen/Gambrinus	39th

1987   Paris, France

Katharine Burdsall/The Natural	1st
Lisa Jacquin/For the Moment	3rd
John McConnell/Sodark	8th
Katie Monahan/Special Envoy	15th
George Lindemann/Sans Pardon	16th
Anne Kursinski/Kino d'Andelou	17th
Beezie Patton/Medrano	18th
Leslie Burr Lenehan/McLain and Siriskia	20th
Deborah Dolan/VIP	22nd
Rodney Jenkins/Play Back	24th
Susan Hutchinson/Livius	26th
Joe Fargis/Touch of Class	32nd
Lisa Tarnopol/Revlon Adam	34th
Hap Hansen/Juniperus	38th

1988   Göteborg, Sweden

Hap Hansen/Juniperus	6th
Chris Kappler/Concorde	14th
Peter Leone/Threes and Sevens	15th
Susan Hutchinson/Samsung Woodstock	16th
Michaela Murphy/Gusty Monroe	18th
Greg Best/Santos	19th
George Morris/Rio	28th
Gary Young/Brillante La Silla	29th
Joan Scharffenberger/Victor	33rd
Katie Monahan Prudent/Bean Bag	37th
Debbie Shaffner/Windsor	38th
Margie Goldstein/Daydream	41st
Norman Dello Joio/Bento	42nd

1989   Tampa, United States

George Lindemann/Jupiter	3rd
Joe Fargis/Mill Pearl	4th
Peter Leone/Threes and Sevens	5th

Chris Kappler/Concorde	6th
Leslie Burr Lenehan/Lenny and Pressurized	7th
Bernie Traurig/Corsair	16th
Hap Hansen/Zadok	18th
Katie Monahan Prudent/Make My Day	19th
Lynn Witte/Zulu	25th
Dina Santangelo/Manassas County	26th
Mark Leone/Costelloe	30th
Greg Best/Gem Twist	33rd
Jeffrey Welles/Webster	36th
Louis Jacobs/Janus de Ver	39th
Rodney Jenkins/Playback	disq.

Dressage

1986 's Hertogenbosch, Holland

Diana Rankin/New Ladykiller	9th

1987 Essen, West Germany

Robert Dover/Federleicht	10th

1988 's Hertogenbosch, Holland

Robert Dover/Federleicht	4th

1989 Göteborg, Sweden

Kathy Connelly/Enterprise	14th

U.S. MAJOR VICTORIES AT CCI

1977 Bramham, Great Britain
Sandy Pflueger   The Abbot

Ledyard, Massachusetts
Michael Plumb   Laurenson

1980 Luhmühlen, West Germany
Michael Plumb   Better and Better

1981 Lexington, Kentucky, United States
Grant Schneidman   Flying Dutchman

Chesterland, Pennsylvania, United States
Bruce Davidson   J. J. Babu

1982 Pratoni del Vivaro, Italy
Bruce Davidson   Beacon Charm

Chesterland, Pennsylvania, United States
Grant Schneidman   Flying Dutchman

1983 Lexington, Kentucky, United States
Bruce Davidson   J. J. Babu

Wylye, Great Britain
James Wofford   Rockingham

Chesterland, Pennsylvania, United States
Bruce Davidson   Pilot Kid

1984 Lexington, Kentucky, United States
Bruce Davidson   Dr. Peaches

Chesterland, Pennsylvania, United States
Peter Green   Tribonius

Boekelo, Holland
Karen Lende   The Optimist

1985 Lexington, Kentucky, United States
Derek Di Grazia   Sasquatch

Chesterland, Pennsylvania, United States
Karen Lende   Castlewellan

Boekelo, Holland
Bruce Davidson   Dr. Peaches

1986 Lexington, Kentucky, United States
James Wofford   The Optimist

Gatcombe, Great Britain
Bruce Davidson   J. J. Babu

Chesterland, Pennsylvania, United States
Bruce Davidson   Noah

1987 Lexington, Kentucky, United States
Kerry Millikin   The Pirate

Stockholm, Sweden
Bruce Davidson   J. J. Babu

Chesterland, Pennsylvania, United States
Kerry Millikin   The Pirate

1988 Lexington, Kentucky, United States
Bruce Davidson   Dr. Peaches

Ridgewood, Canada
Bruce Davidson   Pirate Lion

Chesterland, Pennsylvania, United States
Molly Bliss   Hey Charlie

1989   Lexington, Kentucky, United States

Bruce Davidson   Dr. Peaches

Fair Hill, Maryland, United States

Karen Lende   Nos Ecus

U.S. MAJOR VICTORIES AT CDI

1987   Rotterdam, Holland

| Kür | Robert Dover | Federleicht |

Hanover, West Germany

| Kür | Robert Dover | Federleicht |

Zuidlaren, Holland

| GP | Robert Dover | Juvel |

Zuidlaren, Holland

| Kür | Robert Dover | Juvel |

Aachen, West Germany

| Kür | Robert Dover | Federleicht |

1988   Palm Beach, United States

| GP | Jessica Ransehousen | Orpheus |

Palm Beach, United States

| Special | Jessica Ransehousen | Orpheus |

Tampa, United States

| GP | Belinda Baudin | Christopher |

Tampa, United States

| Special | Belinda Baudin | Christopher |

1989   Tampa, United States

| GP | Robert Dover | Walzertakt |

Tampa, United States

| Special | Robert Dover | Walzertakt |

Stockholm, Sweden

| GP | Marie Meyers | Dimitrius |

Stockholm, Sweden

| Special | Robert Dover | Walzertakt |

GRAND PRIX AND WORLD CUP VICTORIES AT NORTH AMERICAN CSIO

1976   Washington

| President's Cup | Rodney Jenkins | No. 1 Spy |
| | Terry Rudd | Mr. Demeanor |

1977   Washington

| President's Cup | Buddy Brown | Jet Run |

Toronto

| GP | Michael Matz | Jet Run |

1978   New York

| WC | Peter Leone | Semi Pro |

1979   Washington

| President's Cup | Bernie Traurig | Eadenvale |

New York

| GP | Michael Matz | Jet Run |

New York

| WC | Leslie Burr | Chase the Clouds |

1980   Washington

| President's Cup | Michael Matz | Jet Run |

1981   Washington

| President's Cup | Melanie Smith | Calypso |

New York

| WC | Bernie Traurig | Eadenvale |

Toronto

| WC | Bernie Traurig | Eadenvale |

1982   Washington

| President's Cup | Katie Monahan | Noren |

New York

| WC | Mark Leone | Tim |

1983 Calgary

GP	Norman Dello Joio	I Love You

Washington

President's Cup	Rodney Jenkins	Coast Line

New York

WC	Michael Matz	Jet Run

1984 Washington

President's Cup	Joe Fargis	Touch of Class

New York

WC	Joe Fargis	Touch of Class

Toronto

WC	Norman Dello Joio	I Love You

1985 Washington

President's Cup	Michael Matz	Brussels

New York

GP	Leslie Burr Lenehan	McLain

1986 Washington

President's Cup	Katharine Burdsall	The Natural

New York

WC	Rodney Jenkins	Playback

Toronto

WC	Mark Leone	Costelloe

1987 Washington

President's Cup	Katie Monahan Prudent	Special Envoy

1988 Calgary

GP	George Morris	Rio

Washington

President's Cup	Hap Hansen	Zadok

New York

WC	Hap Hansen	Zadok

New York

PC	Greg Best	Gem Twist

GRAND PRIX WINS AT EUROPEAN CSIO AND CSI

1976 Wiesbaden, West Germany

GP	Buddy Brown	A Little Bit

1977 —

1978 Dinard, France

GP	Armand Leone	Encore

1979 —

1980 Paris, France

GP	Melanie Smith	Calypso

Royal International Horse Show, London

John Player	Terry Rudd	Semi Tough

1981 —

1982 Göteborg, Sweden

GP	Bernie Traurig	Eadenvale

1983 Rome, Italy

GP	Anne Kursinski	Livius

1984 Holte, Denmark

GP	Terry Rudd	Donald

1985 Hamburg, West Germany

Derby	Louis Jacobs	Janus de Ver

1986 Royan, France

GP	Conrad Homfeld	Abdullah

Dinard, France

GP	Conrad Homfeld	Abdullah

Mondorf, Luxembourg

GP	Jeffrey Welles	The Girlfriend

Chaudfontaine, France

GP   Joan Scharffen-   Winnipeg
            berger

Donaueschingen, West Germany

GP   Jeffrey Welles   Byron

1987 Lucerne, Switzerland

GP   Katharine   The Natural
            Burdsall

1988 —

1989 Hickstead, England

GP   Joe Fargis   Mill Pearl

U.S. MAJOR VICTORIES AT CAI

1984 Donaueschingen, West Germany

Teams   Emil-Bernhard Jung

1985 Windsor, England

Teams   William Long

1986 Gladstone, New Jersey, United States

Pairs   Larry Poulin

1988 Windsor, England

Pairs   Tucker Johnson

Windsor, England

Teams   Sem Groenewoud

Gladstone, New Jersey, United States

Pairs   Larry Poulin

1989 Windsor, England, Master's Trophy*

Team   William Long
Pair   Lana Wright
Single   Randy MacFarland

*Master's Trophy is unusual because it is the combined results of a team, pair, and single from the nation